About this Book

An admirable book. Margaret Gallagher has collected her vast knowledge of women and the media into a volume that was long overdue. Creativity and persistence appear to be the core features of feminists' struggles all over the world against the onslaught of demeaning images in contemporary media cultures. The book will be an inspiration to activists and theorists, reminding us of the ongoing necessity to combine theory with practice.

Professor Liesbet van Zoonen, author of Feminist Media Studies,
and Gender, Politics and Communication

Across the globe the media disempower people. Among the tools of this disempowerment are stereotyped and damaging images of the human condition including gender, age, race, ethnicity, sexuality, physical and mental illness and disability. Media disempowerment reduces the capacity of ordinary people to control the decisions that others take about their lives and to shape their own futures. This disempowerment affects women in particular. Against the forces of disempowerment, strategies for self-empowerment are essential. Among the creative and effective tools for such strategies are media monitoring and advocacy. Margaret Gallagher's excellent book demonstrates with a wealth of data and analysis how this is and can be done. The book is a must-read for all those committed to a 'gender shift' in the media. It is also essential reading for all those communication researchers and media activists who are concerned about a future which respects the human entitlement to dignity, equality and liberty.

*Professor Cees Hamelink, Professor of International
Communication, University of Amsterdam*

About the Author

Margaret Gallagher is an international media consultant and researcher. Since her first book, *Unequal Opportunities: The Case of Women and the Media* (Paris, Unesco Press, 1981), she has authored numerous analyses of gender patterns in the world's media. Her consultancy work has included projects for the United Nations Statistics Division, UNIFEM, UNESCO, the International Labour Office, the Council of Europe, the European Commission, the European Audiovisual Observatory and the World Association for Christian Communication.

Gender Setting: New Agendas for Media Monitoring and Advocacy

Margaret Gallagher

Zed Books
LONDON · NEW YORK

in association with

WACC
LONDON

Gender Setting: New Agendas for Media Monitoring and Advocacy
was first published by Zed Books Ltd, 7 Cynthia Street, London
N1 9JF, UK and Room 400, 175 Fifth Avenue, New York, NY
10010, USA in 2001 in association with World Association for
Christian Communication, 357 Kennington Lane, London
SE11 5QY.

Distributed in the USA exclusively by Palgrave, a division of
St Martin's Press, LLC, 175 Fifth Avenue, New York,
NY 10010, USA

Cover designed by Andrew Corbett
Set in Monotype Ehrhardt and Franklin Gothic by Ewan Smith
Printed and bound in Great Britain by Biddles Ltd, Guildford
and King's Lynn

A catalogue record for this book is available from the British
Library

Library of Congress Cataloging-in-Publication Data: available

ISBN 1 85649 844 1 cased
ISBN 1 85649 845 X limp

Contents

Boxes and Plates

Boxes

Plates

Acknowledgements

I am indebted to the following people for the time and care they took in providing information about their work, and for answering what at times must have seemed interminable questions about it: Gloria Bonder, Argentina; Helen Leonard, Australia; Sonia Spee and Magda Michielsens, Belgium; Patricia Flores Palacios, Bolivia; Tive Sarayeth, Cambodia; Melanie Cishecki, Canada; Uca Silva, Chile; Feng Yuan, China; Sanja Sarnavka, Croatia; Akhila Sivadas, Anuradha Mukherjee and Leela Rao, India; Dafna Lemish, Lesley Sachs and Orit Sulitzeanu, Israel; Gioia Di Cristofaro Longo, Italy; Hilary Nicholson, Sonia Gill and Suzanne Francis Brown, Jamaica; Toshiko Miyazaki and Masami Saitoh, Japan; Yanghee Kim, Korea; Bandana Rana, Nepal; Bernadette van Dijck, the Netherlands; Gabrielle Le Roux, William Bird, Judy Sandison, Naomi Webster and Farhana Goga, South Africa; María Jesús Ortiz, Spain; Kumudini Samuel and Maithree Wickramasinghe, Sri Lanka; Pius Nambiza Wanzala, Tanzania; Natasha Nuñez, Trinidad and Tobago; Lilián Celiberti, Uruguay; Sheila Gibbons and M. Junior Bridge, USA.

Teresita Hermano and Maria del Nevo of the World Association for Christian Communication supported me throughout the research and writing.

Terry Hermano first raised the idea of this book with me in 1997 and, for the next several years, waited for sufficient schedule space to be cleared. My thanks are due to Terry and to Louise Murray of Zed Books for their patience and encouragement.

Part I

Context

The Case for Monitoring and Advocacy

We were in uncharted territory. And taking on the Jamaican media was close to being a 'Mission Impossible'. But what needed to be done was clear every time Jamaican women switched on their television sets, read newspapers or listened to the radio. (Walker and Nicholson 1996: 96)

Since the 1960s the women's movement has been engaged in a systematic and constant critique of media institutions and their output. In a world in which the media increasingly provide the 'common ground' of information, symbols and ideas for most social groups, women's representation in the media helps to keep them in a place of relative powerlessness. The term 'symbolic annihilation', coined by George Gerbner in 1972, became a powerful and widely used metaphor to describe the ways in which media images render women invisible. This mediated invisibility is achieved not simply through the non-representation of women's points of view or perspectives on the world. When women are 'visible' in media content, the manner of their representation reflects the biases and assumptions of those who define the public – and therefore the media – agenda. More than twenty-five years after the international community began formally to recognise the scale of gender inequality in every aspect of life, and despite the adoption of many measures to redress gender imbalances, the power to define public and media agendas is still mainly a male privilege.

At a global level the United Nations International Decade for Women (1975–85) was an early catalyst for both activism and research. Since the late 1970s this work has revolved round two central axes: a critique of the ways in which media content projects women as objects rather than as active subjects, and an analysis of the institutional and social structures of power through which women are systematically marginalised within media organisations. The limitations of media content have often been linked to women's under-representation and lack of power within the media industry, and one strand of activism has been concerned with increasing women's numerical and decision-making presence in media outlets. The link between media content and the individuals who produce it is of course greatly attenuated by countless factors including institutional policies, professional values and advertisers' demands. So although in most countries more women are entering the media professions than ever before, it would be unreasonable to imagine that this will result in a radical transformation of media content. It is certainly possible to see the mark made by individual media women, as women, on certain types of output. But the fundamental patterns of media representation that preoccupied the women's movement of the 1970s remain relatively intact thirty years later.

What the Research Shows

It is difficult to assess accurately the extent to which these patterns are universal, and the extent to which they might be changing. Studies spanning more than one country are rare. In 1995 the first extensive cross-national quantitative study of women's portrayal in the media ever carried out – spanning newspapers, radio and television, and covering seventy-one countries – found that only 17 per cent of the world's news subjects (i.e. news-makers or interviewees in news stories) were women (MediaWatch 1995). The proportion of female news subjects was lowest in Asia (14 per cent) and highest in North America (27 per cent). Women were least likely to be news subjects in the fields of politics and government (7 per cent of all news subjects in this field) and economy/business (9 per cent). They were most likely to make the news in terms of health and social issues (33 per cent) and were relatively well represented in arts and entertainment news (31 per cent).

This Global Media Monitoring Project, as it became known, also looked at the extent to which the news stories covered ten broad issues which have been traditionally of 'particular concern to women' (for example, violence against women, women's work or health). Overall, just 11 per cent of stories dealt with such issues, and only 6 per cent in Latin America. There appear to be differences in the extent to which the three media – newspapers, radio and television – carry such stories. Stories covering an issue of particular concern to women were most likely to appear in newspapers (25 per cent of all newspaper stories in Central America and the Caribbean), and least likely to appear on television (just 2 per cent of television stories in Asia).

A second, more geographically limited, comparative study of prime-time television content was carried out in 1997 in Denmark, Finland, Germany, the Netherlands, Norway and Sweden (Eie 1998). Women were most often portrayed in roles equated with low social status: 47 per cent of 'ordinary citizens' and 37 per cent of victims were women, whereas men comprised the majority of politicians (72 per cent) and 'experts' (80 per cent). The distribution is striking, given that women's participation in decision-making and public life in these countries is high. Representation of women in the national parliaments, for example, ranges from 31 per cent in Germany to 43 per cent in Sweden (United Nations 2000).

Change in media portrayal is particularly difficult to chart, given the almost complete lack of longitudinal quantitative research in any country. However, it is possible to compare national studies that have used similar methodologies. For instance, a review of research into television advertisements carried out over twenty-five years in Africa, Australasia, Europe, Latin America and North America, did find clear patterns of gender stereotyping across all regions. This analysis concluded that there are small but stable and detectable trends in advertising portrayal, with women depicted less often as dependent or in a purely domestic setting. On the other hand, some gender differences 'seem impervious to change' – for example, women are almost always considerably younger than men, and men are typically shown as more authoritative and knowledgeable than women (Furnham and Mak 1999: 434).

Another review of research since 1990 – this time covering all media – in nineteen European countries concluded that the overall picture of gender portrayal is no longer monolithic stereotyping of the kind described in content studies of the 1970s and 1980s (European Commission 1999). In Latin America, too, some positive changes can be detected. For instance, a 1997 study of the Chilean daily press concluded that the period of total 'blacking out' of women is over. Women are more visible, but usually only as protagonists in spheres defined as important from a masculine perspective: politics, economics, the judiciary. And there is still a tendency to focus on the female magistrate as 'wife', or the parliamentarian as 'mother', rather than as professionals. Representation of men shows little sign of change, though the study reported occasional sightings of male politicians and sportspersons as people with private lives; they are no longer portrayed as the 'head of the family', but as men who make an affective contribution in the family sphere. This, note the researchers, 'is one of the rare illustrations of the small changes taking place in Chilean society' (Silva et al. 1998: 38).

Although greater diversity in images of women and men is recorded in contemporary studies, research also shows that new and highly sexist depictions of female characters now co-exist alongside more unconventional roles for women. For instance, studies of the effects on television images of the German unification process note a new emphasis on women as mothers and housewives, although in the former German Democratic Republic media portrayals generally depicted women as capable of combining paid employment and family life (Rinke 1994). Data from Central and Eastern Europe suggest that the transformations of 1989, and the adaptation of the media to market-oriented demands, have resulted in a new stereotype of women as sexual objects (Zarkov 1997; Zabelina 1996; Azhgikhina 1995).

Media representations in general, and of women in particular, are deeply embedded in political and economic contexts. For instance, in Asia the media in many countries have recently seen a spectacular transformation with the arrival of new commercial cable and satellite channels, and the privatisation of old state-run media has led to new market-oriented content. Current studies from this region highlight the tensions and conflicts that such changes introduce into representations of women. The findings are in line with much of the European data, indicating a greater diversity in women's roles and a move away from the subordinate housewife-mother image. Studies from India and Singapore point to the often contradictory ways in which the media and advertising are accommodating to women's multiple identities in contemporary society. Images of the 'new woman' as an independent consumer whose femininity remains intact, or as a hard-headed individualist whose feminine side must be sacrificed, illustrate new stereotypes of women whose 'femaleness' is always the core issue (Malhotra and Rogers 2000; Munshi 1998; Bajpai 1997; Lee 1998). Others note the emergence of new and highly sexualised images in the commercial media – for example, in Cambodia and Korea – images that are considered shocking and culturally intrusive (Palan 1995; Park 1997; see also *Changing Lenses* 1999: 20–1).

The numbers tell only a tiny part of the story. Behind them lies a power structure – social, political and economic – in which men are considered to be central and predominant. News values intertwine with political priorities to portray a particular view of what is important. For instance, despite China's declaration during the welcoming ceremony of the 1995 Fourth World Conference on Women that 'gender equality is a basic state policy', analysis of the official party newspapers in the four years following the FWCW has shown that this is the least mentioned basic state policy. In 1996 the *People's Daily* (circulation two million) published over 5,000 articles that mentioned education policy, 400 that mentioned environmental protection, and 221 that mentioned family planning. But only twenty articles mentioned equality between women and men (Yuan 1999).

Women, and their voices, may be considered unworthy of serious consideration even in media content that is destined specifically for them. In Tanzania, says one analyst, women's programmes still comprise topics of motherhood, housewifery and lectures from leaders who happen to visit villages or inspect projects. Yet 'I cannot remember listening to any one programme where a leader went to the village and had a dialogue with women villagers. Women are deprived of their right of expression' (Sanga 1996: 110). By extension, issues that are particularly central to women's lives come low down in the scale of what is regarded as newsworthy. At best, they may become 'news' in coverage around a particular event such as Women's Day.

Studies by the Media Monitoring Project in South Africa have shown that while coverage of women's issues increases dramatically in the run-up to National Women's Day (9 August), there is an equally drastic decline immediately afterwards. In 1998 a two-week study covering press and television found that this increase was largely attributable to 'special' newspaper supplements and features. But much of the reporting was about women's victim status in a crime-ridden society. Almost a quarter of the coverage portrayed women as helpless victims of crime or the judicial system. Another predominant image that emerged was that of the wife and mother, happily living within the limited confines of domesticity. So despite the increase in coverage around Women's Day, most of it failed to represent women as active participants in society. For example, the initiatives of civil society organisations were all but ignored. In fact, the overall conclusion from this study was that the sharp increase and decrease in stories around Women's Day, allied with the inadequacy of the reporting, served only to underline the marginalisation of women in society (Media Monitoring Project 1998b).

These kinds of data illustrate just how deeply embedded is the problem of women's representation in the media. It is not simply a matter of notching up a few percentage points in the share of women's time on air or in print. What is at stake is not just the number of women who appear in the media, but the weight of their voices. For instance, a 1997 study of news coverage of women in television, radio and print in Peru found that radio carried more news referring to women (36 per cent of all news). Yet in Peru – and in many other countries – this is the medium that is losing audiences and also influence in terms of setting agendas. The most important medium in Peru today is television, where only 9 per cent of the news referred to women, followed by print (13 per cent). The same study found that news on women was brief, in space or time, with little variety or originality in treatment. The impression given was that these stories are of little interest to the media (Pinilla 1997).

These findings, and those of countless other studies, illustrate clearly that despite the small shifts noted in retrospective analyses, by and large media content still reflects a masculine vision of the world and of what is important. The very fundamental nature of this vision means that women's representation in the media will not be improved by increasing the number of women journalists, or by getting rid of the worst excesses of sexism in advertising. What it actually requires is a wide-scale social and political transformation, in which women's rights – and women's right to communicate – are truly understood, respected and implemented both in society at large and by the media.

This is the starting point for media monitoring and advocacy. Whether or not a critical mass of women working in the media can make an imprint on media content is a secondary question to the need for wider and deeper social change. In any case, despite a widespread perception that the media are rapidly becoming 'feminised', in most countries this is still far from the truth. For instance, 51 per cent of people surveyed in Lima in 1997 thought there were about equal numbers of women and men working in television and 31 per cent thought there were actually more women than men. In fact, this same study showed that women held only about a quarter of jobs in television (Alfaro 1997). And although more women than ever before are entering the media industries in almost all world regions, in general the senior creative and decision-making positions seem likely to be a male preserve for decades to come (Gallagher 1995a). In the end, the crucial question is not who is telling the story but how the story is told. Media advocacy is based on the belief that the public can play a role in determining what stories are told, and how. According to the Centre for Media Freedom and Responsibility, a non-governmental organisation in the Philippines, 'It is not so much who is on top of the journalism totem pole that determines what kind of treatment women receive ... as the prevailing public attitude. Editors make decisions on what they feel the public want to read about or need to know' (Militante 1999: 106–7). The 'prevailing public attitude' is of course a rather fluid and evanescent criterion for editors to try to apply. But the mission of media monitoring and advocacy is to work with the public on defining and expressing that attitude, and to persuade the media to take account of it.

Approaches to Media Change

The nature and scale of women's historical marginalisation in the media, allied with the difficulty of establishing truly performative systems of accountability in an increasingly commercial media marketplace, mean that no single strategy can accomplish a great deal. Ideally, each approach must support and sustain the others. The goal of strengthening women's position within the media industries has already been touched upon. Some organisations of female media workers date back to the 1970s. But it was not until the 1980s that networks and associations of media women really began to flourish, and groups now exist in all regions of the world (Gallagher 1995a).

The main focus of these organisations is on overcoming obstacles to women's career development within the media, but most of them also share concerns about gender portrayal and the adequacy of media representations of women in the wider community.

Some women and media associations pursue these concerns through occasional research or discussion. For example, in 1999 Women in Journalism in the United Kingdom commissioned a study of how national newspapers use photographs of women (Carter et al. 1999). The survey found that out of 12,000 newspaper photographs analysed, women featured in just 30 per cent, compared with 69 per cent for men. Of the photos judged 'not relevant' to the story – i.e. just inserted to give the piece a 'lift' – 80 per cent were of women. Their professional contacts give many women's media associations leverage that other women's groups may not have, and this can be extremely important in focusing media attention on advocacy concerns. For example, Women in Journalism was able to stimulate widespread media coverage and debate when the findings of its study were released. Other women and media groupings like the Journalism & Women Symposium (JAWS) in the United States come together regularly to discuss not only issues of professional career development, but also to consider up-to-the-minute media topics and how their coverage can be enhanced. For instance, the theme for the 2000 JAWS symposium was images of women and girls – a discussion revolving round the depiction of hyper-thin models and how this may influence the self-image of women and girls.[1]

Several women and media associations are actually involved in monitoring activities at some level. For instance, the Zambian Media Women's Association (ZAMWA) has a media monitoring committee that observes the media and takes action when it feels there is cause for complaint. But all of its members are fully occupied with their own jobs, so it is difficult to follow up and see through the many cases that arise – not to mention trying to mobilise community activism to join in protests about objectionable content. During 1999 the monitoring committee was 'swamped by the number of issues that needed to be dealt with … However where we could we responded and got results.'[2] Irregularity and lack of resources for follow-through undermine the effectiveness of monitoring when it is tacked on in this way, though in some situations it is the only alternative available.

A second strategy, extensively used since the 1970s, has been the creation of women's alternative media. Frustrated by lack of access to the mainstream mass media, women have created their own newsletters, journals, radio and video productions. More recently the Internet has allowed the development of e-zines and even online women's newspapers.[3] Often criticised for speaking only to an already committed audience, many of these media have nevertheless given a voice to grassroots women who would never be heard in the mainstream. Through a system of international networking, they have also kept alive and expanded the debate about gender inequality both within activist circles and, increasingly, beyond these circles (Sreberny 1998).

One of the most important contributions of women's alternative media has been to provide space for serious reflection about the nature of women's exclusion from the mainstream. But during the 1990s some women activists – particularly in Asia and in Latin America – began to feel that this reflection had ceased to be productive, and that a new focus was needed. The Uruguayan feminist Lucy Garrido, long associated with the NGO and publication *Cotidiano Mujer*, summed this up in the mid-1990s by calling into question the feminist tendency to privilege the written word (in alternative publications) and to shy away from the image. In Uruguay, for example, figures showed that 45 per cent of people read a daily newspaper, 65 per cent listened to the radio, and 93 per cent watched television. With television overtaking all other media in terms of public outreach and influence, it was no longer possible to ignore it (Garrido 1996). Women activists had concentrated on criticising media content, creating a lack of trust and of interest on the part of media professionals. Worse still, their criticisms had demonstrated a lack of knowledge about how the media operate, their goals, their professional logic and language. Without that knowledge, activists' attempts to intervene could only be very limited.

Other Latin American activists such as Sur Profesionales in Chile were simultaneously thinking along the same lines. Their view was that interaction and dialogue between gender specialists and media professionals was the only way forward. For them, establishing a dialogue meant not simply trying to get certain issues or events covered in the media – the traditional feminist approach – but working to promote an entire perspective, a gender vision within the media.[4] While it did not necessarily mean putting aside women's own alternative media, which were 'absolutely ours', this did mean thinking about ways of reaching a wider public (Portugal and Torres 1996: 13). It represented a completely novel approach for most alternative media groups. One of the first steps taken by many of them was to monitor media content.

From Criticism to Dialogue

In October 1997, searching for elements on which to base detailed discussion with the Uruguayan mainstream media, Cotidiano Mujer monitored ten daily newspapers, 95 hours of prime-time television news across four channels, and 663 hours of radio news and current affairs programmes from five radio stations with the largest national audiences. The study, the first of its kind ever carried out in Uruguay, was an eye-opener even to Cotidiano Mujer. For years the organisation had been arranging meetings and events, as well as using its own publication and its radio programmes, to draw attention to women's portrayal in the media. For example, a 1993 seminar brought feminist activists and researchers together with journalists and advertising executives to discuss the role of the media and advertising in forming public opinion (Cotidiano Mujer 1993). Research was indeed presented at this and other similar events, but its rather academic nature – and perhaps also the formal conference setting of the presentation – meant that it did little to bridge the gap between activists and media professionals.

The much more down-to-earth monitoring study painted a devastating picture. 'We all assumed that we lived in a country where women had little access to the media, but we had no idea of the real dimensions of the problem' (Celiberti 1998: 1). Only 8 per cent of newspaper coverage, and 4 per cent of radio news, referred in any way to women. Coverage of issues that might have informed the public about aspects of women's status or women's human rights was minimal. For example, out of nineteen hours of radio news classified as dealing in some way or other with women, only five minutes in the entire month touched on the economy, education, science or women's rights. Most of the rest of the news covered crime, politics, sport or entertainment. In television news only one woman was interviewed for every seven men. For each hour that a woman journalist spoke on television, male journalists spoke for four. On radio, men were interviewed for 2,384 minutes, women for only 449 minutes – 15 per cent of the total time. Despite the differing political affiliations of the nineteen media, there were no important differences in the amount of space given to women. In fact, there was a serious lack of pluralism in the information sources used by all of the media. Even when it came to issues such as divorce, abortion or contraception, women's voices were not heard. It was as if there was no perception of women as actors in society, with different perspectives to offer from those of the usual official sources (Celiberti et al. 1998).

These findings, which called into question the media's credibility in terms of their mandate to reflect pluralism and balance, were at quite a different level of specificity from earlier generalised criticisms of role stereotyping or discriminatory portrayal of women. The results spoke of absences and imbalances in straightforward terms to which the media could – and did – respond. Meetings were held with editorial staffs, and several newspapers gave detailed coverage to the findings. A prime-time debate was organised on one of the radio stations. A prominent weekly news magazine agreed to give regular space to Cotidiano Mujer during the 1999 election campaign to ensure adequate coverage of women and women's issues. One of the most important current affairs programmes on radio appointed a woman to its staff for the first time. A workshop for thirty journalists was organised. For a small organisation like Cotidiano Mujer, the results were more than satisfying.

The 1997 study had built on their first monitoring experience as participants for Uruguay in the Global Media Monitoring Project of 1995. With partners from Argentina, Chile and Paraguay, they would go on to develop the model in a 1999 monitoring study by the Grupo de Comunicadoras del Sur (Torres 2000).[5] By 2000 it was possible to look back over five years and conclude that these monitoring experiences had helped to develop new social capacities and awareness which could be used to bring pressure on the media. 'We are more demanding about how we see women represented by the media, and journalists – both men and women – have embraced a discourse that is at least more politically correct.'[6] The data had enabled them to move beyond one-sided complaints to constructive dialogue with the media (Celiberti 1998).

Some Monitoring and Advocacy Models

The engagement of Cotidiano Mujer and other alternative women's organisations with the mainstream media was a phenomenon of the late 1990s. But the concept of gender media monitoring and advocacy goes back at least a decade earlier, when organisations like MediaWatch in Canada and Women's Media Watch in Jamaica decided there was need for a constant 'watch' on the media's portrayal of women, and also a channel through which people in the community could voice their views about media content and policy. Later, other organisations were established, each with its own particular emphasis; but the basic premise of all of them is that the creation of effective links between the media and their audiences will lead to more equitable and diverse media systems.

The models that follow encapsulate the range of activities carried out by most gender media monitoring and advocacy groups around the world. Some carry out regular, systematic research. For others, lack of resources makes this impossible and the option is for shorter 'campaign'-type exercises that catch public attention. The overall and defining characteristics of all these groups are to be found in a combination of media observation and follow-up action, allied with public education or media literacy initiatives of various kinds.

MediaWatch, Canada: public advocacy to transform the media environment MediaWatch was the first national organisation set up with the aim of eliminating sexism in media content. Its roots go back to the 1970s, when a growing body of research began to demonstrate pervasive under-representation and stereotyping of women in the Canadian media. Under pressure from the public, in 1979 the Canadian Radio-television and Telecommunications Commission (CRTC) – the agency responsible for broadcasting regulation – convened a task force on sex-role stereotyping in the broadcast media. In 1981 the task force published its report *Images of Women*, containing twenty recommendations to the CRTC, the Canadian Broadcasting Corporation (CBC), private broadcasters, advertisers, the government and the public. In the same year MediaWatch was established with a mandate to work for the necessary changes. Its founding members knew that 'change would come neither quickly, nor easily' (MediaWatch 1993a: 6). Twenty years later MediaWatch is still there, working to 'trans-form the media environment from one in which women are either invisible or stereotyped, to one in which women are realistically portrayed in all their physical, economic, racial and cultural diversity' (MediaWatch 2000: 1).

MediaWatch promotes change through a vast spread of activities, grouped into three broad programmes. The public advocacy programme encourages the general public to take an active part in shaping their media environment. On the one hand, it helps consumers to comment effectively on media content. On the other, acting on behalf of the public, MediaWatch itself intervenes with industry and regulatory bodies, pressuring them to meet their obligations under existing guidelines and regulations on gender portrayal. The education programme helps to make people more aware of how the media operate, and aims to develop media literacy and critical awareness. The research programme commissions regular studies of both media content and audience opinion, and the results are used to lobby the media industry. Although its activities approach the need for media change in different ways, MediaWatch has always operated on the premise that it is ordinary citizens themselves who are the agents of change. Throughout most of its history, the organisation's main effort has been directed to grassroots education and action, its role that of 'facilitating consumers to advocate on their own behalf and to provide leadership in terms of research and analysis'.[7]

Tanzania Media Women's Association: empowering women through media mobilisation   The Tanzania Media Women's Association (TAM–WA) was established in 1987 by twelve women journalists. By 2000 TAMWA had a membership of about 200, of whom 80 per cent were media practitioners. TAMWA has always differed from most women's media associations, whose aims tend to centre on strengthening women's participation in the media industry. From the beginning TAMWA's principal goal has been to use the mainstream media to highlight the issues that prevent women's full and equal participation in all spheres of life. The organisation's point of departure is women's low status in society. This it sees as the root of all other problems. So TAMWA's media advocacy and lobbying has two strands. First it advocates for policy and legal changes that will favour the promotion of women's human rights. For instance, in recent years the association has focused much energy on various aspects of gender-based violence, lobbying for changes in planned and existing legislation. Then it works to increase and improve coverage of these issues in the mainstream media.

TAMWA uses a strategy it calls 'Bang Style' – mobilising its own members and other media practitioners so that a particular topic is covered in most media outlets at the same time. In 1998, for example, 233 stories were published or broadcast on issues around the newly adopted Sexual Offences Act, covering rape, female genital mutilation, sexual exploitation of children, sexual harassment and incest. The association also runs gender-sensitisation programmes to enhance journalistic skills in this kind of coverage. And it monitors the media to keep track of the amount of coverage devoted to its chosen issues (TAMWA 1999, 2000).

Jamaica, Women's Media Watch: challenging sexism and violence in the media Women's Media Watch (Jamaica) evolved out of a 1987 meeting of thirty-four women's organisations in the country who were concerned about the escalating problem of violence against women. As the women discussed the issues and possible long-term solutions, the role of the media surfaced again and again. Women's Media Watch was born, with the twin objectives of raising public awareness about sexual and domestic violence in Jamaican society and changing the portrayal of women and men in the media as one way of reducing violence against women. The focus is therefore not exclusively on violence in the media, but on the entire spectrum of media representations that limit, demean or degrade women. The group's starting point is a belief that consistent gender stereotyping influences both social perceptions and self-images of women and men, and plays a role in normalising violence against women.

From the outset, Women's Media Watch has had a very strong community outreach and public education programme. It organises interactive workshops in urban, rural and inner-city areas for schools, youth clubs, church groups and women's associations. Videos and other audio-visual materials have been produced as resource packages for these workshops. A more formal part of its education programme is the teaching of courses on gender and media for tertiary-level students. Lobbying and advocacy has been the other main strategy. Initially this revolved round letter writing, meetings with members of the advertising and media industries, media appearances and interviews. But as its experience and reputation have grown, Women's Media Watch has been able to focus more of its effort on building a permanent interface with mainstream media and contributing to policy debates. Still a tiny organisation, Women's Media Watch has a high profile in the Caribbean media advocacy sphere. It has worked with women in Trinidad and Tobago and in Barbados to set up media watch groups in those countries, and has contributed to gender mainstreaming training for IPS (InterPress Third World News Agency) journalists in the Caribbean.[8]

India, Centre for Advocacy and Research: a bridge between citizens and media The Centre for Advocacy and Research began life in 1992 as the Media Advocacy Group (MAG). It set out to bridge a gap between two constituencies that at the time were in discord. On the one hand women activists were critical of the media's portrayal of women and women's issues. On the other many media practitioners, although sympathetic to women's issues and concerns, felt the activists were unrealistic and unstrategic in their dealings with the media. MAG's mission was to equip citizens to voice their concerns in ways that would be listened to by the media, and to persuade media producers and policy-makers that there was a case to be answered in terms of their poor representation of women and other disadvantaged groups in media content. MAG was established at a time of radical transformation in the media landscape of India. Between 1990 and 2000 the country's media system developed from a single state-run television network into a forty-channel television environment, dominated by private media companies. By the late 1990s in both urban and rural areas television surpassed print and radio in terms of reach and usage. By 1997 31 per cent of households had cable and satellite television, and most large villages were said to have cable connections (Viswanath and Karan 2000). This phenomenally rapid growth in commercial television with its soaps, serials, films and pervasive advertising, allied to research showing that, as in many countries, women were heavier viewers than men (see Sinha 1996), made television the obvious target for MAG's activities.

Early studies convinced the group that monitoring data could be made more powerful and pertinent if backed up by feedback from viewers. Work with audiences became one of the group's major activities, resulting in the formation of viewers' forums in three cities in 1995. The initial objective, to document viewer habits and preferences, broadened into the much wider goal of building media literacy and public participation in media discussion. A Women and Media Network, spanning four cities, was also developed to

foster co-ordinated media advocacy on issues such as political representation, violence and trafficking, reproductive rights and health. The other
task of the network was to lobby at a national level on media policy issues.
In 1998 the group became formally registered in its present name, the
Centre for Advocacy and Research (CFAR).[9]

**South Africa, Women's Media Watch: bringing diversity into the
mainstream** Women's Media Watch (South Africa) grew out of a
community-based media education and production project set up during
the apartheid years to train communities in the production of graphic
media. When Women's Media Watch was established by its parent organisation Mediaworks in 1995, that grounding in creative protest was clear
in its early eye-catching campaigns against sexism and racism in the South
African media. WMW aims to create communication access for the least
heard women. It has an exceptionally diverse membership base spanning
journalists, artists, independent film-makers, sex-workers, parliamentarians,
community workers, women with disabilities, academics and researchers,
gay rights activists, domestic workers, women working in rape and crisis
centres, youth activists and women who have lived on the streets. Membership diversity is a deliberate goal, a means of bringing the issue of media
representation on to the agendas of all conceivable interest groups in
society, rather than leaving it in the hands of the most obvious ones. The
organisation's aims are also broad, challenging not just sexism but also
racism, classism and homophobia in the media.

All of the work of Women's Media Watch revolves around advocacy
and change, pursued via several different strategies. The advocacy and
activism strand creates channels of communication between citizens and
the media. WMW takes up complaints, lobbies for gender-sensitive media
codes and guidelines, and campaigns on specific issues such the role of the
media in relation to violence against women. The media production strand
includes publishing an information-packed monthly newsletter, creating
posters, producing occasional radio series. In 1999 the group moved into
video production. The consultancy and education strand runs workshops
for WMW members on gender and media issues, and provides gender and
diversity training for media professionals. Media monitoring is the most
recent strand, established because of a growing felt need for empirical data
to support the group's advocacy work.[10]

**Australia, National Women's Media Centre: a focus and a forum for
nation-wide activism** The National Women's Media Centre was established in 1994 to provide a national focal point for the issue of women's
portrayal in the media, following several years of intense government-

initiated activity. The Australian federal government had established a national working party on the portrayal of women in the media in 1989, with a specific focus on advertising. The working party was reconvened in 1991 with broadened terms of reference to include the portrayal of women more generally. During its four years of operation it concentrated on working with the industry to achieve a more realistic portrayal of women in the media. It sponsored research, developed information kits and packages, published a complaints brochure, made a submission on the Broadcasting Services Bill, organised workshops. Its concluding activity was a National Forum on Women in the Media at which it launched a media information kit, aimed at industry members working at the day-to-day decision-making level and including the first contemporary national survey of Australian print and television news.

With the ending of the national working party, the issue of women's portrayal in the media dropped from the government's priority agenda. To fill the void left by this abrupt change of policy, a member of the working party created the National Women's Media Centre. The NWMC co-ordinates and facilitates the activities of women and women's groups concerned about gender portrayal in the media. It advocates for media guidelines and regulation, promotes community education, provides training support for women interested in media portrayal, and acts as a clearing house for information and research. The NWMC has branches in almost all states throughout Australia.[11]

Croatia, B.a.B.e: promoting women's rights in and through the media

B.a.B.e (Be Active, Be Emancipated) is a women's human rights group. It was formed in 1994 by women working at the Women's War Victim Centre, who believed that serious lobbying and advocacy for women's human rights was essential to change women's position in Croatian society. War, an authoritarian regime, and a conservative religious bloc had created an environment in which women's only legitimate place seemed to be in the home.[12] B.a.B.e's major goal is to bring women into positions of power; whether in politics itself, or in other important areas such as the economy, education and the media. At an early stage the group recognised that without the media such an effort would be useless, and B.a.B.e's women and media project started in 1996. The two-pronged project aims both to use the media to further the goal of empowering women, and to change the media by encouraging a more diversified picture of women and women's potential.

B.a.B.e started by monitoring news (B.a.B.e 1998) and then advertisements and newspaper photographs (B.a.B.e 1999). The reports of this work – the first of its kind in Croatia – were distributed to all media organisations, women's groups and members of parliament. They caught the attention of both the public and the media, and for the first time women's portrayal in the media was a subject of debate in the country. B.a.B.e runs media literacy seminars for female and male journalists, organises street protests, and produces videos and television publicity spots. Monitoring of special areas, covering media portrayal of gays and lesbians and the portrayal of women in school textbooks, has been carried out to broaden the picture of how gender stereotypes are produced and reproduced in Croatian society. Backed up with more research, B.a.B.e's media team believes it is better equipped for advocacy.[13]

Feminist Policing or a Struggle for Human Rights?

> The struggle against sexism is a human rights issue. It is not an issue of morality or censorship. (MediaWatch, Canada, brochure)

When the Media Advocacy Group (now known as the Centre for Advocacy and Research) published a study of public reaction to portrayals of sex and violence in Indian film and television (Media Advocacy Group 1994a), there was a huge outcry in the press. Articles accused the group of encouraging curtailment of free speech. MAG found itself aligned with the pro-censorship lobby, attacked for proposing solutions which 'leave space only for the representation of a passionless, sexless female cyborg on the screen'.[14] The group responded that at no point had it advocated more stringent censorship. On the contrary, the study suggested that programming should be made sensitive to viewers' needs. Freedom of expression, it argued, is often no more than freedom of privilege, or of those who have access:

> If television in India began to project sado-masochistic, fascist, racist, casteist images, would we still condone these under the label of freedom of expression? Our stand is that to take an either/or stance here … is simplistic. Rather, what is important is to take account … of audience feedback (a much neglected area in India) and build the best we can on the basis of that …
>
> The concern we bring to this exercise … is not a concern for censorship or morality. It is a concern … for a just and equitable society, and an open and inclusive media.[15]

In the name of freedom of speech, the media claim the right to represent women as they wish. In the name of claiming the right to fair portrayal, women often find themselves denounced as 'feminist police'. Like women's groups in many countries, B.a.B.e fights this double standard in Croatia on a daily basis. 'Bare breasts are used to sell everything, be it beer, jeans, kitchen faucets, cars, medicine, juice. Yet when we try to improve the media, take out sexism, the women at B.a.B.e are regularly ridiculed and called fanatics or extremists.'[16] In 1999 the most popular daily newspaper *Vecernji list* (Evening Journal) attacked two feminists for statements they made on a television show. The journalist went on to say that all feminists are lesbians, communists, Yugo-nostalgic betrayers of Croatia, anti-women pretending to fight for the rights of other 'real' women. Supported by B.a.B.e and other NGOs, one of the attacked feminists sued him. In mid-2000 the case was being heard by the Croatian court.[17]

The situation is complicated by the fact that women advocating media change may indeed find themselves temporarily in the company of some unlikely and unwelcome travellers. Whether it is conservative groups whose aim is to limit sexual expression, or authoritarian regimes that seek to censor media criticism, women striving for genuine diversity in the media must frequently side-step false allies. The shadowy presence of such unwanted company is just one of the things that can make it extraordinarily difficult to explain to media practitioners that feminist advocacy and monitoring have nothing to do with censorship, but everything to do with freedom.

Because the present social and legislative structures do not actually reflect feminist perspectives, when women speak out on controversial and vexatious issues such as pornography, mainstream media practices and interpretations find it difficult to accept that women are not speaking from within the traditional 'conservative' framework. So feminists tend to get pushed into the existing categories with which media people are more familiar. In 1998 Women's Media Watch (South Africa) organised a workshop on pornography which, after the ending of apartheid and the abolition of censorship, had flooded into the country. The workshop aimed to find a WMW position or point of view on the subject. Participants brought and shared whatever pornography they had or could borrow from friends. One of the magazines brought to the workshop was a current edition of *Hustler*. An article titled 'Hustler's Celebrity Urinal Mint' featured the face of Health Minister Nkosazana Zuma inset into the bowl of a men's urinal. The minister had recently announced a decision to regulate smoking in public places. *Hustler's* text was racist, sexist and abusive: 'She looks like the underpaid domestic worker most of us grew up with, but sadly, [she] escaped this degradation during the dark years of apartheid.' Now Dr Zuma was demonstrating her 'inbred nanny skills' by trying to interfere with the rights of smokers. Readers were urged to cut out the picture of the minister's 'sickening' face, set it over the urinal at their workplace and urinate on it.[18]

The viciousness of the *Hustler* attack sparked off a discussion about the political and economic interests that are common to the tobacco industry, the porn industry and the mainstream media. The workshop participants decided that it would be in the interest of freedom of expression to launch a debate about the links between business interests and pornography, and the place of pornography in society.[19] WMW distributed a press release drawing attention to these questions. It received wide coverage in the press, radio and local television, but some of the coverage was misleading and seemed deliberately to misrepresent the group's position. In other cases, journalists chose to make light of the issue. For WMW it was a lesson on the difficulty of getting the mainstream media to represent a feminist viewpoint fairly.

Other lessons were learned when WMW called on the Film and Publication Board to withdraw the edition of *Hustler* 'on the grounds of hate-speech, racism, classism and what amounted to an incitement to cause harm' in the joke about the minister. It emerged that the current legislation did not empower the board to act on hate-speech. The only grounds on which it could withdraw the publication were that it contained too much explicit sex, which was not at all the objection made by WMW.[20] Subsequently, WMW lobbied for changes to the legislation. But the episode was a good example of the struggle faced by media advocates who want to challenge mainstream media definitions of freedom of speech. When the only ground on which objectionable material can be opposed is 'explicit sex', feminists are caught between a rock and a hard place. They can either drop the case or risk being lumped together with conservative groups whose views may be diametrically opposed to their own.

One of the biggest challenges for media advocates is to make clear what lies behind the concept of fair and diverse media portrayal, to explain that it is not just a matter of substituting a 'positive' image for a 'negative' one, however these might be defined. Media people have to grasp the complex problems and limitations in typical media representations of gender, to understand that these are deeply embedded social practices and interpretations, and the part that they themselves play in constructing those representations. Development of this awareness requires dialogue and debate with media critics and activists. To enter into that dialogue, advocates themselves need to understand the language and priorities of the media. They need to be able to talk to media people in terms that resonate, that connect with the routines and practices of media industries. Ideally they need to bring to the debate more than just their own opinions. Facts and figures are the staple food of journalists and programme-makers. In discussions about what is wrong with, or missing from, the pictures of the world we get from media content, hard data – together with concrete examples – will reach media professionals with an immediacy never achieved by theory or abstract argument. This is what media monitoring and advocacy is about.

Notes

1. Information from JAWS website: www.jaws.org

2. Nakatiwa Mulikita, United Nations WomenWatch online consultation on women and the media, 8 December 1999.

3. Accounts of many important women's alternative media initiatives can be found in Riaño (ed.) 1994; Allen et al. (eds) 1996; Portugal and Torres (eds) 1996; Suárez 2000.

4. Uca Silva, personal communication, July 2000; and 'Marco teorico del proyecto Comunicación y Género', 1997.

5. The Grupo de Comunicadoras del Sur (Group of Women Communicators in the Southern Cone) was established in 1997. Its members – from Argentina, Bolivia, Brazil, Chile, Paraguay and Uruguay – reflect the membership of Mercosur, the Common Market of the South. The Grupo de Comunicadoras del Sur is co-ordinated by Isis Internacional, based in Chile.

6. Lilián Celiberti, personal communication, July 2000.

7. Melanie Cishecki, personal communication, July 2000.

8. Information from MediaWatch reports, and Hilary Nicholson, personal communication.

9. Information from MAG and CFAR reports, and Akhila Sivadas and Anuradha Mukherjee, personal communication.

10. Information from Women's Media Watch reports, and Gabrielle Le Roux, personal communication.

11. Information from National Women's Media Centre website, and Helen Leonard, personal communication.

12. When Croatia submitted its first report to the United Nations Committee on the Elimination of Discrimination against Women in 1998, the committee expressed particular concern about this situation (para. 101), and noted 'the need for measures to eliminate stereotypes that restrict women's role to that of mothers and caregivers' (para. 97). Report of the Committee on the Elimination of Discrimination against Women (A/53/38/Rev.1), New York: United Nations, 1998.

13. Information from B.a.B.e reports and website, and Sanja Sarnavka, personal communication.

14. For example, Shohini Ghosh and Ratna Kapur, 'The violence of censoring', *The Hindu*, May 1994.

15. Akhila Sivadas and Urvashi Butalia, 'Airing differences', *The Hindu*, May 1994.

16. Kristina Mihalec, United Nations WomenWatch online consultation on women and the media, 15 November 1999.

17. Sanja Sarnavka, personal communication, July 2000.

18. *Hustler* seems to lack imagination in its campaigns against women in power. It used a very similar approach in its attack on Canadian Heritage Minister Sheila Copps

in 1999 when she questioned the magazine's contents. MediaWatch news release, 'Media Watch out-take awards highlight memorable media portrayals of 1999'.

19. 'Workshop on pornography', *Women's Media Watch Newsletter*, No. 9, 1998: 4-6.

20. 'Women's Media Watch takes on *Hustler*', *Women's Media Watch Newsletter*, No. 10, 1998: 2–4.

2

Catalysts for Monitoring and Action

Although gender monitoring and advocacy groups have existed in several parts of the world since the 1980s, it was not until the 1990s that the potential of the approach became widely recognised and put to use. Several factors contributed to this development. The first and over-arching circumstance was the transformation brought about by changes in the global media system.

Media Trends

What took place in the Philippines in the last decade mirrors what has taken place in many other countries as the market for television programmes is opened up to increased competition, both locally and globally. As the rivalry intensifies, networks do battle by aiming for the lowest common denominator of public taste. As the public becomes bombarded by 'sexy' programming, the networks respond by providing even more titillation: more and more pieces of clothing are taken off, gorier and gorier crimes are shown. (Coronel 1998: 26–7)

As the spread of satellite communication introduced previously unimaginable numbers of channels into many countries, the enormous power of the media to influence ideas and behaviour at all levels of society became fully apparent. During the early years of the international women's movement, media issues had been regarded as of secondary importance to the cardinal problems of poverty, health and education for women. But by the early 1990s, in most regions of the world the media could no longer be dismissed as an elite irrelevance. In many countries media systems had been founded with a mission to educate and inform citizens in the context of social development. But in the post-1989 world order, the acquiescence of governments in the ideology of the free market and deregulation meant that media fast became recognised as potential sources of advertising revenue. These developments had enormous implications for the kinds of content audiences could expect from the media and the kinds of pressure that citizens' groups could exercise.

South Korea is a fairly typical illustration of the profound and rapid changes that took place in many countries in Asia during the 1990s. Until 1990 the country had just two public broadcasting networks, KBS and MBC. Deregulation of the broadcasting industry began with the amendment of the Broadcast Act in April 1990. The first private commercial network, SBS, received a licence in December 1990. The introduction of cable television and local private stations in 1995, satellite broadcasting in 1996, and the removal of restrictions on foreign investment in 1999 meant that by 2000 Korean viewers had access to about forty-five television channels including six foreign satellite networks. In 2001 Korea introduced digital broadcasting, with the potential for hundreds of new channels. In the space of a decade, broadcasting had become extremely commercialised with entertainment programming, especially mini-drama and music variety programmes, leading the change.

South Korea has a strong tradition of citizens' groups, such as the Audience Awareness Movement (AAM), that have been active in monitoring broadcasting since the mid-1980s. To mollify these critics, the television networks promised an end to ratings competition and a reduction in entertainment programmes. However 'they have never implemented these promises in concrete form' (Heo et al. 2000: 625). In fact, the decrease in advertising revenue that followed Korea's economic crisis in 1997 created even more commercialised programming with networks attempting to attract advertisers. In this environment the networks introduced more low-cost programmes such as talk shows, news magazines and situation comedies. These very swift changes in the traditional pattern of broadcasting presented completely new issues for women. The overt commodification of female sexuality, in a country where sexual activity has traditionally happened behind closed doors while the public discourse maintained a high degree of moral austerity, created a situation that was extremely problematic and difficult to confront. Because there was no precedent for activism on these matters, women had to look for new arguments and strategies (Park 1997).

Women have always been a big selling point for the commercial media around the world. The rapidity with which commercialism has taken hold in previously strictly controlled media systems has introduced quite new images and aspirations for women in society. There are both positive and negative sides to this. In Tanzania since 1990 there has been a proliferation of newspapers, magazines and periodicals. For the first time Tanzanians are now exposed to views, opinions and commentaries other than those of the dominant ruling class. The down side is that as newspapers vie for readers, sensationalism and unverified news have become commonplace. In this situation women have suffered most as they are usually the subject of sensational reporting. Because newspaper sales are all-important, 'gender sensitivity has often been sacrificed' (Mtambalike 1996: 135). In China, too, the commercial media have helped to de-politicise the news traditionally presented by established party organs, offering audiences a different, more entertaining type of information. And indeed from the perspective of gender, analysis shows that the commercial media pay more attention to women and women's issues than has been true of the established media channels. But again there is a tendency to sensationalise the portrayal of women as victims and passive objects, and many articles are 'saturated with details of lurid and unnecessary violence and sex' (Yuan 1999: 4).

As state-run media cede control to commercial interests, there are new dilemmas for media activists. The Philippines is a case in point. Under the government of President Fidel Ramos, Philippine media were opened to foreign investment. Today, the owners of Philippine media and telecommunications have alliances with European, Japanese, American, Taiwanese, Hong Kong, Singaporean, Indonesian and Malaysian business firms. The main motivation of these media owners is market share and profit (Militante 1999: 105). What is the prospect for advocacy in this scenario? In the Philippines women were in the forefront of the alternative media and of the movement for general change during the tenure of Ferdinand Marcos. But according to Anna Leah Sarabia of Women's Media Circle, a group producing radio and television programmes, these same women now find it extremely difficult to access either government or commercial broadcasting outlets. 'We do not sell products and lifestyles of the rich and famous, we aren't telling people how great our mostly male political leaders are, so how do small groups like the WMC manage to land one or two hours a week on mainstream television and radio networks that are controlled by powerful men who would rather see women silent and demure?' (Sarabia 1996: 76).

The struggle has indeed become more complicated on all fronts. In their study of the coverage of women's issues in the Indian press, Joseph and Sharma (1994) concluded that the presence of women (and of some gender-sensitive men) had made a difference to the coverage of these issues in a number of Indian publications. But with more recent trends in the market-driven, consumer-oriented media, those contributions are being eroded. While in the 1970s and 1980s many journalists kept in close touch with grassroots movements and organisations, 'today journalists who take strong positions on issues of justice risk derision, if not marginalisation. They are often referred to as crusading, campaigning or "committed journalists" or even "Mother Teresas of the press"' (Joseph 2000: 285). So the paradox is that, as more women enter the media profession, proprietors and managements with profit-oriented agendas are exercising more control than ever on editorial matters, making it difficult for journalists of either gender to swim against the tide.

With this move towards commercialism across the media industries, systems of accountability are also bound to change. Principles of ethics and equality, however tenuously the public or state-run media might have adhered to them, are increasingly put to one side as the media attend to the priorities of the advertisers that provide their revenue. This dependence on advertising not only changes the relationship between media and audiences, but acts as a straitjacket on the media themselves. For instance, in mid-1999 Israel's commercial television network, Channel 2, placed an announcement in the press to say that it was seeking views on how to deal with violence in the media and with offensive advertising. This followed a series of complaints about objectionable advertisements on the channel. Channel 2 contacted the Israel Women's Network (IWN), which had spearheaded the complaints, to say that they intended to organise a conference on advertising and media content in general. But a year later nothing had come of this and IWN members closely connected with the channel reported that the plans had been abandoned in the face of pressure from important advertisers.[1]

These developments change the terrain on which many media activists have traditionally operated. The move from public service to market-driven business means that the media are much less responsive to citizens. But they must listen to consumers. This means working to mobilise communities and organising consumer political action. It means that the ability of the general public to understand, critique and analyse media content has become critically important.

Women's Networking and the Global Media Monitoring Project

Against this background of dramatic shifts in the nature and outreach of media channels, the international women's movement was preparing for the United Nations Fourth World Conference on Women (FWCW) that would take place in Beijing in 1995. At regional and international meetings held to plan for the conference, there was widespread agreement on the need to push for recognition of media issues in the Platform for Action to be adopted in Beijing. Though the media had barely been mentioned in the strategy documents of the first three UN conferences on women, there was by now a strong sense of urgency about the issues raised by recent media developments and a conviction that this area could no longer be neglected internationally.

One of the key pre-Beijing events was an international conference, 'Women Empowering Communication', held in early 1994 in Bangkok. The event was organised by the World Association for Christian Communication (WACC) in collaboration with two women's media networks, Isis International and the International Women's Tribune Centre. It was a unique gathering in that it brought together 400 feminist activists, researchers and media professionals from around the world, and the mix of perspectives was to prove highly effective. The Bangkok Declaration adopted by conference participants outlined a detailed series of measures to address all major aspects of women's relationship to the media. This document played an important part in subsequent regional and international discussions in the lead-up to Beijing, and many of its elements were included in the eventual Beijing Platform for Action.

Apart from the Bangkok Declaration itself, the conference agreed on a number of projects and actions aimed at bringing issues of media accountability to the forefront of the debate on gender inequalities. One of these was to become known as the Global Media Monitoring Project (GMMP). The plan was to monitor the news on television, radio and in newspapers on one 'ordinary' day, and to release the results to coincide with the Fourth World Conference on Women to be held in Beijing. MediaWatch (Canada) agreed to come up with a set of straightforward quantitative measures of media content that could be universally used and that would provide useful research data as well as documentation for lobbying and advocacy work. After a huge networking effort to identify potential participants, groups in seventy-one countries around the world took part in the first-ever global media monitoring day: 18 January 1995.

The significance of this project was enormous. The 1995 Global Media Monitoring Project gave women a tool with which to scrutinise their media in a systematic way, and a means of documenting gender bias and exclusion. The project was unprecedented not simply in terms of its geographical scope, but also in its execution. From teachers and researchers, to activists and lobbyists, to journalists and other media professionals – some with considerable research experience, others with none – groups and individuals from a wide spectrum of backgrounds contributed to the data collection. In some countries disparate groups co-operated for the first time, united by concern about the portrayal of women in their national media. The process of monitoring their news media proved an eye-opening, educational experience for many of those involved. For some it created a new awareness of the pervasiveness of gender stereotyping. For others it provided concrete evidence to support long-held personal opinions (see Gallagher 1999).

Perhaps most important of all, the GMMP was a highly successful actualisation of the links that media monitoring presupposes between research, informed citizenship and action. Gloria Bonder, co-ordinator of the monitoring effort in Latin America, summed this up:

> The results were not surprising, but the insight was that monitoring is a wonderful technique and it's easy enough that we can all do it. The most important insight is that it is necessary and important for women's organizations to start working in citizens' rights in Latin America. And monitoring is a project on the political side, because it's not just the collecting of data – it's the process of involving the audience in the process of acting to change women's images in the media. We have discussed and complained in the past, but this systematic methodology provides proof of the problem, and involves people in education and citizens' rights. (Tindal, n.d.: 19)

Countless comments from those involved in the GMMP showed that the experience had indeed provoked new thinking. When media practitioners themselves were involved in monitoring – as they were in the GMMP – the impact could be considerable. In France the data collection was done by the Association of Women Journalists. Afterwards the co-ordinator, Monique Trancart, reflected that 'the work has already been worthwhile for us. It has changed the way we "read" the media ... and it will help us to show other journalists how and why things need to change' (Trancart 1997: 149). The Association of Women Journalists went on to use the GMMP methodology for a more elaborate study of the French media (Trancart 1999). Indeed, a very great deal of the monitoring carried out by media advocacy groups since 1995 has built on their experience gained in that first global project. Five years later, seventy countries were to take part in a second Global Media Monitoring Project organized by the WACC. Fifty-two of the countries that monitored their news media on 18 February 2000 were part of the original milestone study – a sign that the enthusiasm provoked by the first GMMP was still alive, and that the approach had proven its usefulness in generating data and documentation for effective media advocacy.

Beijing and the Culture of Monitoring

By the time the GMMP results were launched at the Beijing FWCW in September 1995, the media had indeed found a place on the international women's agenda. Intensive lobbying – especially in Asia and Latin America, regions that had been particularly affected by the media trends of the early 1990s – helped to ensure this. In the Platform for Action the media were identified as one of the twelve 'critical areas of concern' in which priority action was needed for the advancement and empowerment of women. In a set of thirty-two recommendations, the Platform addressed ways of increasing women's participation in the media and of promoting a balanced media portrayal of women. Although there was quite a lot of overlap and repetition between the proposals, they were surprisingly comprehensive and specific. As a package of measures, they provided the basis for a reasonably coherent approach to many of the problems long since identified by media advocates.[2]

Monitoring and advocacy were recognised as important strategies in the Platform for Action, specifically in relation to the media but also more generally in terms of holding governments accountable to the commitments they had made at Beijing. In fact, in the years after 1995 an entire monitoring 'culture' developed as the United Nations – particularly through its Division for the Advancement of Women (DAW) and the United Nations Fund for Women's Development (UNIFEM) – encouraged women's organisations to monitor, lobby and network to ensure implementation of the Beijing recommendations. After Beijing UN-DAW and UNIFEM set up an Internet gateway site known as WomenWatch to help women keep in touch with news, research and meetings on the follow-up to Beijing. As part of the preparation for the Beijing review conference in 2000, in addition to the usual government reports NGOs were invited to submit their own alternative assessments of developments since 1995, and both the official and the alternative reports were published on the WomenWatch website. WomenWatch helped to finance an international information, communication and media network known as WomenAction 2000, with a special focus on women and media, whose mandate was to ensure maximum NGO involvement in the Beijing review process. In late 1999 WomenAction 2000 moderated an online discussion on Women and Media – one of a series organised by WomenWatch covering all twelve 'critical areas of concern' identified in the Beijing Platform for Action. On the basis of this and other information provided by NGOs around the world, WomenAction 2000 produced an alternative report on progress in implementing the media recommendations of the Beijing Platform.[3]

All this activity contributed to an environment in which media monitoring by women's organisations was not just encouraged, but was often financially supported, as part of the Beijing follow-up. In that sense the Beijing process helped to promote a context in which monitoring could be presented as a means of pressing for accountability rather than as an attempt to sanction or control. The Fourth World Conference on Women had many other repercussions. For all kinds of reasons it received massive media coverage – twice as much as the combined coverage for all three previous UN women's conferences (Gallagher 2000). Few people involved in governmental and non-governmental circles around the world could have been unaware of Beijing, the issues that were debated there, and the hotly contested Platform for Action that it finally produced. This gave women's groups considerable leverage to push for measures to support their own initiatives within a framework of the follow-up to Beijing (Garrido 1996: 135).

In terms of media monitoring and advocacy, one of the swiftest reactions came within China itself. Just before the Fourth World Conference on Women (FWCW), the Chinese government promulgated a Programme for the Development of Chinese Women (1995–96). Paragraph 11 called on the media to focus public attention on women's social contribution, and on women's equal rights and status; to curb media portrayals that insulted or denigrated women; and to work towards transformation of discriminatory attitudes against women in society at large. This provided a useful context, though in the months after the FWCW it became clear that no government initiatives were planned to implement the programme.

At the same time, the FWCW introduced two new concepts into the public domain in China: NGO and gender. 'In Chinese political jargon, there were only the government and anti-government organs; if someone were to talk about "non-government" it would be thought of as some sort of anti-government organ. Now, for the first time, non-governmental organisations were being accepted by the authorities and by the public' (Yuan 1999: 6). This opened a new space for women's groups in China. During the lengthy preparations for the FWCW, and in the intensive discussions during the conference itself, constant references to gender-based indicators, gender-based discrimination and gender-based inequalities were another eye-opener for Chinese women. According to the orthodox ideology of the Chinese Communist Party, men and women were guaranteed equal rights and treatment. But with no gender-based analysis of the male-dominated, hierarchical structure of the party, women's rights to knowledge and expression were never actually explored or acknowledged. 'Now, after the long-time legacy of integrating women's interests into the party-state's agenda, women in China started to claim their own needs and rights separately' (Yuan 1999: 8). Media women, influenced by the new ideas generated at the FWCW, were among the first to realise their own gender interests.

In March 1996 China's first gender media monitoring group was established. Known as the Media Monitor Network for Women, it has members from *China Women's News* (a national daily newspaper directed by the All China Women's Federation), the Institute of Journalism and Communication, the Institute of Women's Studies and various major media organisations. The network has status and credibility and its connection with *China Women's News* gives it nation-wide outreach. One of the group's first activities was to survey the coverage of women in the main pages of eight major newspapers. Using the method followed in the 1995 Global Media Monitoring Project, whose results they had seen launched at the FWCW, the network found that less than 1 per cent of news was relevant to women's issues, and just 13 per cent of news had female major news actors. In summary: men's identities were those of the authorities; in contrast women's identities were more diverse, but more 'unidentified'. It was more likely for their images to appear than their opinions, and their ages were more obvious. Men were twice as likely to be quoted. Women were more likely to be photographed, and 54 per cent of all female images in photos were of young women. 'While men are speakers to the readers, women tend to be gazed at by readers' (Yuan 1998: 4)

The Media Monitor Network surveyed the chief editors of the eight dailies that had been monitored. Most acknowledged that the percentage of stories featuring women was not in proportion with the role Chinese women play in social development. After a seminar in 1998 to launch the results of the survey, most of these chief editors reported having had no sense of gender awareness in the past. For the network it seemed clear that the survey had acted as a wake-up call to decision-makers of China's mainstream newspapers ('China' 1998: 57).

The lack of awareness is widespread. 'Chinese people, both officials and ordinary people, men and women, are unaware of and insensitive to gender inequities. They are afraid of the word *quan* (right and/or power), especially *nuquan* (women's right and/or power)' (Yuan 1998: 7). To change this, women themselves need to understand the gendered social structure and gendered power relationships. The Media Monitor Network has been running several gender training programmes, not only for its own members but also for groups such as minority women journalists, and women journalists outside Beijing. Another strategy has been to launch two columns 'What we think of media' and 'Media observation' in *China Women's News* to carry critical reviews about media and coverage of gender-related issues. Articles, many of which are written by general readers, have challenged gender discrimination in news reporting, women's magazines, karaoke, fairy tales, pop songs, soap operas, cartoons, literary works and films (Wei et al. 1999).

In such a vast country, it is almost impossible to keep track of what is happening in the media throughout the nation; but general readers can provide valuable news clues. For example, one reader from Guangzhou, in the south of the country, commented that she had seen newspaper reports in which a woman was being blamed for the defeat of the national football team because she had been with the team on their bus. The article, entitled 'Is It Feminine Fatality?', was published in *Football* – a very popular newspaper published by *Guangzhou Daily*. Several widely read media reprinted the article. The MMN opened a debate space in its 'What we think of media' column, and contributions flowed in. They also published reports following up the issue (the woman sued the author of the original article). All this aroused immense interest in the media and in society, and the network discussion was quoted in mainstream publications, including *Digest*, *Sports Digest* and *Beijing Evening News*.

In its first phase the Media Monitor Network concentrated on monitoring and critiquing media output, based on studies such as 'Gender Issues in Chinese Established Media' and 'How to Cover Domestic Violence Against Women'. Since 1999 it has put more emphasis on trying to influence the process of media production and on developing new ways of arguing, persuading and lobbying decision-making levels of media and other relevant bodies. A small example: one of the editors of *China Women's Daily* was given the copy for a public service advertisement about girls' education whose slogan read 'For the future mothers'. The ad was to be published in the following day's edition. When she contacted the editor and producer of the advertisement and asked them to change the text, they were baffled. After considerable discussion about traditional stereotyping of women, they seemed to understand. The slogan eventually read: 'For the future of the girl, for the future of our country, please support girls' education'. In these ways the MMN tries to encourage media professionals to recognise the routine frameworks of media portrayal and to step beyond them.

Until very recently, gender and media was a completely blank area in China. According to Wei et al. (1999) the Media Monitor Network for Women has given the issue visibility and credibility, and has had an important influence on China's media through positive criticism based on gender-sensitive criteria. Without the Beijing Conference, this might not have happened.

Notes

1. Orit Sulitzeanu, personal communication, July 2000.

2. United Nations (1995), *Beijing Declaration and Platform for Action*, Section J: Women and the Media: available at www.un.org/womenwatch/daw/beijing/platform

3. 'Alternative assessment of women and media based on NGO reviews of Section J, Beijing Platform for Action', compiled by Meena M. Shivdas, and co-ordinated by Isis-International-Manila on behalf of WomenAction 2000: www.womenaction.org/csw44/altrepeng.htm

Part II

Experiences

3

Policy Development

The Policy Vacuum

> Discussing the policy and practice of Indonesian mass media is like discussing myth and reality. There is a code of ethics for journalists, as well as a code of ethics for advertisers, plus a Broadcasting Act of 1997 ... However, disparagement and violation continue. This may be attributable in great measure to the ambiguity of the Act and the codes, with the latter not containing any article dealing with violence against women or the issue of women's dignity. (Siregar 1999: 64)

In their report on the implementation of the Beijing Platform for Action's media recommendations, WomenAction 2000 concluded that one obstacle common to all regions is the lack of adequate media policy on fair gender portrayal. Where they exist, media codes and guidelines are generally framed round questions of indecency, obscenity and morality rather than issues of gender equality. In many countries a strong ethos of freedom of expression means that action is left to voluntary measures on the part of media enterprises or to ineffective compliance/complaints authorities, who often lack monitoring capacity and whose policy framework rarely includes any consideration of gender. 'Too often, the task is left to private citizens to watch, challenge and litigate.'[1]

One of the problems in mounting successful challenges is that media codes tend to be too general to allow unambiguous interpretation. A review by Isis International of existing codes in nine countries in Asia and the Pacific concluded that concepts were not clearly defined and guidelines were vague, with the result that they can be easily side-stepped (*Changing Lenses* 1999:146–55). This is a universal problem. A survey of sixty broadcasting organisations in twenty European countries found that only nine had any written policy on gender portrayal, and most of these were too vague to be made operational. Just four companies had truly specific written policies on gender portrayal (Gallagher 1995b). All of these were public service broadcasters in – Finland, Sweden and the United Kingdom. As a general rule, public service companies tend to have more specific codes of practice in this area than the commercial media. For example, the Australian Broadcasting Corporation's clause on portrayal of women and avoidance of stereotypes is precise in relation to the portrayal of women's roles and physical characteristics, demeaning or discriminatory stereotypes, and the need for gender balance in interviewees and experts.[2] The code used by the Federation of Australian Commercial Television Stations simply proscribes material that will seriously offend on grounds of gender. And even this is hedged around with so many caveats that it would be practically impossible to invoke the code in any challenge (Leonard 1999). It is not surprising that codes and guidelines are more explicit in public than in commercial media organisations; but the growth of the commercial sector and the shrinking of the public service ethic in most parts of the world means that it will be even more difficult to develop effective codes of conduct in the future.

Because most existing codes fail to include principles that permit evaluation of portrayal from a gender perspective, they are of little value to feminist media advocates. Women's Media Watch (South Africa) discovered the implications of this in a case it pursued in 1999. While the group was gathering information for a resource guide for journalists on the reporting of violence, the story emerged of a young woman who had charged four men with rape in October 1998. Sensationalist newspaper coverage of the case had caused the woman deep distress. Stories headlined 'Girl a "willing partner"' and 'Sex party' had given the men's version of events. The woman's voice was not heard. When the state decided to drop the case in May 1999 because of 'lack of evidence', another story ran in the press. The four men were said to have been living in 'sackcloth and ashes' for the past seven months, and had been greatly upset at being accused of rape. The report included a picture of the men, fully clothed. Another picture showed the girl naked – in a still from a video taken on the night of the event. The entire episode raised many questions about biased coverage, including the use of video material. WMW decided to take up the case, and contacted the editor of *Rapport*, the newspaper that had run the story including the video still. His reply ignored the specific criticisms made by WMW, and dismissed the matter as one that did not 'merit further discussion'.

WMW then contacted the press ombudsman. In a detailed letter, which they copied to the Commission on Gender Equality, the Human Rights Commission, the Western Cape Network on Violence against Women, and the owners of *Rapport*, WMW dissected the newspaper reports, arguing that they had violated the South African Press Codes. The Ombudsman neither conceded nor refuted this reading of the codes. His response was that he could only take up a case more than ten days after publication if he had 'good and satisfactory' reasons as to why he should look into a late complaint. WMW's reply referred to the circumstances surrounding the case, and called on him to investigate the matter. 'To the best of our knowledge it was the first time that the Press Codes had been challenged from a feminist perspective and we were keen to get a response from him. Instead he referred us back to the editor of *Rapport*.'[3]

The Commission on Gender Equality, an independent statutory body, agreed to take the case further. Eventually, in 2000, the Department of Communication, the public service arm of the Ministry of Communication, agreed to set up a working group to examine all existing media codes and guidelines, and to write in a clear gender component in each case. This was regarded as a major step forward by WMW. Although the ombudsman had not actually taken the case far enough to support or reject their interpretation of the press code, their own reading had convinced them that many of the clauses they cited could have been interpreted differently.

Another major problem for feminists is that when codes are specific *vis-à-vis* the portrayal of women, this tends to be expressed in moralistic terms in relation to the use of provocative or obscene imagery. Often these exhortations reflect obsolete interpretations of public taste. For example, the Broadcasting Standards Code of the National Association of Commercial Broadcasters of Japan includes a section on 'Sex' whose portrayal must not, *inter alia*, 'cause feelings of unpleasantness or consternation' and must not 'arouse undue passion on the part of the audience' (code reproduced in Venkateswaran 1996: 195). Yet in Japan today, the depiction of female nudity is commonplace in magazines read by the general public. The two most popular weeklies, *Post* and *Gendai*, have circulations of around 800,000. They have been selling particularly well since 1993 when a court judgment lifted a ban on the publication of photographs showing pubic hair. Each issue of these magazines includes several pages of nude women with exposed pubic hair (Miyazaki 1999: 73).

Women media advocates in several countries have been pushing for the revision of outdated codes of this sort. For instance, in India the only relevant legislation is the Indecent Representation of Women (Prohibition) Act, 1986. The Act was passed in response to pressure from women's groups in Delhi and Bombay. One of their targets of criticism was the hoardings and posters that had mushroomed all over these cities, particularly near cinemas. The Act forbids 'indecent representation' of women in print media, including advertisements. In 1997 as part of an intensive lobbying effort to influence a proposed new Broadcasting Act, the Media Advocacy Group called into question the efficacy of the Indecent Representation of Women Act. The first problem is that it covers only print, when in fact television and film images have become much more influential.

The second is that it has not been implemented in spirit and letter. 'Its virtual disuse and in some instances even misuse means that the violation of women's dignity and rights needs to be addressed in a far more systematic, informed and long-term manner' (see Media Advocacy Group 1997a). But the Act has not been amended and remains an obsolete irrelevance in India's current media scenario.

The limitation of obscenity laws is not simply that they are incapable of dealing with the many aspects of gender portrayal that concern media advocates today. The more profound problem is that if they are invoked they help to maintain an extremely conservative system of values to which many women do not subscribe. So there are difficult choices to be made when no adequate policies are available. For instance, a case arose in the mid-1990s in Israel, when a television advertisement for oranges showed a man peeling an orange and fantasising about a woman who was passing by. Every time he removed a bit of peel, in his mind he would peel off a part of her clothing. Complaints that the advertisement objectified and dehumanised women achieved nothing. Then Anat Hoffman, one of Israel's best-known feminist activists, decided to analyse the ad frame by frame. She found one frame that showed the nipple of the woman in the advertisement. With that evidence she filed a complaint based on legislation that forbids 'obscenity' on television. This time the complaint was accepted, and the ad had to be re-edited in a major way. But for feminists the victory was hollow and in some ways absurd in that they were forced to resort to an outmoded law, with which they did not agree, to obtain a result.[4]

Lobbying for Policy Change

Some codes and laws were framed many years ago. But even newly developed codes do not necessarily take account of gender. In Thailand, where 'yellow journalism' is widespread, the establishment of the Press Council of Thailand in 1997 was regarded as a historic event (Ekachai 2000). The initial draft of its 1998 Code of Ethics tackled standard issues of accuracy, balanced reporting and the right to reply. But although the portrayal of women as sex objects is prevalent in the Thai press, this was not covered by the code. Eventually, after close monitoring and pressure by the group Media Consumer Power, a new clause was added to the original proposal, stating that news reports must not victimise women or violate their dignity (Siriyuvasak 1999).

Of course, efforts to influence media policy go far beyond pushing for the inclusion of clauses on gender portrayal into existing or new codes of practice. In countries where there are no mechanisms through which women can become involved in the process of policy-making and regulation, lobbying is directed at their establishment. In Japan the Forum for Citizens' Television and Media (FCT) has since 1992 been proposing the creation of an independent regulatory body such as a broadcasting committee, through which the public would be able to participate in policy development and monitoring (Miyazaki 1999).[5]

The FCT believes strongly in the power of media literacy. It takes the view that it is better to work towards public understanding of gender portrayal issues than to impose ill-conceived controls on the media. So the FCT tries to focus attention on gender in the context of very broad policy discussions. For instance, in 1998 public voices in Japan began to call for the introduction of the V-chip as a means of giving viewers technical control over violent television content. The FCT opposed this. It was concerned that if the V-chip were introduced without adequate consideration, it would create the illusion that all problems with television had been solved. 'We opposed a too-easy introduction of the V-chip while there was a neglect of such issues as the media and human rights, bullying of the weak, gender stereotyping, and the commercialisation of sex. Instead we argued for promoting media literacy initiatives ... We also urged the TV broadcasters actively to take up these matters and deal with them in concrete ways' (Suzuki 2000: 9). By 2000 the Japanese Ministry of Posts and Telecommunications (MPT) had moved away from the V-chip option and was recommending the introduction of media literacy in the school curriculum.[6]

Lobbying for policy and legislative change can be immensely time-consuming and there is no guarantee of success. In 1996–97 the Media Advocacy Group in India lobbied intensively for gender and human rights perspectives to be part of the terms of reference of an independent authority which was to be established under the new Broadcasting Bill. MAG played a pivotal role in organising the depositions of groups around the country, and in ensuring that the groups made both oral and written statements. In the event, changes in government and weakened parliamentary majorities during the year led to the establishment of a body whose powers and accountability are unclear (see Viswanath and Karan 2000). The experience left MAG convinced that in the context of this constantly changing political and institutional environment, an incremental approach to advocacy would not suffice and that it needed to build stronger mechanisms such as citizens' initiatives that would help to make advocacy more broadly based.[7]

The chances of success may be higher when lobbying for policy change is at the media institutional level, particularly if allies can be found within the senior echelons of the organisation concerned. In 1992 the Israel Women's Network persuaded the country's public service broadcaster, the

Israeli Broadcasting Authority (IBA), to include a new section on gender portrayal in its existing programme guidelines. The process of persuasion began with research into women's portrayal, and continued with workshops for senior IBA staff, all of which helped to build a receptive climate within the organisation. The additions to the guidelines – which applied not just to the IBA's own radio and television programmes, but to all agreements with clients – covered both non-sexist language and content dimensions.[8] The IWN considered this as a breakthrough (Sachs 1996). Looking back almost a decade later, it did seem that the guidelines had been an important step in building awareness.[9]

In Sri Lanka, research was also an initial stepping stone in the development of the country's first ever Code of Ethics for Gender Representation in the Electronic Media, launched in 1999. The Women's Education and Research Centre (WERC) organised a three-month monitoring study of five television channels in 1998. The findings showed a well-known pattern of traditional gender portrayal, and suggested that television was not in touch with a contemporary Sri Lanka in which women were often breadwinners, significant economic contributors, and had an increasing share in decision-making. WERC established a consultative forum to make recommendations and draft a set of guidelines. To try to ensure that these would be taken seriously, the chairperson of the state television corporation (SLRC) and the programme director of one of the private television stations (MTV) were invited, and agreed, to become members of the consultative forum.

The code includes policy recommendations for media managers, a set of guidelines for television producers, guidelines for formulating advertising policy, and an action plan for gender equity in the media. One recommendation in the action plan was the establishment of a monitoring committee to ensure adherence to the Code of Ethics (WERC 1999). It remains to be seen what impact this may have on television content in Sri Lanka. But it did represent a step forward for the women's movement in terms of bringing gender portrayal into the arena of public debate.

The WERC tactic of involving senior members of the media community in consultations is extremely wise, when it works. But instinctive media reaction to the idea of any kind of regulation, even voluntary, tends to be negative. In 1995 the Jamaican government announced its intention to ask media houses to develop self-regulatory guidelines on the portrayal of crime and violence in the media. But in the face of strong media opposition, the plan came to nothing (Walker and Nicholson 1996). The focus then shifted to revision of the broadcasting law itself. Following several unsuccessful attempts by Women's Media Watch to invoke legal sanctions in relation to offensive television content, in 1997 WMW made a submission to the Jamaican Broadcast Commission, which regulates the country's electronic media. The WMW submission suggested the development of content standards that would take into consideration portrayals of gender, gender-specific violence, violence in children's programming and the use of sexist language. Anticipating serious resistance by the very powerful broadcasting lobby, the Commission decided to collect research data and to examine levels of popular support for the reform. This work began in 1999 and the results were discussed in a series of consultation forums around the country beginning in 2000 and involving key interest groups including broadcasters, producers, educators and social activists. The plan is that the research and consultation findings will feed into a new detailed content standards code, which will be applied to all broadcasters and cable operators directly through their licences, and by the Broadcast Commission.[10]

Influencing and changing policy, as the Jamaican experience shows, requires both stamina and strategic thinking. But if the people empowered to develop policy are not receptive or sympathetic towards the pursuit of gender-sensitive standards, advocates face an almost impossible struggle. Women's Media Watch was fortunate to find a crucial ally in the (female) assistant executive director of the Broadcast Commission. Support at this level can make all the difference between certain failure and possible success. Strategic alliances and planning – knowing where, when and how to apply pressure – are crucial if lobbying is to bear fruit in terms of policy change. A very different example of how this can work comes from South Korea where until the mid-1990s gender and media was a blind spot in terms of policy development. Since then, due in part to pressure from the Korean Women's Development Institute (KWDI), a whole series of measures has been implemented in new legislation. KWDI is a government-established research institute. Its main function is to provide input to policy development for women. KWDI reports to the Ministry for Political Affairs (II), the government department that until 1998 was responsible for development of these policies.[11] KWDI has studied women's representation in the media for many years and, concerned by developments in the Korean media system since the early 1990s, it began to focus attention on the fact that there was no media dimension in any existing women's policy.

As a follow-up to the Beijing conference, in October 1995 the institute and the ministry jointly organised a seminar on policies for women's development. One of the outcomes was a set of Ten Policy Priorities for Women. This provided the framework for the Basic Act for Women's Development, legislated in December 1995. The elimination of gender discrimination in the media was included in the Ten Policy Priorities, which state that:

- women's participation in media decision-making processes should be increased to 30 per cent by the year 2005
- an objective standard to assess the degree of gender discrimination in the media should be developed
- production and distribution of public advertisements on women's issues should be increased

The Basic Act for Women's Development (Article 28) requires that national and local bodies should make efforts to eliminate gender discrimination in, and to promote gender equality through, the mass media. Responding to the call for an objective standard to measure gender discrimination in the media, KWDI went on to develop a gender discrimination indicator (GDI) for the mass media (Kim and Min 1997).

These debates and activities brought the entire issue of gender and media into the mainstream and when the Broadcasting Act was revised in 1998, new clauses were introduced prohibiting any media representation that discriminates on the basis of gender.[12] Time will tell what impact these developments have on media content in Korea, but the speed with which the measures were introduced shows what can be achieved when institutional influence is clearly focused within a receptive political context.

Self-regulation: Testing Citizens' and Media Interests

Of all countries in the world, Canada stands out as having the most detailed codes of conduct on gender portrayal and the most effective mechanisms for their implementation. Backed by a strong culture of public participation in policy development of all kinds, Canadian citizens are exceptionally well positioned to advocate fair and balanced media content. Proximity to the United States with its potential to flood Canadian airwaves with American programming is one reason why self-regulation has been taken more seriously in Canada than in most other countries (Cishecki 1998). In the early 1980s the broadcast industry voluntarily drafted Sex Role Portrayal Guidelines. These cover:

- the changing interactions of women and men in society
- diversity in terms of roles and occupations
- demographic diversity
- avoidance of exploitation
- non-sexist language
- gender balance in voice-overs, experts and authorities

The guidelines are detailed, requiring that the various elements should be respected in programme development and acquisition, and also in commercials.[13] In addition, there is a Code on Violence in Television Programming that contains a general provision concerning violence against women.

In 1986 the Canadian Radio-television and Telecommunications Commission (CRTC) made compliance to the Sex Role Portrayal Guidelines mandatory, and a condition for the renewal of radio and television broadcasting licences. However, in 1992 responsibility for enforcing the guidelines was transferred to the Canadian Broadcast Standards Council (CBSC), an industry watchdog created by the private broadcasters. Since its establishment in 1981 MediaWatch has made regular representations to regulatory bodies such as the CRTC when it believed that gender portrayal guidelines were being flouted. The results have been variable. One case that developed in the late 1990s illustrates both the scope and the limitations of citizen intervention, even in a country like Canada with its strong tradition of public participation in the self-regulatory process.

Howard Stern, an American broadcaster with a sensationalist style (known as 'shock jock') began to air a syndicated radio programme in Toronto and Montreal in September 1997. From the outset Stern deliberately provoked women, ethnic minorities and French Canadians in his daily programmes, which were broadcast live. He graphically described violent sexual acts against women, and repeatedly targeted women (and other groups) with ridicule, humiliation and verbal attacks. There was an enormous public outcry, with complaints flooding in to MediaWatch, the CRTC and the CBSC, as well as to the radio stations that were airing the Howard Stern Show. In two formal decisions – October 1997 and March 1998 – the CBSC acknowledged that the show was in breach of the industry codes. Both stations broadcasting the show agreed to engage additional production staff and to install digital time-shift recorders that enabled them to monitor and edit out objectionable material. Despite this, the show continued to provoke public condemnation. Eventually the Montreal-based station dropped the Howard Stern Show, and also abandoned plans to broadcast a television version. The Toronto-based radio station Q107 continued to air the show.

At this point one of the CRTC commissioners raised publicly some highly pertinent questions about the relative strength of broadcasters and private citizens in cases such as Howard Stern: 'Do complainants become worn down while the broadcaster in question has endless resources to keep up the fight? Do complainants give up on the CBSC and by extension the CRTC?'[14] MediaWatch did not give up, and started to monitor the radio programme systematically throughout 1999. In April 2000 MediaWatch made a presentation of its findings to the CRTC, detailing how, despite the digital time-shift editing, the Howard Stern Show continued to violate the Sex Role Portrayal Guidelines almost on a daily basis. They also presented findings from a national opinion poll of community attitudes towards standards of taste that they had commissioned in spring 2000, and from a pilot study of reactions to the Stern television show (available to Canadian viewers via American satellite channels).[15] In spite of all this evidence, the CRTC showed itself unwilling to act. In the summer of 2000, Q107 signed a new three-year contract to broadcast the Howard Stern Show on radio. Still MediaWatch refused to give up, submitting another complaint to the CBSC and urging members to continue with their protests.[16]

Whatever the final outcome, the arduous process demonstrates how unequally the odds are stacked in favour of commercial media interests. But with tenacity, and with access to publicly available channels of pressure, MediaWatch and other concerned organisations were certainly instrumental in having the radio show dropped in Montreal, and in preventing transmission of the television version.

Notes

1. 'Alternative assessment of women and media based on NGO reviews of Section J, Beijing Platform for Action', compiled by Meena M. Shivdas, and co-ordinated by Isis-International-Manila on behalf of WomenAction 2000: 19; see: www.womenaction. org/csw44/altrepeng.htm

2. Australian Broadcasting Corporation, ABC Code of Practice, Clause 3.4 'Portrayal of Women and Avoidance of Stereotypes'; see: www.abc.net.au/corp/codeprac.htm

3. 'Refusal of Ombudsman to Take up the Case', *Women's Media Watch Newsletter*, No. 6, 1999: 6.

4. Dafna Lemish, personal communication, July 2000.

5. The Ministry of Posts and Telecommunications directly oversees Japan's broadcasting and telecommunications industry. There is no independent regulatory body such as the FCC in the United States or the CRTC in Canada. Given the country's very strong national ethos of freedom of expression, this is something of an anomaly.

6. Toshiko Miyazaki, personal communication, July 2000.

7. Akhila Sivadas, personal communication, July 2000.

8. 'Guidelines for Public Service Broadcasters', additions of 21 July 1992. Information provided by Dafna Lemish.

9. Lesley Sachs, personal communication, July 2000.

10. Sonia Gill (Assistant Executive Director, Broadcast Commission), personal communication, July 2000.

11. Since 1998 this responsibility has passed to the Presidential Commission on Women's Affairs.

12. Yanghee Kim, personal communication, February 2000.

13. For complete text and background information on the Sex Role Portrayal Code for Television and Radio Programming see: www.ccnr.ca/english/codes/sexrole.htm

14. CRTC commissioner Andrew Cardozo, quoted in MediaWatch *Action Bulletin*, August 1998: 1.

15. MediaWatch submission to the Canadian Radio-television and Telecommunications Commission, CRTC-Corus Entertainment, April 2000, unpublished document.

16. 'Stern renewed for 3 more years', MediaWatch *Action Bulletin*, summer 2000: 2.

4

Fact and Fiction in Media Content

It matters profoundly what and who gets represented, what and who regularly and routinely gets left out; and how things, people, events and relationships are represented. What we know of society depends on how things are represented to us and that knowledge in turn informs what we do and what policies we are prepared to accept. (Hall 1986: 9)

There is a great contrast between news or factual media and fiction or entertainment media in terms of what and who gets represented, and how they are represented. A 1997 study of prime-time television in six European countries showed that men consistently dominated the factual categories of news, current affairs and documentary (Eie 1998). Although there was no category in which women outnumbered men, in relation to their overall share of appearances (32 per cent) women's representation was relatively high in television fiction or drama (38 per cent) as well as in music, variety and other types of entertainment programming (36 per cent). Above all, women were most likely to be found in children's programmes (44 per cent). Although they only scratch the surface of the complexities of gender representation, figures like these already tell a certain story. The two central content types – news and factual, entertainment and fiction – present quite different issues in terms of gender portrayal and require different approaches from media activists. However, monitoring and advocacy efforts have devoted much more attention to the absence or non-representation of women in news than to their presence or misrepresentation in fiction and entertainment. Given that a central, enduring preoccupation of many women activists has been to find ways of airing issues generally ignored in the mainstream media, news monitoring was a natural point of departure.

Patterns and Priorities in the News

News monitoring studies have been launched in a number of countries since 1995, when the first Global Media Monitoring Project demonstrated to activists that quantitative data could be generated relatively easily and that the results could attract media attention. In some cases these studies have produced quite devastating evidence of women's exclusion from national news agendas. An extensive comparative monitoring in Argentina, Chile, Paraguay and Uruguay in 1999 found very little news linked, in any way, to women. In Paraguay just 3 per cent of radio news, and in Uruguay only 4 per cent of television news items referred to or included women. Although Chile was an exception with 21 per cent of television news related to women, half of these items were crime stories in which women were victims of abuse, assault or fraud. Interviews account for a lot of time in radio and television programmes. For example, in this study interviews took up 62 per cent of Chilean radio news time. Yet women were practically absent as interviewees. Not a single woman was included in radio interviews in Chile or Paraguay. Even in cases where women were cited as spokespersons or sources of news stories, frequently they were not seen or heard (Torres 2000).

Monitoring studies have also shown how women's invisibility and under-representation in the news is linked to traditional news priorities. Much less space and time is allotted for education, health, social development, sexual and reproductive rights (in which women tend to appear as sources) than for politics and government (in which they tend not to appear). This was clear in a one-week monitoring of the five main Bolivian newspapers that compared women's distribution across news themes with the proportion of all news devoted to these themes. News about social development – for example, human rights, community and rural development – accounted for only 5 per cent of all news, yet 20 per cent of news featuring women was in this category. Not only did most of these news stories occupy very little space – a couple of columns or less – but many were presented as brief 'miscellaneous' items, without any background or context (Flores 1999a). So even if such stories are read, their placement and treatment encourages the public to regard them as relatively insignificant.

These patterns in the news media are deeply entrenched. MediaWatch has been monitoring women's representation in Canadian newspapers since 1990. Its most recent study, looking back across almost a decade, found that women were 18 per cent of newsmakers in 1990 and only 20 per cent in 1998. In fact, there had been no increase since 1992. Even new media outlets seem to make no dent in the established pattern. The 1998 MediaWatch study covered the first day of publication of the *National Post*, but only 10 per cent of newsmakers in this brand-new daily were women (MediaWatch 1998). These monitoring studies confirm in very concrete ways that 'news is not only about and by men, it is overwhelmingly seen through men' (Hartley 1982: 146). Two decades after Hartley's assessment, the world represented through the news still seems almost impregnably male. It is a world in which women become visible and validated primarily when they make a mark within a traditionally male context – politics, business, or the law. These news values mean that women's contributions in many contexts – for example within small enterprises, the rural economy, the educational and cultural spheres – are hidden (Flores 1999a; also Pinilla 1997; Silva et al. 1998).

What use can media advocates make of this kind of information? In Canada, for at least a decade, female newspaper readership has been declining at an even faster rate than men's. Arguing that this may be related to the very male world perspective that women encounter in the daily press, MediaWatch has been trying to convince editors of the need for more female points of view and analyses (Cisheki 1998). In countries where the debate about gender representation has only recently begun, news monitoring data can often be a first step in engaging the attention of the media. One example is Cambodia, where the Women's Media Centre used the findings from their extensive quantitative studies to start a dialogue with editors and journalists about women's treatment in the news.

Using Data to Launch Debate

After decades of war, peace came to Cambodia in 1991. Press freedom was introduced in 1993. Media watchers have summed up Cambodia's years of press freedom as 'free but foul-mouthed' (Clarke 2000: 254). There has been a huge increase in the number of papers, most of them privately owned and dependent on advertising. Many are crude publications, illustrated with violent or sexual drawings, graphic pictures of mutilated corpses or pornographic scenes. A handful of professional newspapers exists alongside the popular press. So the representation of women in the Cambodian press is particularly problematic. While sensationalist and voyeuristic portrayals of women are used to sell the popular papers, standard news priorities mean that women are barely visible in the pages of the quality press.

Because of the long war, women are 64 per cent of the adult population in Cambodia, head one-third of all Cambodian families and form about 55 per cent of the country's workforce – the highest female participation in the labour force anywhere in the world. Yet in a two-week survey of three daily newspapers conducted for the International Federation of Journalists (IFJ) in 1995, the Women's Media Centre of Cambodia discovered that only 6 per cent of news items were about women (Palan 1995). As a result, the WMC established a media monitoring group in January 1996. The monitoring group successively studied the main print, television and radio media in the country (Sarayeth 1996b, 1997; Women's

Media Centre of Cambodia 1999). The picture that emerged from these studies was troubling in many respects. In the press, only 4.5 per cent of news stories mentioned women. In television news and sport, between 7 and 9 per cent of items focused on women. Just 8 per cent of radio news featured women. But while Cambodian women were virtually absent in the news of all media, some 22 per cent of items about women in the press were categorised as 'obscene', and women were almost always portrayed negatively in photographs (84 per cent) and cartoons (94 per cent).

With these findings, the WMC started trying to convince media managers and journalists that something needed to be done. It was an uphill struggle, at least in the beginning. In the early days there was often complete incomprehension about what the monitoring was trying to achieve. For example, at a press conference held to release the findings of the first monitoring study in 1996, journalists working for one of the worst offending newspapers responded that the media monitoring group should be trying to resolve the problem of prostitution rather than monitoring the media (Sarayeth 1996a). They simply did not understand the role of monitoring in focusing attention on the link between journalistic practice and media content. When editors were challenged about the amount of sensational material in their publications, initially they could see no problem. This was quite simply a taken-for-granted way of reaching the market and of increasing sales. But a debate did develop. Two years later, when the WMC organised a high-level workshop on women and media, they invited one of the foremost editors-in-chief to react to their findings. His recommendation – that activists and concerned citizens should submit good articles to displace objectionable content from the newspaper pages – completely ignored the issue of editorial responsibility for change. But the mere fact that he felt compelled to make a suggestion, however inadequate, showed that media management was vaguely starting to see that there was a genuine case to be answered.

Gradually, things improved. By 2000 several newspapers had set aside space for articles on women and women's concerns. There was much less sensationalism in the daily press. The state television channel had launched a weekly programme dealing mainly with women's place in society. The Cambodian Communication Institute had introduced topics on ethics and gender awareness into its journalism training courses. In May 2000 the WMC organised a discussion forum on gender-sensitive media production. Journalists and editors-in-chief from all media attended in reasonable numbers. Despite some resistance, when media examples were analysed in the group there was a relatively positive reaction to the critical comments and the suggestions for change. The Women's Media Centre believes that the intensive work of its media monitoring group since 1996 has strengthened its lobbying and has had a real impact on thinking about media portrayal of women. Without it, there could have been no debate.[1]

Detecting Bias in Reporting

A lot of monitoring activity goes no further than charting what is present in news content: the amount and type of coverage given to women and men, in relation to which issues. Some monitoring goes on to extrapolate from that, drawing attention to themes that could be covered and are not. But there is yet another way of looking at news coverage, which is to analyse how the news media are skewed in sometimes quite subtle ways towards certain points of view rather than others.

Monitoring and advocacy groups tackle this in various ways. B.a.B.e in Croatia includes a weekly press review on its website to highlight the routine ways in which the news sidelines or stereotypes women. Each story is briefly analysed, and where possible there is a hypertext link to the full article in the newspaper concerned. The National Women's Media Centre (NWMC) in Australia uses part of its website to publish articles, editorials and readers' letters on topics to which newspapers give a particular angle or slant, often to women's disadvantage. For instance, in late 1999 and early 2000 a debate began in *The Australian* – one of the country's major dailies – about the activities of the Family Court. In cases of divorce or separation, this court decides which parent will have custody of any child of the relationship. In most cases, custody is given to the mother. On 24 December 1999 the paper ran a lengthy article headlined 'Court out: one man's battle for his kids' written by a man who, on the basis of his own experience, argued that men do not get a fair hearing in the cases that come before the court. On the same day, the paper published a report by one of its own journalists criticising the court and supporting the views in the article. Three days later it published an editorial on the same subject titled 'Families need new ways of ending strife'. This too was critical of the court. Over those days *The Australian* published six readers' letters on the topic. Five of them applauded the newspaper for its reports and editorial. Only one – from the Chief Justice of the Family Court – condemned the paper for publishing what he described as a 'sensational account' that undermined faith in the judicial system 'in a most irresponsible manner'.

The Australian probably could not refuse to publish a letter from the Chief Justice, but it did ignore other similar points of view. Several critical letters – including one from the president of the Sole Parents' Union – were sent to the newspaper, with copies to the NWMC. None of them was published. Instead, when a columnist for *The Australian* discovered that someone had used a women's e-mail list to object to the way the issue had been handled in the paper, he wrote two opinion-pieces condemning this 'feminist'. Letters were sent to *The Australian* responding to the columnist's remarks. These were not published either. However, in two final (anonymous) news briefs, *The Australian* noted that it had been 'flooded with angry rants' from 'the sisterhood' about its 'mild support' for 'one man's battle'.[2]

In this and similar cases the NWMC lists all the material, without comment, chronologically in three adjacent columns: published articles, published responses, responses not published (but sent to NWMC). The approach is an excellent way of drawing attention to the techniques used by certain media to promote a specific and one-sided version of what are often complex questions, and of raising questions about media commitment to free speech. Detailed analyses like this can help media activists to understand and identify the many levels at which 'media portrayal' works. The task of uncovering these levels goes much further than counting bylines, comparing the numbers of women and men who are interviewed, or categorising the topics that are covered in the news.

Another organisation that focuses on bias in the news is FAIR (Fairness and Accuracy in Reporting) in the United States. FAIR's Women's Desk monitors the mainstream print, cable and broadcast media for instances of sexism, racism or homophobia. When examples of skewed reporting are found, the desk issues 'Action Alerts' to a nation-wide network of activists and media professionals. Each Action Alert contains a detailed analysis of the report or programme in question, together with contact details of the individuals and media concerned.

Typically, the Action Alert will conclude with one provocative statement or question against which people can frame their response to the media organisation. For example, on a hot day in June 2000 dozens of women were 'gang-groped' at a parade in New York's Central Park. Crowds of young men surrounded the women, hosed them down with water, stripped their clothes off, and molested them. Media coverage was intense. Much of it showed repeated images of nearly naked women crying, screaming and trying to cover themselves. FAIR's analysis of coverage in the major print and television media was particularly critical of the NBC television network's programme 'Dateline'. In an Action Alert that summarised the main points of its news analysis, FAIR issued a call for action: 'Please ask "Dateline" why it felt it was appropriate to repeatedly run exploitative images of women being stripped and groped against their will, and why the show framed its investigation with the question of "what responsibility" victims bear for such assaults.'[3]

If the Action Alerts draw attention to specific cases of news bias, some of FAIR's actions are on a much larger scale. In 1999 the Women's Desk organised a coalition of thirty organisations to put pressure on the Public Broadcasting System (PBS) for more gender-equitable programming. The campaign started when PBS aired a series of programmes in April 1999 about the 'gender wars', claiming that gains in girls' and women's rights had begun a 'war on boys' that could lead to a 'gender Armageddon'. FAIR prepared detailed documentation outlining inaccuracies in the programmes as well as conflicts of interests between the series' funders and some of its participants. Armed with this, in November 1999 the coalition met PBS executives. It also provided PBS with documentation on across-the-board gender imbalance in the network's news and public affairs programming. To address the specific problems posed by the 'gender wars' series, the coalition suggested a television series on gender equity hosted and produced by feminists. To redress the overall imbalance, they asked for at least one weekly news or public affairs programme with a progressive feminist host, and the publication of a clear plan to increase the numbers of women and people of colour appearing as sources, guests and hosts in PBS programmes. The company promised an investigation. In May 2000 PBS wrote to FAIR discounting most of the charges about the 'gender wars' series, but promising a formal change to its procedures 'to further ensure' that funders were prevented from influencing programme content. The suggestions made by the coalition were ignored. In mid-2000 the campaign continued, with FAIR continuing to press PBS to fulfil its 'mandate to present balance over time' along the lines suggested by the coalition.[4]

As part of its Media Activist Kit, FAIR includes a number of questions to bear in mind as a means of detecting bias:

- Who are the sources?
- Is there a lack of diversity?
- From whose point of view is the news reported?
- Are there double standards?
- Do stereotypes skew coverage?
- What are the unchallenged assumptions?
- Is the language loaded?
- Is there a lack of context?
- Do the headlines and stories match?
- Are stories on issues important to the public interest featured prominently?

The kit expands on these questions with examples to illustrate common types of bias, and suggests a series of steps that activists can take to challenge bias in the news media.[5]

Using Data to Change Journalistic Practice

Much of FAIR's work is aimed at getting journalists to think afresh about professional practices they tend to take for granted. Other groups too use qualitative news analysis to raise questions about news-gathering and reporting routines. In an early monitoring exercise, the Media Advocacy Group in India analysed news and news magazine programmes (Media Advocacy Group 1994b). The quantitative results showed the familiar pattern found in many other countries. Women were only 14 per cent of those represented in the news and 20 per cent in news magazines. Men dominated in all categories, accounting for 90 per cent of experts and 76 per cent of ordinary (non-expert) contributors. Women predominated only as victims (58 per cent). Men were shown in a much greater variety of roles, and were provided with more opportunities to present their viewpoints. Thus they were portrayed as persons of influence. Even when the news was about development issues such as advocacy of breast-feeding, the eradication of leprosy or national environment concerns, women were generally shown as passive bystanders while men were the active agents.

The pattern is a familiar one, but the question is what can be done to change it? Presented with findings like this, media people often respond along the lines of 'but that's the way it is', 'I can't distort reality', or 'if the Prime Minister is a man, I can't change that'. But in fact while some of this patterning is unavoidable – particularly given standard definitions of what and who is newsworthy – some of it could actually be changed, with a little reflection and effort.

This is what the Media Advocacy Group set out to demonstrate in a workshop where it presented its findings to media professionals in 1994. After discussing the overall quantitative results, a number of news items were selected and analysed to start a discussion about how the stories could have been presented differently. For example, the wide coverage given to issues such as the flood situation in the country offered plenty of scope to examine its impact on people's lives. In fact, repetitive and unimaginative visual and textual coverage of different rivers flooding, with ministers conducting aerial surveys and committing themselves to short-term relief measures undermined the potential of these news items. Negotiations around the GATT coincided with the news analysis period, and extensive coverage was given to these. Here again, the impression given was that it was a matter only for a few key politicians. But – particularly given the number of stories run – there was ample opportunity for inputs from the agricultural community, small and medium-sized entrepreneurs, and consumers of many kinds. The inclusion of these viewpoints would not only have helped to give a voice to women; it would also have resulted in more rounded and in some ways more credible information.

The lessons for media practitioners from this kind of analysis are two-fold. Not only is there a systematic pattern in which women are ignored, or are stereotyped.; there is also a tendency towards lazy journalism. The first is exemplified by resort to clichés about how women and men are expected to behave. MAG gave the example of a news profile of the first female mayor of Bombay. The commentary noted with relief that she 'doesn't fit the stereotype of someone in a position of power. On the contrary she behaves like a typical housewife, rather than an aggressive hungry go-getter.' And viewers were reassured that although she was pro-women, 'unlike rabid feminists she is not anti-men'. So much time was spent establishing her as a happy housewife that viewers never got to hear about her plans or goals in her new position.

This kind of stereotyping feeds into and relies on routines and easy solutions that simply amount to bad journalism. For example, MAG pointed out how, in stories about prostitution, the constant use of visuals of sex-workers turning away from the camera and covering their faces was partly just a lazy use of library archive footage. But it also told its own story about these women, who were invariably presented in an extremely limited way as culprits, when there was so much more to be said about their lives and occupations. Reacting to this kind of analysis, media profes-sionals naturally defend their ways of working. Time is short. Deadlines are pressing. Resources are few. No one is available to give an alternative point of view on the issue. Such was the case at the workshop organised by MAG. But while 'some absences were beyond the control of media producers, others were not so easy to explain away'.[6] There was much food for thought. This 1994 workshop was one of several factors that led to the creation of the women's current affairs programme 'Sampark' to which MAG acted as editorial consultants in 1995.

Patterns in Entertainment Media

In late 1999, during an online discussion on Women and Media organised by the United Nations WomenWatch, a heated debate developed about the exploitation of women in popular music. This unexpected and lengthy exchange of views centred on rap and hip-hop, and the penchant of some of its practitioners for sexually violent messages and imagery. The par-ticipants had very divergent viewpoints as to where responsibility lies for these images, but the debate was largely subjective. Although music and other types of entertainment media raise important questions in terms of gender portrayal, so far these genres have received little systematic attention from gender media monitoring groups.

There is a small but important body of academic work on gender imagery in popular music. However, like most academic research in the public domain it originates mainly from North America and Western Europe. The collection edited by Whiteley (1997) looks at the construction of femininity and masculinity in popular music, at misogyny and sexism, at gender and sexuality.[7] Sut Jhally's powerful video *Dreamworlds II* (1995) argues that music video works systematically to deny women subjectivity and to construct them through a discourse of 'nymphomania' as ever-available objects in an endlessly repetitive adolescent fantasy world. The original *Dreamworlds* (1991) caused such uproar that MTV tried to halt its distribution with the threat of legal action (subsequently dropped). But the limitation of all these materials is that they focus on 'mainstream' pop-rock music originating in North America and, to a lesser extent, the United Kingdom. There is almost nothing available that analyses popular music of other countries – even those that export widely such as Jamaica.

One exception is Zambia, where findings from a study of popular Zambian songs in the early 1990s (Longwe and Clarke 1992) were shared in a workshop with some of the musicians involved. Many of the most popular songs moralised about women's behaviour – how they should behave if they want a husband, and how they can keep a husband. Other songs put women down, or depicted the woman as an evil seductress preying on unsuspecting men. Some picked on the theme of the independent woman, whose assertiveness seemed often to include an urge to steal other women's husbands. The results of this survey were something of a revelation to the musicians, who had never been faced with a systematic analysis of the content of their songs. Promises were made to do better, but follow-up activities were not consistent enough to ensure a real impact. Zambian songs today are still said to carry these very traditional messages, though perhaps not as blatantly as before.[8]

Variety shows are another frequent target of feminist criticism and, given the enormous popularity of the genre, it is unfortunate that almost no data yet exist to support claims that these shows are deeply sexist and exploitative. One limited analysis was made in Bolivia, as part of a wider monitoring study in 1998. The show selected for study, 'Sábados Populares' (Popular Saturdays), is a much-imitated national production, which itself emulates many features of productions from other Latin American countries such as Argentina. In that sense the conclusions are rather wide-reaching. The analysis found 'dramatic abuse of the dignity of young women', using all manner of camera techniques and angles. The young female hosts almost never spoke. They were just moving bodies, scantily and sexily dressed.

Misogyny and machismo were present throughout the episodes studied, sometimes obvious and almost lacerating, sometimes more subtle. Female contestants were invariably addressed as good mothers, wives, cooks, and servants to their husbands. One of the novel aspects of the study was its analysis of camera movement. This was found to operate as an active instrument in the exploitation of the show's female participants. So much so, that 'the aggressive techniques of camera operators and directors amount to a kind of violence against women, which is accepted and approved in each broadcast – by hosts, directors, and viewers' (Flores 1999a: 134–5).

It may not be surprising that gender media monitoring has not yet systematically addressed these rather spectacular genres. But even the area of popular television fiction, which presents quite different gender portrayal patterns, has been relatively little studied by activists. One of the few monitoring groups to have tackled this genre in detail is the Media Advocacy Group in India. In its comprehensive 1995 study, MAG analysed 105 hours of television fiction across the country's four leading channels (Media Advocacy Group 1995a). Most of the serials revolved around the life-styles of the rich. Altogether 60 per cent of characters represented the elite, cosmopolitan class. The middle class got some representation, though usually in comedies. Lower-class homes were a rarity. Looking at the types of character represented, the analysis found that in contrast to the submissive, sacrificing woman of the past, the typical woman in these soaps and serials was portrayed as modern and with a mind of her own. Strong women held centre-stage, with many soaps and serials built around them. Professional women were predominant, though the housewife or homemaker role was still prevalent, accounting for 32 per cent of all women. These women too were typically portrayed as modern and ambitious. Even if they were at home, they had something to say, often influencing their husbands' decisions with regard to business. Overall the women represented a range of complexity in terms of characterisation – from the negative and/or stereotypical woman to women in new situations, raising new issues. At the same time the latter were often portrayed as being at the root of familial or social tension and conflict.

This study led MAG to the conclusion that for many Indian viewers such serials probably presented problematic images, in terms of viewers' ability to identify with and evaluate the characters. The group later organised a series of discussions with women viewers spanning the full socio-economic spectrum. The most important point to emerge was that all groups appreciated the new, bold woman. There was widespread approval for this woman who could not be taken for granted by anyone, and who would fight for what she wanted. Nevertheless, there was a great deal of disagreement over the specifics of portrayal, the issues and how they were treated, and the stance taken by the protagonists. These perspectives stemmed from the realities inhabited by the various groups, with low-income women feeling distanced, even though they appreciated the strength of the characters. It was also clear that many of the women reflected on, and evaluated their own real life predicaments through the serial format (Media Advocacy Group 1997b). These discussions were instrumental in confirming MAG's view that media literacy was a key tool in citizen empowerment, and they would later make this operational with the creation of their Viewers' Forums.

Pushing for Change in Prime-time

One of the reasons advocacy groups focus more on news than on entertainment media is that the latter present an even bigger challenge when it comes to pushing for change. Most news is still locally or nationally produced, and journalists are relatively accessible. In many cases journalists do subscribe – at least in principle – to an ethic of social responsibility, and some are quite open to discussion and indeed interested in critique. With the entertainment media the situation is altogether different. In most countries a fair proportion of television entertainment content – particularly popular drama and comedy, but even some game shows and music – is imported from abroad. In these cases there is no local producer, director or scriptwriter to talk to. Activists can try to develop a dialogue with programme buyers or production executives, but leverage is very limited. Even when material is locally produced, commercial criteria tend to over-rule issues of culture or aesthetics. As long as audience ratings show – as they often do – that sexism and sensationalism appeal to the general public, there is little hope of persuading media managers to consider doing things differently. Instead, many activists tend to put their faith in media literacy – hoping that in the longer term people will turn away from offensive drama, variety programmes or game shows.

To achieve more immediate or direct change, advocates need to be able to convince media executives that public opinion is sufficiently strong for consumers to pressure advertisers into withdrawing advertisements and their revenue. Very few media advocacy groups have the networks and organisational capacity to contemplate this route. But one that has an exceptionally large and influential membership is the National Organisation for Women (NOW) in the United States. Since its establishment in 1966, NOW has been energetic in media advocacy and, with a membership of 500,000 organised into more than 600 local chapters, it is able to combine grassroots activism with national lobbying. In February 2000 NOW launched a nation-wide 'Watch Out, Listen Up!' campaign. 'We are putting the four major networks on notice,' said NOW president Patricia Ireland. 'Feminist viewers across the country will decide if ABC, CBS, FOX and NBC measure up when it comes to treatment of women.' The campaign would be 'another step toward making television more relevant to women's lives and more responsive to women's needs'.[9]

Teams of viewers across the country monitored 165 prime-time television programmes spanning the four networks. The programmes included popular drama, comedy, game shows and films. Each show was analysed according to four criteria:

- Violence: number and severity of violent acts.
- Gender composition: percentage of women in the cast, with bonus points for diversity and positive role models, and deductions for stereotypes.
- Sexual exploitation: programmes were ranked in a range from very respectful treatment of women/girls, to substantial exploitation with no positive value.
- Social responsibility: shows were ranked in a range from strong social content with relevance to people's lives, to irresponsible content with no redeeming values.

Every programme was assigned a numerical score in each of the categories. Not surprisingly, male-oriented action drama performed poorly across all categories, with few positive female characters and much violent and sexually exploitative content. Comedy appeared to have no place for strong women, except as the targets of sexual comment and advances. Game shows were found to be very male-centred – from the contestants to the hosts to the silent women assistants. The game show 'Who Wants to Marry a Multi-Millionaire' ranked at the bottom in three of the four categories, because of its 'stereotypical, exploitative and irresponsible presentation of 50 women competing for a man'. In all shows, but particularly in comedy, there was little diversity in terms of race and ethnicity, sexual orientation, age and body type. The top score for any programme went to the drama series 'Family Law' and the overall results showed that 'the strongest, most fully drawn female characters were in such dramas'.[10]

Based on the programme scores, an overall result was worked out for each of the four networks. At the bottom came FOX, which scored lowest in all categories except violent content. When NOW released the results in May 2000, FOX found itself named a 'Network of Shame'. NOW organised 'Network of Shame' protests at FOX affiliate stations in several cities across the country, and the in-coming female president of Fox Entertainment held a meeting with the president of NOW, promising to work from within to address feminist concerns. 'Cautiously optimistic' about possible future improvements, NOW declared its intention to continue monitoring television output and lobbying network executives. It would also contact advertisers to encourage them to support women-friendly programmes.[11] Whatever the real impact of the on-going campaign, NOW's immediate success was to alert the networks that 'feminists will be watching', and in sufficient numbers to merit some attention.

Notes

1. Tive Sarayeth, personal communication, July 2000.

2. 'Family Court media coverage, December 1999–January 2000, *The Australian*'. See National Women's Media Centre website: www.nwmc.org.au/FEATURES/family_court.htm

3. FAIR Action Alert: 'Dateline NBC Exploits Central Park Victims', 23 June 2000: www.fair.org/activism/dateline-central-park.html

4. 'National Desk: FAIR's Women's Desk challenges biased PBS series, campaigns for greater diversity and balance on PBS': www.fair.org/feminist-coalition.html

5. FAIR's Media Activist Kit, 'How to Detect Bias in the News Media': www.fair.org/activism/detect.html

6. Media Advocacy Group, Annual Project Report 1994: 8.

7. Other useful sources are Goodwin (1993) and Frith (1996).

8. Nakatiwa Mulikita, United Nations WomenWatch online consultation on women and the media, 8 December 1999.

9. 'NOW issues warning to networks during sweeps month: Watch Out – Listen Up!' NOW press release, 14 February 2000.

10. 'Watch Out, Listen Up! Feminist Primetime Report'. See National Organisation for Women website: www.now.org/issues/media/watchout/report

11. 'NOW cautiously optimistic following Fox meeting', NOW press release, 6 June 2000.

5

The Advertising World

What's the problem? No woman ever went broke from seeing a fashion ad.

Can you imagine a world without advertising? ... Would we have the same overwhelming choice of dozens of mobile phones, car brands, types of food, holiday destinations? ... Almost certainly not ...We are of the opinion that restricting advertising restricts a whole lot more than advertising alone. The independent press, for example. The development of the Internet and e-commerce. The range of affordable consumer goods. The democratisation of culture. In short, your quality of life. That's why we think that the only fair restrictions on advertising are those imposed by your interests, your desires and your common sense. And last but not least, through our respect for all of the above. (Extract from the European Publishers' Council 'Adfreedom' campaign, 2000)[1]

Throughout the 1990s European media corporations struggled to promote 'freedom of commercial speech' in the face of relatively light-handed attempts to regulate certain forms of advertising in the European Union. Resolutions on the portrayal of women in advertising were adopted by the Council of the European Union in 1995 and by the European Parliament in 1997. *Inter alia* these called on member-states to encourage advertising agencies and the media to formulate new ideas that would reflect the diversity of gender roles, to develop and implement voluntary self-regulatory codes,[2] and to adopt measures to prevent any form of pornography in the media and in advertising.[3] A Resolution has no legal status in the European Union. It is essentially an aspirational guideline, to which member-states may or may not adhere. Yet the reaction of organisations like the European Publishers' Council – a lobby group with representatives from many of Europe's most powerful commercial media – to any voicing of concerns about advertising is unfailingly hostile. European politicians are cast as paternalistic, with a tendency to 'try and protect consumers from themselves ... To all those who are eager to regulate advertising, we would say that the most effective regulation possible is the common sense of the consumer.'[4]

In fact European legislation on advertising is restricted to a few quite specific matters covering, for example, the ways in which tobacco and alcohol can be marketed. For the rest, in Europe as in many other parts of the world, advertising is subject to self-regulation by the industry itself. In relation to gender portrayal, some countries do have mechanisms or procedures that in principle allow the public to lodge complaints about objectionable advertising content. But often they are not as effective as activists would wish. In most cases this is because the guidelines are too vague to provide a clear framework for decisions. This vagueness may itself be linked to a lack of commitment to take seriously the issues that many citizens would wish to address. A brief tour of the bodies that regulate advertising in three countries – Australia, the United Kingdom and Canada – shows how different levels of commitment are reflected in the self-regulatory procedures themselves and the decisions that result from them.

Self-regulation and Advertising

In Australia, despite intensive government and industry lobbying by the National Women's Media Centre and a wide range of women's organisations, the self-regulatory system that was launched by the Australian Association of National Advertisers in September 1998 pays no specific attention to gender portrayal. Its Advertiser Code of Ethics contains only a general clause stating that 'people' must not be portrayed in a way that discriminates 'on account of race, ethnicity, nationality, sex, age, sexual preference, religion, disability or political belief'.[5] Similarly broad clauses cover the portrayal of violence and of sex, sexuality and nudity.

The Advertising Standards Bureau (ASB), which is funded by the advertising industry itself, oversees implementation of the code and considers complaints from members of the public. The ASB does not make it easy to complain. The Advertiser Code of Ethics is not posted on its website, and it provides little guidance for consumers. Complaints must be made in writing, and e-mail complaints will not be considered.[6] Given that the Advertiser Code of Ethics is so vague, and that the ASB publishes only very general information about the complaints it receives, it is impossible to know how significant issues of gender portrayal are in terms of complaints made and upheld. However, it is clear that women are particularly dissatisfied with advertising in Australia. They accounted for almost three-quarters (73 per cent) of complainants in 1998 (the latest year for which figures are available). The board of the ASB upheld only 5 per cent of all complaints received in that year.[7]

By contrast, the British Advertising Standards Authority (ASA) upheld

10 per cent of the complaints it received in 1999. The ASA covers all advertisements apart from those on television and radio, which are overseen by the Independent Television Commission (ITC) and the Radio Authority respectively. The ITC upheld some 5 per cent of complaints in 1999. Both the ASA and the ITC give a moderate amount of information on their procedures as an aid to potential complainants. The relevant codes are published on their websites, as are electronic versions of the complaint forms. Complaints can be made in writing or by e-mail. The ASA highlights certain categories of complaint, including 'portrayal of women'. The proportion of complaints in this category is usually around 4 per cent.[8]

Like the Australian Advertiser Code of Ethics, the British codes on advertising standards are very general in relation to gender portrayal.[9] For example, the main objective of the ITC code is to ensure that television ads are not misleading, harmful or offensive. These are the three overall criteria used by the ITC. Thus the scope for interpretation is broad. It is almost unknown for the Commission to uphold complaints on grounds of sexism. A few examples:

- May 1998: Citroën Xsara, in which model Claudia Schiffer progressively takes off her clothes, and drives away naked. This was the subject of 121 complaints (the average number of complaints is three per advertisement). Complainants found it 'degrading to women, that it was sexist, that it was unacceptable and gratuitous to use a woman's body to sell cars'. The ITC judged that 'the nudity in this light-hearted, tongue-in-cheek advertisement was not explicitly filmed' and 'did not consider that most viewers would share the complainants' view that the tone of the advertisement was unacceptably offensive, degrading or sexist'. Complaints not upheld.
- August 1998: Gillette Male Body Spray, in which a skydiver wearing the body spray crashes through a roof into a hospital bed. He is immediately surrounded by attractive nurses, drawn by the scent of the spray. Most of the twenty-five complaints came from nurses, 'who felt that this was a stereotypical portrayal of female nurses as sexually available'. Some complainants argued that the ad would lead to an increased risk of sexual harassment for nurses. The ITC 'understood' the objections but did not think that 'this obviously ridiculous … scenario' was likely to affect most viewers' attitudes to the nursing profession. Complaints not upheld.
- April 2000: Fiat Punto. This was a pair of ads. In one a young man pontificates to an imaginary female audience about the car's suitability for women – for example, praising its 'satellite navigation system

because, let's face it, with your sense of direction, finding the way out of the garage is a bit of a challenge'. In the other ad a young woman describes the car's suitability for men – its 'satellite navigation system because, let's face it, how are you going to find your way around Birmingham when you can't even find your way around a woman's body'. All seventy-four complainants objected to the 'strongly sexist tone of the commercials'. The ITC 'agreed that the commercials were sexist in tone, but noted that this did not automatically put them in breach of the Code'. Complaints not upheld.[10]

Reaching a conclusion about whether or not an advertisement is offensive is, of course, hazardous. The first question is: offensive to whom? The second question is: who decides? The answers to both will undoubtedly affect the final evaluation. What is clear from the ITC decisions is that they contain many value judgements about, and on behalf of, the general public. Yet these value judgements are obviously not shared by the sometimes numerous people who complain. For example, the Citroën Xsara ad attracted a very large number of complaints by ITC standards. Nevertheless, the assessment was that 'most viewers' would not be offended. In the opinion of the ITC the ad was 'light-hearted' and therefore inoffensive. But the viewers who complained apparently did not share the ITC's sense of humour. Indeed, since perceptions of humour are well known to be extraordinarily variable, this seems a dubious measure on which to base an assessment.

As it happens, this same advertisement provoked a high level of public protest when it was shown in Spain in 1998. The Advertising Observatory – a public watchdog – decided to act on the complaints. Unlike the ITC, the Advertising Observatory is run by women, for women. Given the large number of complaints lodged in both countries, the two different decisions cannot really be ascribed to broad cultural factors – for example, as between what 'most viewers' in Spain and in the United Kingdom might find objectionable. But another type of cultural difference – one based on gender – does seem to be at work. When Citroën ran the same advertisement again on Spanish television in early 2000, the Advertising Observatory announced that it would intervene for a second time. Press clippings at the time of the announcement show a clear gender difference in the reactions of journalists. A number of men ridiculed the Observatory's decision. Like the ITC, they described the advertisement as simply 'humorous', 'idiotic' or at worst 'in bad taste'. However, the women journalists either did not comment specifically on the ad, or called into question its intention: 'Would you really buy a car because a well-known model decides she doesn't need to wear her expensive lingerie when driving it?'[11]

This small example illustrates at least two things. First, although there are no simple answers in this domain, gender seems to play a role in different evaluations of certain kinds of advertising. Therefore, it matters who is making the decisions. Second, since this is a terrain in which personal value judgements are inevitable, the decision-making process will be helped rather than constrained by guidelines that are as specific as possible. Extremely broad criteria such as those used by the ITC and similar bodies in most countries, that merely refer to 'human dignity' or 'standards of taste and decency', are open to such wide interpretation as to be almost meaningless.[12]

Canada is the country that leads the way in terms of the specificity of criteria, and the transparency of procedures available to members of the public who wish to complain about offensive advertising. Advertising Standards Canada (ASC) covers advertisements in all Canadian media. In 1999, 17 per cent of the complaints it received were upheld. The Canadian Code of Advertising Standards provides the basic set of criteria by which all complaints are evaluated. In relation to gender portrayal, the most relevant section is Clause 14 on 'Unacceptable Depictions and Portrayals'.[13] However, in addition, the ASC uses detailed gender portrayal guidelines 'designed by and for the advertising industry to help advertisers develop positive images of women and men in commercial messages'.[14] In 1999 11 per cent of all complaints raised issues under the guidelines, and 24 per cent of these complaints were upheld; 34 per cent of complaints raised issues under Clause 14 of the code, and 18 per cent of these were upheld.

The ASC provides very detailed information on its website about all review and adjudication procedures, publishes the texts of the code and the guidelines in full, and gives examples of complaints upheld under each of these. In some cases, a single complaint is sufficient to result in a complaint being upheld. In 1999 the ASC embarked on a new Canada-wide consumer awareness campaign, using a media release and a print and radio public service announcement (PSA) with the slogan 'Everyone Has Something to Say about Advertising. And We Listen'. A free telephone line was also established to provide ready access to ASC information. In fact, the number of complaints received by the ASC in 1999 was up 30 per cent on 1998, and was double the number received in 1997.

The overall impression is of a self-regulatory mechanism that is taken seriously by those responsible for its implementation, and is regarded by members of the public as worth using. Nevertheless, even this example has limitations in terms of its potential to address public dissatisfaction with advertising. In a survey of Canadian women and men carried out for MediaWatch in 2000, only 6 per cent said they had tried to complain to someone when they were offended by something they saw or heard in the media. This suggests that a complaints-based system of regulation will catch only a very small proportion of those who encounter offensive content, and that other channels for public criticism are needed.[15]

The Complexity of Advertising Images

> If you let me play sports, I will have more self-confidence. If you let me play sports, I will be more likely to leave a man who beats me. If you let me play sports, I will be less likely to get pregnant before I want to. (Nike advertisement, quoted in Stabile 2000: 193)

As image of girl after girl moves across the screen, their voices are heard making statements that pay homage to the women's movement and its concerns. Nike's use of this feminist discourse implies a commitment to women's liberation and empowerment. It is part of a wider rhetoric of social responsibility in which Nike projects itself as a corporation that cares deeply about fundamental issues such as gender and racial inequality. By providing 'positive' images and messages – wonderfully exemplified in its slogan 'Just Do It' – Nike presents itself as a sensitive and ethical company. Yet Nike is a multinational enterprise that sells outrageously expensive sports shoes produced in sweatshop conditions in South-East Asia.

So what are we to make of these advertising images? Taken at face value, it is hard to conclude anything other than that they are 'positive'. Indeed, when the National Organisation for Women in the United States surveyed their members' views on positive body images of women and girls in 1998, the Nike advertisement 'If you let me play sports' was one of very few examples cited.[16] Yet there is a profound disjunction between the surface message of these images and the reality they conceal. The idea that Nike supports women's empowerment can only be believed 'as long as the Vietnamese women who make Nike shoes, working 12-hour days for a wage of between $2.10 and $2.40 a day, are kept off the screen' (Stabile 2000: 199).

In fact, studies show that even young consumers can produce quite sophisticated readings of corporate advertising messages and are able to understand their inherent contradictions. In a MediaWatch study of eleven- to fourteen-year-old girls in Canada, Nike was specifically singled out for criticism:

> What they were doing was they were showing all these people with dis- abilities and problems and stuff and you go 'oh you poor people and all that' and you just sit and watch it and think that it's really good and effective.

And then I found out it was for Nike and Nike has children working for them in their factories and stuff, and then I felt no sympathy for them after that, you know, it's people they put on, they use. I felt like they were using, not only were they using the people with disabilities and stuff for their ads to make people want to buy it, but they're also using kids to make us buy it. I just hate that so much. I never, never buy anything. (Fourteen-year-old girl quoted in MediaWatch 2000: 20)

Kim Christian Schrøder's study of the reactions of British adults to corporate responsibility advertisements showed a similar cynicism and indeed a feeling that by creating more and more sophisticated messages, advertising is shooting itself in the foot. As one informant put it: 'they are really training people to be sophisticated in the way they receive the ad, and in the end that works against advertising as whole' (Schrøder 1997: 289). On the other hand, corporations employ some of the brightest minds in the world to keep one step ahead of the public, and advertising messages become ever more complex. This means that advocates must develop concomitantly sophisticated techniques of analysis and critique. For instance, Adbusters, a Canadian activist organisation committed to exposing and undermining corporate power by 'culture jamming',[17] concluded that at the beginning of the twenty-first century, its approach to the advertising industry needed reinvention if it was successfully to lay bare the often subtle and nuanced messages of contemporary ads.

In the 1990s one of the techniques used by Adbusters was the 'spoof ad' or 'subvert'. These would parody advertising techniques so as to bring into focus the values, and undermine the messages, of the product companies (see Plate A). The great global advertising campaigns of the 1990s – Absolut (vodka), Marlboro (cigarettes), Calvin Klein, Nike – were easy targets for the Adbusters culture jamming techniques. But while some of those campaigns lasted for years, leaving time and space for the development of subversive responses, by 2000 the pace had changed completely with a new ad campaign every few months. 'They're fast moving targets, hard to shoot down. The ads are more complex, abandoning catch phrases in favour of irony, mood and emotional nuance … Corporate marketing has borrowed some of the jammer's techniques and gone guerrilla – small, fast-moving, everywhere.' In mid-2000 Adbusters called for a shift of tack: 'Subvertising must evolve; social marketers must come up with new ideas and an edgy, new, slick-subversive style. It's a never-ending cat and mouse game.'[18]

These few examples demonstrate that for effective media advocacy the monitoring of advertisements must go far beyond simple counting. Of all the areas in media content, advertising in particular embodies levels of

PLATE A Reproduced by courtesy of www.adbusters.org

complexity that will be barely scratched by a purely quantitative analysis. Indeed, from some perspectives it is arguable that the images of advertising deserve less attention than the realities those images are designed to conceal. The Nike 'If you let me play' series is a case in point. As Carol Stabile argues, by analysing what multinational corporations make visible in the form of advertising and corporate propaganda we are just looking at what these companies want us to see: 'Unless our goal as critics is to contribute to their market research and to add further sophistication to their advertising techniques, it might be more useful and politically effective for us to concentrate on making visible those practices and realities that are routinely kept out of sight' (Stabile 2000: 200).

Creating Critical Consumers

> The power of the consumer is not to be underestimated. Our experience
> has shown that the media care about what their audiences think. If ad-
> vertisers, stations or the print media are threatened by an exodus of the
> consumers their profit margins depend on, they are very likely to change or
> remove the offending material. (Cishecki 1998: 7)

Studies carried out during the 1990s suggest the steady growth of a form
of consumer politics in many countries. A survey of Canadian women
found that 53 per cent had at some time refused to buy products from
advertisers who offended them (MediaWatch 1994a). In the United Kingdom about 50 per cent of shoppers are said to operate product boycotts
of one form or another (Nava 1991; Schrøder 1997). In Denmark, recent
research shows that people frequently resort to consumer choice as a way
of expressing dissatisfaction (Phillips 2000). Some are optimistic about the
power of consumerism, for example in relation to environmental activism
(Nava 1991). Others discount the likelihood of consumer politics having
any fundamental impact on social power structures. In this view consumer
behaviour does not represent an effective form of political action. Consumption gives people a sense of freedom and control over their lives. But
the ability to consume is unequally distributed, and consumerism gives
freedom only within the terms of the market, not freedom from the market
(Bauman 1997). Radical media activists like Adbusters would tend to agree
with this position. In their view the proliferation of advertising in so many
social and public spaces means that 'the job now is to constantly find space
to send out the message: we are free'.[19]

While some aim to topple the corporate establishment, others take the
quieter route of incremental change. In fact, these approaches are not
antagonistic, and can be mutually reinforcing. Advocacy groups like B.a.B.e
in Croatia and MediaWatch in Canada believe passionately that active,
critical consumers are central to the struggle against unwanted advertising
messages. Both of these organisations use parts of their websites to analyse
offending ads, and encourage people to send in additional examples with
their own critiques. MediaWatch in particular has a long history of urging
consumer complaints about advertising, and has had many successes. There
are two sides to its strategy. One is to develop critical awareness, to help
consumers recognise sexism in advertising and other media content.
Through its quarterly newsletter *action Bulletin* and its website, the
organisation regularly publishes examples of sexist and disturbing advertisements, each accompanied by a critique. The addresses to which letters
and comments should be sent are given, with a request that copies of

letters should be sent to MediaWatch. On the basis of all this, MediaWatch keeps an archive of successful campaigns. Each item in the archive contains a description of the product, an analysis, a section on 'what to do' (addresses of all relevant contacts, of which there may be many), and a 'results' section describing the outcome.

This contributes to the second part of the MediaWatch strategy – to convince people that taking action can make a difference. The organisation works hard to stress that 'average citizens' can help to shape their media environment, and that sometimes it takes only a few letters or phone calls to convince a media producer to print an apology or withdraw an ad. Indeed, many of the examples in the MediaWatch archive demonstrate that this is true. MediaWatch believes that, over the long term, it is this ongoing communication between consumers and media producers that will bring about change.

The flow of sexist material continues nevertheless, prompting the question of how much genuine communication is actually achieved in this process. In its spring 2000 newsletter MediaWatch drew attention to an advertising campaign for Skyy Vodka that portrayed an image of male physical and sexual domination of women. It urged consumers to 'let Skyy Vodka know that this message is dangerous for women and disrespectful to their (potential) female customers'.[20] In its next newsletter MediaWatch was able to report that the company had dropped its advertisement. But in that same newsletter it published a picture of an ad for Gucci clothes, again suggesting consumer action.[21] The image – of a woman on her knees, with much of her body exposed, crouching beneath a man whose crotch was his focal point – projected a message of male domination which was almost identical to that in the Skyy Vodka advertisement.

The seemingly endless flood of this kind of imagery in advertising might suggest that advertisers and product manufacturers are not yet poised for truly fundamental change as a result of consumer action. MediaWatch and other advocacy groups maintain that the very process of taking action is itself an empowering experience for citizens and can contribute to a climate in which public participation will spread. There is bound to be truth in this, though citizen action faces a mammoth struggle given the resources now available to corporate advertisers determined to maintain the status quo.

More than sixty years ago journalist and press critic George Seldes wrote in *Freedom of the Press* that advertisers, not government, determine the limits of free speech in the United States. His insight is clear today, not just in the United States but in other countries where the commercial media have taken strong root. Since the mid-1990s Adbusters has been pioneering the development of citizen-produced advocacy messages –

'uncommercials' – intended to give the public an alternative slant on advertising. By 2000 they had still had no success in airing these messages on Canada's public service broadcaster CBC, or on networks including CBS, NBC and CNN in the United States. One of their hardest-hitting messages is a thirty-second uncommercial called 'Obsession Fetish'. Its reference point is fashion advertising of the Calvin Klein type and its aim is to raise public consciousness about anorexia and bulimia. The soundtrack evokes a fashion catwalk. A sexy, barebacked woman undulates alluringly – until it becomes clear that she is vomiting into a lavatory bowl. The voice-over adds 'Obsession – fascination – fetish … Why are nine out of ten women dissatisfied with some aspect of their bodies? The beauty industry is the beast.'

This uncommercial was turned down by CBC on the grounds that it violated standards of taste, and that the images comprised 'unacceptable exploitation of sex and nudity'. CNN was not enthusiastic either. The executive whom Adbusters contacted said that although he personally liked 'Obsession Fetish', the sales department probably wouldn't. 'Will CNN risk angering its big time sponsors by airing "Obsession Fetish?"' asked Adbusters in mid-2000, 'stay tuned'.[22] So in their bid to create critical consumers, while activists may have some success through their own communication channels it seems that the national airwaves – through which millions of citizens could be reached – are out of bounds.[23]

An Advertising Observatory

According to a survey of prime-time television advertisements in five major cities [in China] in the early 1990s, there are two dominant images of women. One is 'traditional' – the complacent housewife and caring mother. The other is 'modern' – the consumer or desirable sex object. About one-third of all ads were said to be blatantly discriminatory (Bohong and Wei 1997: 46)

Market reform generated an advertising bonanza for the Chinese press during the 1990s. In the early 1980s, advertising was virtually insignificant. Nationally, the growth rate of advertising revenue from 1986 to 1996 surpassed that of the gross national product several times. According to Yan (2000: 508) advertising grew thirty-one times over that decade. For societies undergoing rapid social or economic change, advertising images often embody the contradictions of transition from past to present.

One example is Spain, which emerged from authoritarian rule only in the late 1970s and became a member of the European Union in 1986. Rapid changes in Spanish society have produced a kind of schizophrenia in much popular media content. A decade of research helped to document the co-existence of traditional and outmoded images of women (the house-wife enthralled by detergents) and highly sexualised content in which women's bodies are objectified (for example Balaguer Callejon 1985; Ferrer 1995). Against this background the Advertising Observatory was established in 1994 within Spain's Institute for Women, the body responsible for implementation of the government's equal opportunities policy.[24] The Observatory provides a channel through which Spanish citizens can protest about advertisements they believe are sexist or degrading to women. If the Observatory decides that an advertisement contravenes Article 3 of the Spanish Law on Advertising by offending against the dignity of the person or violating the values and rights of the constitution, 'particularly with regard to children, the young and women', it will contact the advertiser and ask for the ad to be withdrawn or modified.[25]

A national free telephone line operating twenty-four hours a day, every day of the week, is the main route through which complaints are received. The Observatory also includes a complaint form on its website, and e-mail has been growing as a means of transmitting protests: 12 per cent of all complaints received in 1999 came via e-mail. Between 1994 and 1999 the Observatory received on average just under 400 complaints per year, usually referring to about 100 advertising campaigns. The number of individuals is larger than the number of complaints, as complaints submitted by groups or by several people are counted as single cases. The typical complainant is female, aged twenty-six to forty-five, well educated, single, urban-based and in paid employment. However the proportion of complaints from men has increased, from 8 per cent in 1994–95 to 11 per cent in 1999.

The Observatory's detailed statistics put it in almost a unique position to evaluate trends in both advertising and in public reaction to it. One point of note is that it seems that encouraging people to express their views about advertising can help to build awareness of other, less im-mediately obvious, sources of discrimination in media content. For example by 1999 8 per cent of all complaints received by the Observatory related to general press and television content. Television news, talk shows, game shows, variety shows and popular drama series have all come in for criticism. Internet content first surfaced as a target of criticism in 1999, accounting for 2 per cent of all complaints.

In its 1999 report the Observatory noted that in some respects there has been an undeniable improvement in women's portrayal in advertising, with an increasing number of campaigns that show flexibility in gender roles. But ads that depict women in the active, public roles or that – very occasionally – show men occupied with domestic tasks are still a tiny minority compared with the replay of traditional stereotypes and the continued use of women's bodies in sensational ways. In fact, in that year the Observatory followed up complaints relating to sixteen advertising campaigns – twice the number pursued in 1997. Three of the 1999 campaigns were considered to normalise or trivialise violence against women. For example, in one television commercial a female secretary was shown with a blackened eye, after her boss threw a telephone directory at her. The reason? She should have provided him with the 'best' telephone directory, produced by QDQ, sponsors of the campaign. This 'humorous' use of violence against women was one of five broad categories of advertising about which citizens protested in 1999. The Observatory labelled these:

- *To be a woman*. The woman who is born to seduce, with a sixth sense for fashion and who seeks physical perfection so as to be desired.
- *A body to be explored*. Mainly directed at men, advertisements such the one for a Citizen wristwatch with the tag-line 'only for great explorers', showing a man's hands 'exploring' a woman's buttocks.
- *Super woman*. Women's increased buying power has made them the target of campaigns for chic cars and financial services previously aimed only at men. Populated by young, attractive women, most of these ads simply dress up old stereotypes in new clothes.
- *Only for men*. Ads that show men struggling to preserve territory that seems in danger of intrusion by emancipated women – such as the IWC wristwatch campaign: 'This titanium IWC is hard. Especially with women. It's only for men.'
- *Gender violence – with humour*. Using a context of gender violence to sell products with humour, with the result that domestic violence and sexual harassment are trivialised or ridiculed.

This panorama of advertising types from 1999 may not seem particularly encouraging. Nevertheless, the Observatory believes that one of its most important achievements has been to enable Spanish citizens to find, and use, their voices and thereby to create an awareness of the possibilities for public action. In its negotiations with advertisers and product manufacturers, the Observatory can thus bring two kinds of pressure to bear. One is its own official status as an adjudicator of material that infringes the law on advertising. The other is the weight of consumer opinion. Typical arguments used by agencies to defend their campaigns are that their pre-tests showed no objections to the advertisements, that the design team included women, that they did not intend to offend women, or simply that they do not agree with the Observatory's assessment. But in many cases they do agree to withdraw or modify a campaign. Whether this is through fear of public protest, or concern that bad publicity will affect product sales, or because they have been genuinely taken aback by a new interpretation of their message, is not clear.

One limitation of the Observatory's approach is that in focusing on the citizen-consumer, there has been no sustained dialogue with the advertisers themselves. The risk is that changes may be superficial or cosmetic, based on an irritated wish to avoid problems rather than on a real understanding of what lies behind the criticisms. The Observatory's annual report certainly generates a great deal of media attention, but without a context of detailed analysis and discussion press coverage can be superficial, doing little to enlighten readers about the issues at stake. Some journalists try to undermine the enterprise as a kind of 'feminist policing', subjecting it to irony or ridicule. And of course any discussion of women's portrayal in advertising can provide those who want it with yet another opportunity to publish the very images that are the subject of criticism. This may involve not just reproducing pictures from offending national advertising campaigns, but gratuitously using even 'worse' examples from other countries.[26] Conscious of these hazards and of the need to engage advertisers themselves in discussion, the Advertising Observatory planned the development of closer professional links and dialogue with the advertising industry in a new phase of activity beginning in 2001.

Creating a Dialogue with Advertisers

I just wanted to take a beautiful shot. (Lisa Trindle, National Marketing Manager of Windsor Smith Shoes, Australia)

In early 2000 a billboard advertisement appeared in Australia. It showed an image of a large-breasted woman seated with her legs apart, and her lips pursed. Her head, cupped by a man's hands, was being drawn down to his genital area. The advertisement was for shoes.

This billboard provoked a huge outcry and great controversy. The national marketing manager of the shoe company was interviewed on a morning radio show. When asked what this image had to do with selling shoes, she replied: 'I just wanted to take a beautiful shot ... I didn't see myself as using that woman ... he's not forcing her in any way, she's resting her head in his hands, and she's sitting really strongly and confidently.'[27]

People in the advertising industry frequently make use of language associated with the women's movement, though that language is often associated with images that many women would find objectionable. For example, an Italian advertisement for Wampum jeans carries the slogan 'pari opportunità' (equal opportunities), apparently suggesting that women have just as much right as men to wear these jeans (see Plate B). Yet the ad reproduces the kind of exploitative imagery that a lot of women would

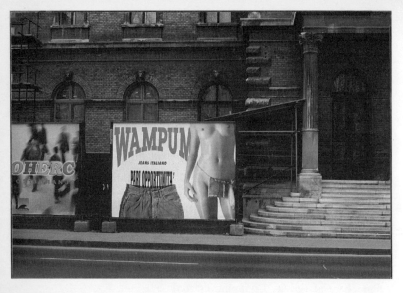

PLATE B Reproduced by courtesy of Kristina Mihalec/B.a.B.e, Croatia

interpret as one of the obstacles to their pursuit of equal opportunities. It shows a glistening female torso, without a head but with breasts exposed, and only a loincloth covering the genital area. From the loincloth dangles a small fish. The brand name Wampum suggests a cultural reference to Native Americans. The advertisement manages to convey racist and sexist messages simultaneously.

What was the motivation for this advertisement? Was it a cynical abuse of women's aspirations to equality? An effort to associate the jeans with images of modernity (equal opportunities) and independence (the wide-open spaces inhabited by Native Americans)? An attempt to be humorous or provocative by using conflicting textual and visual images? And when the national marketing manager for Windsor Smith shoes says that her advertisement showed the woman as strong and confident in her positioning *vis-à-vis* the man, does she truly read the image that way? Is she offering an interpretation based on the view that images of women taking pleasure in their sexuality are liberating? Or is she rather desperately casting around for a response to unanticipated controversy? And if it had not occurred to her that this advertisement would provoke controversy, what does this imply about her views as a woman and a professional?

Many advertisements raise questions to which there are no clear answers.

For activists seeking change in the content of advertisements, it is self-defeating to dismiss advertising executives as irredeemable cynics who sift through feminist discourse, appropriating ideas and turning them into marketing slogans. It is also over-simplistic. Like all media practitioners, advertisers work within a particular framework of ideas, routines and assumptions. This framework reflects both professional and cultural values. One has only to look at advertisements in different countries to see that their images and messages vary according to the current cultural and economic climate. Countries in political and economic transition – such as those of Central and Eastern Europe – experience this very dramatically. The website of the Croatian advocacy group B.a.B.e gives examples of advertisements from mainstream media – magazines, newspapers – that would certainly be rejected as pornographic by media in some other European countries. Cultural shifts on this scale naturally affect professional values. People begin to think differently about what is acceptable, admissible. But the relationship between cultural and professional frameworks is constantly shifting and – particularly in the field of advertising – the search for novelty, and the need to reach new markets, opens a small space for dialogue. Some media activists believe that if they can draw advertisers into this space, self-reflection and discussion on both sides will produce real, grounded change.

One organisation pursuing that approach is ZORRA in Belgium. This has its roots in academic research into women's portrayal in the media and advertising carried out by the Women's Studies Centre of the University of Antwerp. Presentation of the findings at a public meeting in November 1996 provoked tremendous interest and a desire for action among the women who were there. They formed a network called ZORRA (Zien, Opsporen, Reageren op Reclame en Advertenties: Looking, Detecting, Reacting to Advertisements and Publicity). Co-ordinated by the Women's Studies Centre, ZORRA's purpose has been to raise awareness among advertisers and publishers. With funding provided under the post-Beijing ministerial budget, ZORRA has developed into a focal point for channelling complaints. Its quarterly newsletter is distributed to the entire advertising community in Flemish-speaking Belgium, as well as to members of the ZORRA network itself. A website posts advertisements with a brief analysis of each one, and a discussion between members of the public and advertisers responsible for the ads ensues. ZORRA's strategy is to provide a forum for friendly debate, believing that many advertisers simply have not thought about the issues and that they need to be encouraged to question taken-for-granted advertising strategies.

The lack of awareness is at times staggering. In October 1999, a poster campaign was launched for the weekly Antwerp city magazine *Apart*, in

which businesses and services can place advertisements. This three-poster
campaign began with a close-up picture of an attractive young woman
with a bruised and blackened eye. A second poster showed another young
woman with a bloody nose. The third – designed to attract local businesses
to advertise in the magazine – declared '*Apart* beats everything'. A ZORRA
press release about the ads received national media coverage and, following
a large number of complaints, the advertising agency issued an apology
and stopped the campaign. The manager responsible stated that they had
thought the campaign was clever, and had not understood its potential to
cause distress. But if this seems difficult to credit, it is a mind-set that
other advertisers share. For example, in 1999 the British Advertising Standards Authority upheld complaints about an advertisement for hair removal
cream. The ad showed a sensually positioned woman in underwear. It was
headlined, 'I like my men rough, not my legs'. In response to the ASA the
advertisers said they had not intended to offend or to trivialise violence
against women. The ad was intended to be light-hearted and humorous.
They argued the advertisement sought to reflect that women were 'confident, feminine and empowered' after removing unwanted body hair.[28]

ZORRA's philosophy is to regard such reasoning not as an excuse, but
as a reflection of ignorance. By engaging advertisers in discussion, and by
motivating them to create more 'women-friendly' messages through an
annual award, they hope to create fundamental change – something they
believe will not happen by simply imposing sanctions, or by putting the
advertising industry on the defensive.

Dialogue is also the motivation for the Award for Non-Sexist Publicity,
created by the Centro de Estudios de la Mujer (CEM) in Argentina and
supported by UNIFEM. The idea is to introduce discussion about sexist
images in advertising within one of the most famous festivals of advertisers
in Iberoamerica – the Iberoamerican Festival of Advertising (FIAP) which
takes place every year in Argentina. The event attracts about 1,500 delegates
and some 5,000 television, radio and print advertisements each year from
all over Latin America, Spain and Portugal. The non-sexist advertising
award started in 1998 as an annual event. Three awards are given for print
ads, and three for television. One of the most interesting features is the
process used to select the prize-winning ads. First the general festival jury
is asked to make a pre-selection from all the ads submitted in the competition. In 2000 this jury consisted of seventeen very senior advertising
executives, all of whom were men. Seven basic criteria are used to make
this selection (Garrido 1999). The ads should:

1. Present non-stereotypical and non-violent images of men and women.
2. Respect the personal dignity of men and women and avoid their use as
   sex objects.

3. Show the diverse range of life-styles which men and women follow today.

4. Reflect the capacity of women and men for personal development in all roles and functions.

5. Express the creativity and contributions of women and men in all social spheres.

6. Promote relations based on equity, respect and co-operation between men and women.

7. It is important to highlight the participation of boys, girls and young-sters according to the listed criteria

On the basis of the pre-selection made by the festival jury, a specialised jury of seven – including feminists, journalists and advertisers – choose the winners. This two-stage selection means that the general jury has to give some thought to the question of what non-sexist advertising is, or could be – something most of them would never otherwise consider. So this is quite a novel strategy for introducing different viewpoints and values into the advertising community. It is always difficult to evaluate the impact of initiatives of this sort, but the organisers believe that advertisers certainly value the prize more highly than they did when it began. They are proud to win an award. And there does seem to be a larger number of non-sexist – or at least less sexist – advertisements from which to make the selection.[29]

Notes

1. See www.adfreedom.com

2. Resolution of the Council and of the Representatives of the Governments of the Member States on the Image of Women and Men Portrayed in Advertising and the Media, 5 October 1995 (95/C 296/06), para. 2.7.

3. Resolution of the European Parliament on Discrimination Against Women in Advertising, 16 September 1997 (A4-0258/97), para. 5.

4. See www.adfreedom.com

5. Australian Association of National Advertisers, *Advertiser Code of Ethics*, para. 2.1.

6. See Advertising Standards Bureau website:www.advertisingstandardsbureau.com. au

7. The issue that attracted most complaints (39 per cent) in 1978 was 'portrayal of people', but the lack of detail provided by the ASB makes it impossible to know whether gender was a significant factor in this category. See: www.advertisingstandards.bureau. com.au/bureau/facts/stats.htm

8. Recent figures show 3 per cent of all complaints in this category in 1995, 7 per cent in 1996 and 4 per cent in 1997, 1998 and 1999. See 'The ASA in Figures': www.asa. org.uk/guide/figures.htm

9. The relevant codes are the British Codes of Advertising and Sales Promotion administered by the Advertising Standards Authority (see www.asa.org.uk), section 5.1

'Decency'; and the ITC Code of Advertising Standards and Practice administered by the Independent Television Commission (see: www.itc.org.uk), rule 13 'Taste and Offence'.

10. ITC Advertising Complaints Reports, see: www.itc.org.uk

11. 'Sigue la publicidad sexista, pero ¿es la más inquietante?, *El Mundo*; 'Sexo-gilipollez', *Diario 16*; 'La provocación', *Diario 16*; 'Azafatas minifalderas, conductoras desnudas y mujeres maltratadas', *El Mundo*; all articles published 18 April 2000.

12. A reform of all the ITC's advertising and sponsorship operations and policies was taking place during 2000 though it was unclear how, if at all, this might affect complaint criteria and evaluations.

13. Until May 1999 this clause was known as 'Taste, Public Decency'. For full text of the code, see: www.canad.com/asc/ccas.html

14. Advertising Standards Canada, '1999 Ad Complaints Report': 6 (see www.canad.com/asc/Complaints/1999ReportE.pdf). The Canadian Gender Portrayal Guidelines were originally developed in 1981 and have been revised several times since then. The most recent version dates from 1993. The guidelines (available at www.canad.com/asc/gender.html) are currently the most thorough set of standards for the self-regulation of gender portrayed advertising anywhere in use.

15. MediaWatch submission to the Canadian Radio–Television and Tele-communications Commission, CRTC-Corus Entertainment, April 2000, unpublished document.

16. 'Reader Survey Results: Fall 1998 – Body Images'. See: www.now.org/nnt/winter-99/surveyresults.html

17. 'Culture jamming' is Adbusters' term for a wide range of campaigns and activities aimed at changing the way meaning is produced in society. 'We believe culture jamming can be to our era what civil rights was to the '60s, what feminism was to the '70s, what environmental activism was to the '80s. It will alter the way we live and think.' See 'The culture jammers network' at: www.adbusters.org/information/network

18. 'Creative resistance: is the spoof ad dead?' *Adbusters Magazine*, No. 31, 2000. This issue of the Adbusters magazine prints a series of 'subverts' (the Red Cross series) that illustrates their new, more subtle approach. See: www.adbusters.org/campaigns/first/toolbox/creativeresistance/03.html

19. Ibid.

20. 'The Skyy's the limit', *action Bulletin*, spring 2000: 1.

21. 'Gucci keeps women on their knees', *action Bulletin*, summer 2000: 1.

22. See 'Obsession Fetish': www.adbusters.org/uncommercials/obsession

23. In its magazine *Extra!*, FAIR (Fairness and Accuracy in Reporting) regularly documents how the American mainstream media are pressured by advertisers – for example to ignore consumer boycotts, or to refocus or drop stories that could portray products unfavourably. See: www.fair.org/extra/index.html

24. Spain has played a leading role in putting advertising and the media on to the agenda in European Union discussions of equal opportunities. It was under the Spanish presidency that the European Council adopted the first resolution on the Image of Women and Men Portrayed in Advertising and the Media in 1995; Resolution 95/C 296/06.

25. Information about the Advertising Observatory is taken from its Annual Reports

for 1997, 1998 and 1999, and from María Jesús Ortiz, personal communication, July 2000.

26. When the Observatory's 1998 report was launched in April 1999, *La Voz de Galicia General* used a French advertisement to accompany its article ('Más de cien campañas publicitarias han sido denunciadas por sexistas', 28 April 1999); the following year *Ideal de Granada* used a Brazilian ad ('Aumenta en un 12 per cent el número de denuncias por anuncios publicitarios de carácter sexista', 18 April 2000). Both ads featured female nudity. In neither case was there any reference to these images in the articles themselves.

27. Tamara Stowe, 2 June 2000, 'That Windsor Smith Billboard'. See National Women's Media Centre website: www.nwmc.org.au/Articles/stowe.htm

28. ASA 1999 report: www.asa.org.uk/reports/staff_adj_99.htm

29. Gloria Bonder, personal communication, July 2000.

6

Gender, Politics and the Media

Birds of Parliament. Fine feathers flutter on Thabo's big day. (Headline in *Cape Times*, South Africa, 26 June 1999)

In 1994 in South Africa's first elections after the end of apartheid, women were returned to 25 per cent of parliamentary seats. This put South Africa among the world's leading countries in terms of women's political representation (United Nations 2000). With six women at ministerial level, they had enjoyed a high profile in public life and political decision-making by the time of the 1999 national elections. On this occasion women were returned to 30 per cent of the seats. Yet for the media, women in parliament still seemed to be some kind of exotic species. The *Cape Times* report was typical of how women were depicted in press reports on the opening of parliament on 25 June. Picture spreads showed women in colourful regalia, or side by side with their children. Given the high proportion of women elected, this might have been reported as a big day for them. Instead they were projected as the 'birds of parliament', fluttering their feathers to grace the 'big day' of President Thabo Mbeki.

The Media and Women Politicians

The dignity with which [Hillary Rodham] Clinton conducted herself during her husband's impeachment seemed at first to be an asset ... The mere fact of her humiliation ... had elevated a vaguely unpopular first lady to an ideal ... But then she took the dignity thing too far. She wouldn't show bruises ... She is not willing to change that one crucial thing: she will not show weakness. In a way this makes her a feminist icon, a chilling feminist heroine: a woman who refuses to be vulnerable, who deftly manipulates power, who does not allow love to get in the way of her career goals. (Katie Roiphe, 'It's a girl thing', *Guardian*, 1 August 2000)

Women entering the political arena provide the news media with a problem. As women they embody a challenge to masculine authority. As active, powerful women they defy easy categorisation. Often the media attempt to contain the threats they pose by trying to situate them as 'women' rather than as 'politicians'. Studies show that while the media emphasise the political record and experience of male politicians or political candidates, with women the focus is more on their family situation and their appearance. This pattern is true even in countries with a strong tradition of women in political office such as Finland (Koski 1994), Norway (Skjeie 1994) and Sweden (Börjesson 1995). And while certain types of popular media tend to stress the family relationships of all politicians, men and women are not necessarily presented in the same way in terms of their families. For instance, van Zoonen (2000) found that the Dutch gossip press depicted the families of male politicians as a source of support, while the family was portrayed as a source of conflict for women pursuing a political career.

When women disobey the rules of feminine behaviour, they may be portrayed as 'iron women', aggressive or belligerent. South Africa's Nkosazana Zuma is one example. She is said to be the 'antithesis of the obedient woman. Her position and her role have brought her into frequent and turbulent contact with the media. Zuma embodies all the qualities that are frequently admired in male politicians' (Media Monitoring Project 1999a: 165). Media coverage of such women at times shows clearly how parallel evaluations – of the politician and the woman – run side by side in a way that rarely occurs in the case of men. And while at one level journalists and editors may be aware that these evaluations lead to contradictory conclusions, at another level the framework is hard to resist. In their study of women in South African politics, the Media Monitoring Project illustrated how this dilemma can be simultaneously acknowledged and downplayed by the media. 'Zuma has been one of the most effective cabinet ministers in the Mandela government' ran an editorial in the *Independent on Saturday* (1 August 1998). 'It is precisely because of her strong character, and the fact that she feels very passionately about her job, that Zuma has attracted the kind of negative publicity that surrounds her.' Yet the editorial failed to compare Zuma's treatment with that of male politicians with similar strength of character and passionate commitment. At the same time it distanced the media from the coverage of Zuma by labelling it as 'publicity' rather than news reporting.

Several studies of media coverage of Hillary Rodham Clinton demonstrate the force of traditional gender interpretations in slanting media coverage. As a 'first lady' (wife of the incumbent president), she was constructed as a kind of 'gender outlaw' because she stepped outside the conventional dichotomies of citizen and wife, public and private (Brown and Gardetto 2000: 22). As a political candidate in her own right, she was depicted as over-ambitious and power-hungry. Only when portrayed as a victim, in the aftermath of her husband's confession in the Monica Lewinksy case, did Hillary Rodham Clinton attract sustained sympathetic coverage from the media. This leads to a troubling conclusion: 'we are to fear women with power, yet admire women with the status of victim' (Parry-Giles 2000: 221).[1] Other studies in the United States have found that the public seems to have a more positive attitude towards political candidates when they act in a way considered gender-appropriate (Chang and Hitchon 1997) and that female politicians may actually choose to play to gender stereotypes (Kahn and Gordon 1997). Indeed, research in the United Kingdom shows that women in politics are conscious that the images and language used to describe them are different from those used to describe their male colleagues, and that this can have an impact on their ways of dealing with the media (Ross and Sreberny 2000).

All of this adds up to a complicated scenario that presents few straight-forward courses of action for media activists. For although it is clear that the image and language of politics as mediated by television, radio and the press 'supports the status quo (male as norm) and regards women politicians as novelties' (Ross and Sreberny 2000: 93), it is not at all clear how women can most effectively intervene in and change that system of mediation. A good example of the contradictions comes from Israel, where in 1997 a group of four women – all mothers of combat soldiers – initiated a call for Israel's withdrawal from the occupied territories of southern Lebanon. A year later, the movement included 600 activists and could muster 15,000 signatories on a petition (Lemish and Barzel 2000).

The protest was quickly dubbed the 'Four Mothers' movement by the Israeli press, which used several strategies to frame it as a 'mother's' voice rather than a 'civic' one. But the activists themselves conformed to gender stereotypes: 'they adopted the name (and with it the frame) proposed by the media; they voiced their motherly concern; they invoked their own sons as their driving force; they talked in a form of emotional "motherese"; they vacated the stage in favour of the men who joined them; they ap-pointed an official spokesman, and so on' (Lemish and Barzel 2000: 166). Yet in a context in which women's voices and concerns are perceived as irrelevant to the debate over security and war, because they are not active participants in combat, how is the women's movement to intervene? This study concluded that the very process of news management that seemingly depoliticised women in fact resulted in the voicing of a female political alternative that would otherwise have remained silent.

Women's Politics and the Media

[There is] a depressing stability in the articulation of women's politics and communication ... The underlying frame of reference is that women belong

to the family and domestic life and men to the social world of politics and
work; that femininity is about care, nurturance and compassion, and that
masculinity is about efficiency, rationality and individuality. And whereas
women's political activities try to undermine just that gendered distinction
between public and private, it seems to remain the inevitable frame of reference to understand it. (Sreberny and van Zoonen 2000: 17)

In this introduction to their edited collection on gender, politics and
communication, Annabelle Sreberny and Liesbet van Zoonen point to a
paradox in women's attempts to break down the public–private division
that characterises gender definitions and relationships in social and political
life. By accepting the public vs private divide as the framework through
which gender differences are analysed and interpreted, women help to
confirm the very divisions that they seek to undermine. Nevertheless, a
good deal of media monitoring and advocacy in relation to the public
sphere is motivated by a belief that women's perspectives and agendas
must be given more importance in politics, precisely so that current gender-
based divisions in relation to public and private will be eroded.

One of the battles in this struggle is to change media perceptions of the
newsworthiness of female politicians and of issues of particular concern to
women. In election campaigns female politicians and candidates tend to
receive significantly less media coverage than their male counterparts. For
instance, a study of television news leading up to the 1997 British general
election found that, although at the time 9 per cent of members of the
British parliament were female, women accounted for only 5 per cent of
national politicians appearing in the news (Garner 1997). The pattern seems
widespread. As part of its monitoring of television coverage of the 1998
national elections in India, the Media Advocacy Group made a special study
of how gender and social development issues were covered in news and
current affairs programmes. A total of twenty-nine issues – covering
questions such as women's status, education, health, water, civic amenities,
housing, rural development, poverty – was identified. They had prominent
coverage on television, accounting for 53 per cent of television time. Issues
specifically concerning women's status and gender accounted for some
8.5 per cent of development matters raised in the programmes. Yet of the
170 politicians who spoke on any of the twenty-nine issues, only nine (5 per
cent) were women. Of forty-five people invited to contribute as experts, just
seven (15 per cent) were women. Thus there was a paradox in that, even
though gender and development issues dominated the political broadcasts,
women's representation was still negligible (Media Advocacy Group 1998).

Monitoring of media coverage of the 1999 South African elections
showed that only 9 per cent of news sources were women. Compared with

less than 1 per cent female news sources in the 1994 elections, this could be seen as some improvement (Mthala 1999). But given the relatively high proportion of women who hold political office in South Africa, the result is poor. Institutionalised racism during apartheid meant that other forms of oppression received less attention in South Africa's early political reforms. For example, the Commission on Gender Equality was set up only in 1997. So the marginalisation of women in the 1994 election coverage could be interpreted within this context (Media Monitoring Project 1999a). No such explanation would prove adequate five years later.

A two-month monitoring study of the 1999 election coverage found that out of 14,100 items monitored, only 95 (less than 1 per cent) focused on gender. Part of the explanation was the events-driven nature of the election coverage, which tended to draw the focus away from election issues and towards party leaders. Even when issues were covered, there were few attempts to look at them through the prism of gender. Although crime was one of main items covered during the election campaigns, crimes of violence against women were seldom covered and there were few attempts by the media to establish party positions on this issue. Discussions on HIV/AIDs and on poverty similarly ignored the particular situation of women. Political parties that presented the issue of employment equity legislation as 'reverse discrimination' or 'high cost labour' for industry and agriculture went unchallenged by the media. Gender stereotyping of female candidates – described as 'Mrs so-and-so' or 'wife of so-and-so' – and of other women associated with the election (for example, Graça Machel, whose wardrobe was extensively analysed) were 'sad indictments on the media's treatment of women' (Media Monitoring Project 1999b: 57).

Reviewing this and earlier research into election coverage, the Media Monitoring Project conclude that 'a distinction needs to be drawn between what the media can reasonably do to access women sources, and what responsibility lies with political parties' (Media Monitoring Project, 1999b: 57). Party ideologies play a role in this. The African National Congress (ANC) which has a 30 per cent quota for women had by far the largest number of women quoted in news reports in 1999. Few other parties demonstrated any commitment to gender equality in their party lists or campaigns, and this was reflected in the media coverage. On the other hand, the media play a large role in the selection of issues, and gender stereotyping of female politicians is something entirely within their control. The MMP sees this not as a conspiracy on the part of the media to exclude or marginalise women, but as a result of taken-for-granted newsroom practices in which it 'makes sense' to do things in a certain way. So change is needed in media newsrooms. Standard perceptions of newsworthiness need to be challenged in training sessions with working journalists. Gender-sensitive training can also help journalists to understand how stereotyping works through the choice of language, descriptions and so on. In South Africa several such training initiatives have been launched. The Institute for Advanced Journalism runs an annual two-day workshop on 'Human rights – gender in the media'. The South African National Editors' Forum (SANEF) began a series of workshops on gender and diversity in late 1999, organised by Women's Media Watch.

Increasing Women's Power through the Media

Monitoring over time shows that, without specific actions to encourage it, election coverage of women and women's interests is unlikely to break free of media definitions that place men at the centre of political activity. The Israel Women's Network commissioned a study of the portrayal of women and gender equality issues in the 1996 television election broadcasts. They wanted to compare findings with an earlier study of the 1988 elections (Lemish and Tidhar 1991). In the intervening eight years women's organisations, in particular the IWN, had achieved several breakthroughs for women by legislative and political lobbying. Women's lives and status, for example in relation to equal labour rights and marital rights, had improved significantly. It seemed reasonable to expect favourable changes in the portrayal of women in the 1996 elections. The study looked at the representation of all women who appeared on television on behalf of the various political parties, and analysed the ways in which women and women's issues were constructed by party ideology (Lemish and Tidhar 1999).

Contrary to expectations, no significant difference was found between 1996, when women accounted for 17 per cent of all those who appeared, and 1988 (13 per cent). In both years women accounted for a much greater proportion of ordinary citizens, as opposed to party leaders or members, than men. Women and men were also treated differently, with a much higher proportion of women appearing as anonymous figures, without any formal introduction. Men were on screen for a significantly longer period of time, on average. In the months leading up to the election campaign the IWN had distributed to all political parties a platform specifying seventeen issues that in their view should be addressed. Only six of these emerged at all in the election broadcasts: economic equality, welfare, the need for special public bodies for women, issues of marital status, women's representation in religious bodies, and violence against women. Overall, women's issues were addressed by only 1.3 per cent of persons who appeared on television. There was a gender difference here. Although 7 per cent of women addressed one or more of these issues, less than 0.5 per cent of men did so. Out of the long list of possible issues of specific interest to women, the theme of battered women was the only one to which an entire broadcast was devoted. Although there was no sensationalism or over-emotionalism in the programme, women were once again cast as victims.

There were also differences in the way that female and male politicians were portrayed. For instance, none of the women was shown in any form of political work or surrounded by admiring voters, though many of their male counterparts were. In fact, the image of women as mothers was a much more dominant message in 1996 than it had been in 1988. Women with babies in their arms and children by their side talked about peace, the future, education, equality, personal safety, poverty, military service and much more. 'It seemed that their roles as mothers provided legitimacy to their presence on screen and to the message they were delivering' (Lemish and Tidhar 1999: 403).

These disappointing findings led the IWN to two general conclusions. First, the political parties still largely ignored women's achievements and their specific concerns. Second, female politicians were overshadowed and sidelined in the election coverage, to some extent reflecting a political reality in which women's parliamentary representation was extremely low – 9 per cent before the 1996 elections (United Nations 2000). To try to redress the situation, the IWN launched an extensive public awareness campaign aimed at getting more women into political office. In the run-up to the 1999 general elections, it commissioned a series of advertisements to draw attention to women's invisibility in Israeli politics and to encourage politicians to include women on their electoral lists. These ads all used role reversal messages, showing very well-known male political figures in women's dress and – in some cases – doing women's tasks. The first advertisement (see Plate C) was issued with a press release in June 1999. It caused a minor sensation in the Israeli media. The text of the ad reads:

Gentlemen!
It's impossible without the ladies!

OK, you're all born leaders – well known, smart and talented. Real men. But no matter how qualified you are, you're still men. It doesn't matter how aware you are, or how hard you try. Only women – in realistic slots on your electoral lists – can represent women and the rest of the Israeli public.

Don't forget that every second voter is a woman.

This advertisement was printed in almost all Israeli newspapers, was shown on television and was discussed on talk shows. Two other ads followed, and the campaign was a huge success in raising a wide and animated public debate about women's place in politics. The campaign did not really

PLATE C Reproduced by courtesy of Danny Mayer/Vieder Sigawi, Israel

achieve its objective of persuading the political parties to position more women, more prominently, in their electoral lists. But in the general election women were returned to 12 per cent of parliamentary seats, a higher percentage than ever before. Perhaps the general public had moved a little ahead of the parties themselves in accepting women's eligibility for political office.[2]

Media strategies to increase the number of women in electable positions have also been at the forefront for advocacy groups such as B.a.B.e in Croatia. In the run-up to the 1995 parliamentary elections, B.a.B.e initiated the Women's Ad Hoc Coalition for Monitoring and Influencing Croatian Elections. The aim was to promote women and women's agendas during the election campaign, and to increase the number of women elected. At that time, women were only 5.7 per cent of members of parliament – among the lowest percentages in Europe. This initiative was renewed for the 1997 elections, when 7.8 per cent of those elected were women, and again for the elections held in early 2000. Over time, a great deal of expertise had been built up in terms of media strategies. Street activities, posters, leaflets, badges, T-shirts with the logo '51%' had all helped to draw public and media attention.

For the 2000 campaign, the group extended its activities in several important directions. One of the aims of the campaign was to encourage citizens, especially women, to give their vote to parties that showed commitment to gender equality. A Women's Amendment to the Electoral Law (governing the conduct of the elections) was drafted, requiring all parties to ensure that their electoral lists included at least 40 per cent women. Although the amendment was not accepted, it received considerable media attention and a number of parties did promise to include more women on their lists.

To draw attention to women's lack of visibility in media coverage of politics, a media monitoring day was organised on 1 October 1999. It covered television news, political programmes and the most popular daily newspapers. In the 419 relevant media items on that day, 88 per cent of those who spoke or were mentioned were men, 12 per cent were women. Women were the main actors in only 5 per cent of items related to the economy. Issues discussed only by women were pension benefits, employment, schools, refugees and the family. Issues not discussed or even mentioned were sex education, sexual harassment, contraception, abortion, single parenthood and gender equality.

In the immediate run-up to the elections, B.a.B.e's Elektorine team monitored five of the most important daily newspapers and three weekly magazines, as well as election broadcasts on national television and radio. The aim was to react immediately to the interpretation of women's issues in the media. Four reports were issued in December 1999 and a further three in January 2000. They were widely distributed to media organisations, women's groups and political parties. Women's representation – in terms of numbers appearing or mentioned, numbers quoted – as well as the campaign issues covered, were analysed in these reports. Women were 15 per cent of those who appeared or were mentioned, and 21 per cent of those quoted. The subjects that women typically talked about included regional politics, youth, the economy and the progress of the election campaign itself.

All this was interpreted by B.a.B.e as an indication of women's increased visibility in relation to politics, and of a move away from stereotypical associations in which female politicians tend to be linked primarily with social policy (B.a.B.e/Elektorine 2000). The elections on 3 January 2000 resulted in a female parliamentary representation of 21.2 per cent and the defeat of the conservative HDZ party which had been in power since 1991. For B.a.B.e, and other women's NGOs in Croatia, an important step forward had been made.[3]

Both B.a.B.e and the Israel Women's Network organise training for women in public positions to help them improve their communication skills. In October 1999 B.a.B.e held a five-day seminar on Women in Politics, during which a journalist and a television producer ran workshops for women to develop their media skills. Four of the participants were candidates for the seats in the elections. Each participant did a to-camera presentation, after which the performance was analysed and then repeated. In every programme the IWN holds for women in senior public and private sector positions, a part is designated for media skills development: how to write press releases, how to be interviewed effectively on radio and television, and so on. More than 2,000 women have gone through these courses and many have gone on to hold public office. The first openly gay woman to be elected to a public position – as a mayor – in Israel is one of them. For her the course was an eye-opener, increasing both media skills and self-confidence, and leading her to ask 'Why not me?'[4]

Notes

1. This study concluded that media coverage has contributed to a 'mediated collective memory' of Hillary Rodham Clinton which is 'reductionist, iconic and hyperreal' (Parry-Giles 2000: 205). That the iconic status of HRC has indeed lodged itself in the public imagination was underlined in comments about another powerful woman, Cherie Booth, made by a British member of parliament in summer 2000. When Ms Booth, one of Britain's foremost lawyers, spoke publicly in defence of a new Human Rights Act, she was described as 'a cross between First Lady and Lady Macbeth'. Cherie

Booth's husband is the British Prime Minister Tony Blair. 'Tories aim barbs at PM's "Lady Macbeth"', *Guardian*, 9 August 2000.

2. Orit Sulitzeanu, personal communication, July 2000. The campaign was so successful that the advertising agency responsible for it later reprinted all three ads in a promotion to attract new clients.

3. 'Introduction to Croatian Election Results' 2000, *B.a.B.e. up-date*, No. 8: 1.

4. Orit Sulitzeanu, personal communication, July 2000.

7

Media, Violence and Women

The nature and extent of violence against women in society surfaced as a powerful issue on the international agenda only during the 1990s. The 1993 United Nations Declaration on the Elimination of Violence against Women was the first international human rights instrument to deal exclusively with the question. In March 1994 the UN Human Rights Commission appointed a Special Rapporteur on Violence against Women. The 1995 Beijing Platform for Action included 'Violence against Women' as one of the twelve critical areas of concern to be addressed by governments and other actors. It also drew attention to the media dimensions of violence: 'Violent and degrading or pornographic media products are ... negatively affecting women and their participation in society.'[1]

In the years that followed Beijing, discussion of the links between the media and violence against women crystallised around two focal points. One was the extent to which negative and stereotyped women's images in the media – particularly in fictional content – might contribute to gender violence in society. In 1998 Isis International and representatives from other women's non-governmental organisations met at the forty-second meeting of the UN Commission on the Status of Women in New York to consider these questions and to debate media strategies for addressing violence against women (see *Changing Lenses* 1999).

The second major area of discussion concerned media coverage of actual incidents of violence against women. This was one of the main agenda topics at a 1999 global video conference organised by the United Nations Development Fund for Women (UNIFEM), in collaboration with other UN agencies. During a six-week online virtual working group held in preparation for the video conference, the media were highlighted both as a means of enhancing the effectiveness of other strategies to end violence against women and as a specific focus for anti-violence advocacy. The working group stressed the need for activists to work with the media 'to promote coverage that exposes violence against women as a human rights violation and that challenges the social, cultural and political norms that support it. Media have a key role to play in stimulating public debate, exposing the severity and prevalence of violence against women, and providing a forum for exploring strategies in other areas.'[2]

Fictional Violence and Gender

> With more media, the amount of media violence has increased. This is due not only to the cumulative effects of the creation of new media, but also to the increased competition between the media and their globalisation and privatisation ... What drives media violence, then, is not primarily popularity but global marketing. Concentration of media ownership ... makes it difficult for newcomers, smaller firms and alternative production companies to succeed on the home market. They are therefore forced into the video branch and foreign sales. Their products need a dramatic ingredient that requires no translation and fits as many cultures as possible. That ingredient is often violence. A study in the USA indicates that American programmes exported to other countries contain more violence than American programmes shown in the US. (von Feilitzen 1998: 45–6)

One of the results of media globalisation is that almost 90 per cent of children around the world are acquainted with violent action characters such as *Terminator* and *Rambo*. This finding, from the largest ever intercultural study on the impact of media violence on children, indicates the extent to which children the world over are immersed in a media environment in which violence is rewarded and normalised. More than 5,000 twelve-year-old children from twenty-three countries from all world regions took part in this questionnaire-based study (Groebel 1998). One of the innovative features of the research was that it included children living in both 'crisis' environments (war zones, high crime areas) and low-aggression milieux. This allowed the researchers to examine the links between media preferences, environmental influences and aggressive tendencies.

Among the issues addressed by the study was the question of gender differences, and indeed these were found to be extremely marked. Boys in particular were fascinated by aggressive media heroes. While boys named media action heroes as role models (30 per cent of all models mentioned by boys), girls mentioned pop stars and musicians (27 per cent of all models mentioned by girls). The fascination with media violence was linked to the fact that aggressive behaviour is rewarded in the media. For boys especially, media violence helped to create a frame of reference for attractive role models. The study found a clear link between the preference for media violence and the wish to be involved in aggression itself, particularly among boys: 47 per cent of those who preferred aggressive media content, compared with 19 per cent of those with other media preferences. The overall conclusion was that, although the social and economic conditions in which children grow up are probably more important than the media in terms of influencing behaviour, 'the extent and omnipresence of media violence contributes to the development of a global aggressive culture. The "reward-characteristics" of aggression are more systematically promoted than non-aggressive ways of coping with one's life ... When violent content becomes a common phenomenon ... the probability that children develop a new frame of reference, and that problematic predispositions are channelled into destructive attitudes and behaviour increases immensely' (Groebel 1998: 198).

While this twenty-three-country study confined itself to the gender dimensions of media preferences and aggressive tendencies, several media monitoring groups have looked into the gendered characteristics of violent media content itself. In 1995 the Media Advocacy Group's study of soaps and serials on Indian television concluded that a high degree of violence had become one of the most important hooks in ensuring the success of these programmes. Of the 210 episodes monitored, 151 (72 per cent) showed instances of violence. Sexual violence was prevalent. Although only one actual instance of rape was noted, there were frequent verbal, threatening references to this form of violence (Media Advocacy Group 1995b).

In a later study, the group found that this trend was increasingly showing up in programmes popular with children. Across more than fifty-six hours of content monitored, there were some 750 acts of violence. Family drama serials – usually predicated on conflict – depicted violence in a domestic context. Crimes of passion, in which a love triangle was the source of violence, were common. There were also cases in which sexual violence was linked to psychotic behaviour. One example, centring on the rape of a schoolgirl by a psychopath, was transmitted at 18.00. Most of the aggressors were male (79 per cent). Much male violence in these serials was directed at women (34 per cent of the depictions). And while in some cases the perpetrator of violence was punished, in many instances violence was depicted in a rewarding context – to settle issues or resolve conflict (Centre for Advocacy and Research 1998). Very similar patterns were found in a 1998 study carried out by Women's Media Watch in Jamaica. The research covered 166 hours of programming on two television stations over seven days. Children's programmes and cartoons accounted for over 48 per cent of all violent scenes. The initiators of violence were mainly men (80 per cent), and violence was often used as the first response to dealing with problems. The use of violence to solve problems was condemned in only 30 per cent of cases.[3]

This is not an easy area for direct activist intervention. Organising complaints about specific examples of gender violence in the media, or boycotting products advertised on shows with highly violent content, may occasionally bring short-term results. But to achieve more fundamental change, strategies need to be broadly based, along the lines pursued by Women's Media Watch (Jamaica) for whom media violence has been a principal focus since its establishment in 1987. For example, public debate involving citizens, educators, media professionals and politicians can try to reach common ground on acceptable standards. Professional guidelines and codes of conduct are especially important in this area. Perhaps above all, media education is essential so that audiences can be helped to create a critical distance between their own life struggles and the violent solutions so often presented in the media.

Advertising and Sexual Violence

Sexual objectification of women is one of the most serious and recurring charges against advertising. When portrayed as objects, women are represented as available for use, exploitation, and mistreatment. Hints of violence run through a great deal of advertising. However, the ever-present quality of promotional culture in most societies means that in many cases advertisements are scanned obliquely rather than carefully observed by members of the public. At the same time, advertising's very pervasiveness means that people may experience contradictory feelings of immunity from and vulnerability to it.[4] For instance, a study of young adults in the United Kingdom found that although they were active, sophisticated consumers of advertising, they also felt unable to escape it. There was a belief that even 'blindfolding and deafening people' would not be enough to prevent exposure to ads, 'that advertising would somehow still seep through into people's consciousness' (O'Donohue 1997: 268). Overall, these young people expressed a sense of enjoyment of advertising, even though they were frequently angered by it. This additional level of complexity – the attraction of advertising – is something that activists have increasingly recognised must be faced in any critique of advertisements (and indeed other forms of media content). For if feminist critique does not acknowledge the basis of advertising's attraction, then the attack on advertising becomes an attack on the people who enjoy it – the very people whose support activists want to enlist (Walker 1999).

The power of advertising often rests on its ability to connect us with some aspect of our own reality. This is particularly true of advertisements that address us along gender lines. Yet most of these messages are hyper-ritualistic. Designed for instant communication, they draw on certain very limited codes of gender display. Reflecting on advertising's 'obsession' with gender and sexuality, Sut Jhally points out that although gender could be defined in many ways, in advertising it is equated almost exclusively with sex. 'Women are defined primarily in sexual terms. What is important about women is their sexual behaviour ... Viewing women from this narrow perspective can result in treating women as less than truly human' (Jhally 1990: 138).

Jhally maintains that while it is difficult to criticise a single advertisement in isolation (even those that objectify women), effective criticism can and should be addressed to the 'system of images' that equates women with sexual availability, and at the cumulative effect of these messages.[5] This was the approach taken by a group of women in Israel, who developed a toolkit on how to recognise and analyse sexually violent themes in advertising. The kit was used in training and awareness-raising workshops for people from all walks of life. Using ads from the Israeli mainstream media, the group identified five major themes that will be widely recognisable across most countries.

- *Fragmentation:* only part/s of the female body is/are presented.
- *Bondage:* women are tied, limited in their movement or restricted in their freedom in other physical ways.
- *Forced contact:* women are shown being forced by men.
- *Symbolic violence:* women are associated with violence, though no actual aggression is presented.
- *Potential violence:* women are presented in situations that are known to be potentially dangerous (Lemish 1998).

At the workshops, examples of each theme were presented and then discussed by participants to arrive at an interpretation of the ads. Although the participants spanned a very wide range of social groups, many shared the same associations and found similar meanings in the images. A common sensation expressed in analysing these ads was a sense of danger. The advertisements projected two overall views of women. First, women seemed oblivious to violence, or indifferent to it. Often they appeared to be enjoying it. Second, women were often presented as provoking violence. They were dressed and positioned as if to invite an 'innocent' male; their body language was meant to be arousing. Although there can be no clear answer to the question of causality, 'the question remains: to what degree can such images be associated with perpetuating myths of violence against women? From a feminist perspective, the mere existence of such images is problematic' (Lemish 1998: 291–2).

The workshops reached hundreds of people, and the materials were eventually housed within the Israel Women's Network where they had a tremendous impact on the network's own strategy. The IWN started to organise 'media events' – for example, on 25 November to mark International Day on Violence against Women. In fact, the IWN's first and most successful campaign was on the issue of violence against women. This mobilised funds, legislation, NGOs, and led to many initiatives including the establishment of Israel's first rape crisis centre. So the effect of these workshops went far beyond raising public awareness about violence in advertising – important though that was – and triggered a number of fundamental social and political actions to tackle violence against women in society at large. In addition, the IWN used the workshop material to organise seminars on the portrayal of women in advertising for staff of the Independent Broadcasting Authority (IBA), Israel's public service broadcaster. These seminars were part of a broader discussion in which the IBA eventually agreed to the introduction of a section on gender portrayal in its guidelines on programme content.[6]

Reporting Violence against Women

In early June 1998 the news media of Indonesia, Australia, the USA, Hong Kong and Singapore started to release stories about the mass rape of ethnic Chinese women during the May riots in Indonesia. Women's groups played a crucial initial role in bringing the facts to public and media attention. After more than fifty days of silence in the Chinese national media, the *People's Daily* published a first brief report on the subject. In the days that followed several more articles appeared. All of them ignored the women's rights dimension and gender aspects of the events, focusing instead on race and economic issues. In the only commentary on the subject, the *People's Daily* referred to the 'plundering of people's property, raping people's wives and daughters'. Angered by the blinkered and sexist coverage, women applied to hold a demonstration in Beijing, but their application was turned down. Nevertheless, about a hundred women – most of them journalists – got together informally to refocus the issue around women's rights. The All-China Women's Federation (ACWF) sent a statement to the *People's Daily*, pointing out that the rapes constituted a violation of the human rights of women. This was the only women's voice on the subject that appeared in the *People's Daily* (Yuan 1999).

During the late 1990s, media activists in many countries began to monitor and critique the amount and type of coverage given to cases of violence against women. One of the most extensive projects was in Sri Lanka where the Women and Media Collective's Women's Rights Watch monitored thirty newspapers between 1997 and 1999. The conclusions of the two-year project were discomfiting. Many incidents of violence, particularly those relating to rape, wife beating and sexual harassment, were ridiculed or sensationalised in press reports. Most of the substantive elements were either omitted or hidden within spectacular accounts, frequently based on speculation. In fact, the opportunity to speculate often appeared to be the main reason for covering stories. Except for cases considered important by the press – usually those dealing with important personalities – reports were seldom followed up. The press rarely initiated any substantive debate about the causes or consequences of violence against women, and there was little comment on laws, law enforcement or policy. Some newspapers disregarded the privacy of victims of violence, publishing names and photographs, speculating on life-styles and past sexual history in the case of rape victims, and indulging in biased commentary. Male correspondents filed the vast majority of reports on violence against women and many of the more sensational features were written by men (Samuel 1999).

These findings are echoed in studies from very different countries. For example, research covering twenty Canadian newspapers concluded that stories about violence against women generally lacked analysis or context, depicting the crimes as the isolated, freak actions of a 'serial killer' rather than as being part of a larger problem. Statistics from Status of Women Canada painted a very different picture about crimes against women from the one presented in the press. In 1991 80 per cent of such crimes were committed by individuals the women knew, particularly husbands or ex-husbands, and 62 per cent occurred in the home (MediaWatch 1993b). Another problem is the tendency to use language and images that underplay the dimensions of violence against women – for example, presenting it as a 'family scandal' or a purely private matter. For instance, in Japan the word 'rape' (*gokan*) is avoided in rape stories. Instead, the word used is the Japanese term for 'assault' or 'violence' (*boko* or *ranbo*) in relation to adult women and 'mischief' (*itazura*) in relation to young girls. The rationale for this is that the victims will suffer social and mental disgrace when the word 'rape' is used. At the same time, press reports routinely publish the names of victims (Miyazaki 1999).

Media advocacy groups in these and other countries work hard to draw attention to the limitations of media reporting that decontextualises the problem of violence, depicting it as a series of isolated and often sensational incidents. In Sri Lanka Women's Rights Watch has recommended training for media policy-makers and journalists in gender-sensitive reporting and feature writing, and has called for more women journalists to be assigned to cover incidents of violence against women (Samuel 1999). In 2000 MediaWatch launched a new campaign to draw attention to the way in which the Canadian media continue to slant reports on violence against women, by creating a 'blame the victim' attitude. Members were urged to write to the editors/publishers of the media in which they found objectionable reporting.[7] In Japan, responding to protests from women, some newspapers have begun to use the term *gokan* (rape) and to maintain the anonymity of victims. For example, a group called Workshop on Gender and Media (GEAM), which has been monitoring Japanese newspaper content and newspaper style manuals since 1989, published a set of non-sexist guidelines for the media in 1996 (Ueno et al. 1996). This immediately influenced a number of newspapers such as the *Asahi Shimbun*, the second largest daily in Japan, which stopped using the term *itazura* in 1997.[8] In the Philippines, too, pressure from women activists and journalists following a series of violent rape cases that made sensational news in print and radio in late 1993, resulted in the creation of Guidelines on the Coverage of Crimes against Women and Minors. Among the most important provisions are recognition of the victims' right to decide whether to be identified or not; recognition of the victims' right to dignity, especially in death; and recognition of the responsibility of media to report factually and seriously crimes of violence against women and children (Militante 1999).

Probably the most comprehensive and sustained campaign to influence news reporting of violence against women has been in South Africa, where the incidence of violence is higher than in any other country in the world. This was recognised by South Africa's broadcasting regulator, the Independent Broadcasting Authority (IBA) in 1999, when it introduced a revised Code of Conduct for Broadcasters: 'The issue of violence in broadcasting, and particularly on television, is a world-wide concern. In South Africa, with our legacy of violence and abuse of human rights, this issue is of even greater concern, particularly in relation to violence against women.'[9] The IBA's new provisions dealing with violence against women – a much condensed version of guidelines developed by Women's Media Watch in conjunction with the Commission on Gender Equality and other groups[10] – acknowledged the degree of national concern attached to the issue. For media advocates, the IBA's inclusion of special clauses in its Code of Conduct for Broadcasters was one of several important outcomes of two years of dedicated effort through monitoring, action and education.

One of the first initiatives of the Commission on Gender Equality (CGE) after its establishment in 1997 was to commission a study of how violence against women was being covered in the media. The two-month monitoring study of the daily press found that the amount of coverage was very low, with most items focusing on dramatic incidents of rape and murder. Domestic violence barely featured. Organised events held to protest against the abuse of women were all but ignored. The most frequent representation was of women as victims, with violence depicted as dramatic and brutal, and women as helpless against it. The few reports on domestic violence were poorly handled, with incidents depicted as avoidable love triangles. The woman's perspective was seldom reported, and her dignity and privacy were frequently abused (Media Monitoring Project 1998a). These results, presented at a CGE workshop in late 1997, prompted Women's Media Watch to draw up a first set of general guidelines for reporting violence against women.

In 1998 an alliance of NGOs came together in a movement called Transformation for Women in the Media (TWM). TWM dedicated 1998 to the issue of violence against women. A second monitoring study was carried out, covering a wider range of media including television. The findings confirmed those of the 1997 research, although one positive note was an increase in the representation of women as survivors (Media Monitoring Project 1998c). Nevertheless, women as victims still predominated in the media coverage. The results of the study, together with more elaborate editors' guidelines, were launched during the 16 Days of Activism against Gender Violence in late 1998.[11]

Throughout 1999 Women's Media Watch worked to popularise the guidelines through its regular workshops and in meetings with journalists and editors. At the same time, a comprehensive resource booklet for journalists was produced in a collaborative venture by the Soul City Institute for Health and Development Communication, the National Network on Violence against Women, the Institute for the Advancement of Journalism, the Commission on Gender Equality and Women's Media Watch. The booklet includes facts, figures and information on violence against women in South Africa. It deals with common misconceptions surrounding domestic violence, rape, femicide (murder specifically targeted at women) and sexual harassment. It presents some of the findings on how the media currently cover violence against women, and gives extensive suggestions for improving coverage of VAW. Now widely circulated throughout South African newsrooms and training institutions, the booklet gives working and aspiring journalists practical help in an accessible form. The culmination of two years of co-ordinated monitoring and action in one of the most contentious areas of media advocacy, the booklet and the IBA's adoption of special provisions in its Code for Broadcasters illustrate how planned monitoring and action, together, can bring results at the level of media policy and practice.

Good reporting can make a difference. Women's Media Watch, South Africa, claims that stories about women who escape abusive relationships are often inspirational to women still caught in the cycle of violence.

'Many women leave relationships on the strength of articles or radio programmes that tell a story of a woman they can relate to who leaves. Most often these women do not tell the journalist that their article was a life-line; perhaps journalists need more positive feedback to write other, similar stories' (Le Roux 1999: 25).

The Media, Violence and Women's Human Rights

Women activists can also build highly effective media strategies to focus public attention on women's rights violations. The Tanzania Media

---

Box 1 Guidelines for Reporting on Violence against Women

Sources

- Use more than one source for your report wherever possible.
- Use people opposed to violence against women as sources, rather than relying solely on the police.
- Use different kinds of story. Crime round-ups and briefs are useful in providing an overview; feature stories will introduce new perspectives and understanding of the nature of violence against women.

Language Language can influence people's perceptions of violence against women. Describing someone guilty of sexual harassment as a 'sex pest' trivialises the offence. Harassers should be called harassers. Someone who kills his wife should be called a murderer, not a person who has committed a 'crime of passion'.

Descriptions Focusing on the physical appearance, attractiveness or clothing of women who have been sexually victimised may inadvertently reinforce the myth that sexual assault is caused by lust, or that women are responsible for it.

Victims vs survivors Challenge the depiction of women as helpless victims by describing them as survivors. Where possible, emphasise women's coping skills and their survival strategies.

Focus of the story Often news stories revolve around the perpetrator of violence and marginalise the survivor. If it is not possible to obtain the woman's side of the story, contact an organisation that can provide information from a survivor's perspective.

Women's Association (TAMWA) has developed a particularly comprehensive approach to lobbying and advocacy in the area of gender-based violence. For instance, in 1998 it launched a campaign to lobby for amendments to the Law of Marriage Act which, according to research commissioned by TAMWA, condones domestic violence, denying women and children their rights – including inheritance and property ownership. Workshops were organised to sensitise journalists to the deficiencies in the Act and to help them report convincingly on the needed amendments. Using what it calls a 'Bang Style' strategy, TAMWA mobilised media coverage. In the weeks following the workshops, sixty-four stories were

---

Type of case highlighted Reports tend to focus on stranger rape, reinforcing the misconception that rape is usually committed by strangers in public places. Challenge police media liaison people to provide details of other kinds of rape case and information about domestic violence cases.

Looking for other angles Look for alternatives to the 'woman-as-victim' stories so as to highlight other sides to the problem of violence against women. These might include:

- Cases that result in successful prosecutions.
- Information about new legislation, which you can simplify for your audience.
- Initiatives to prevent violence against women or to deal with its aftermath.

General suggestions for reporting on violence against women

- Highlight VAW as a fundamental human rights violation.
- Recognise VAW as equally significant to other crimes and treat it as 'hard' rather than 'soft' news.
- Remember the media's public education function; this includes reporting on positive role models for women and debunking myths about VAW.
- Include analysis and contextualisation of events in news stories.
- Provide information about services for survivors of VAW for readers, listeners and viewers.
- Name perpetrators of violence wherever legally possible.

Adapted with premission from *Violence against Women in South Africa: A Resource for Journalists*, 1999

produced, covering aspects such as the lack of protection offered by the law with respect to spousal battery. Lobbying and advocacy for review of the Law of Marriage Act remained a priority for the association in 1999 and 2000.

TAMWA regularly sends teams of journalists from print and electronic media to the country's regions to conduct journalistic surveys and interviews on practices that adversely affect women. In 1997 the association began to highlight a practice, based on beliefs about witchcraft, that was leading to the killing of elderly women in one particular region. In 1998 the association produced a documentary video to shed light on the facts and myths surrounding these killings. The documentary was screened on four television stations in Dar es Salaam. TAMWA's media monitoring showed that the number of press reports on this issue increased from 128 items in 1998 to 576 in 1999. In September 1999 alone, after a field trip for journalists to the region in question, 141 hard news stories, editorials and feature items were published and broadcast on witchcraft-related killings of elderly women. Intense public debate followed, through newspaper columns and radio programmes. Encouraged by the reaction and concern expressed at all levels of society (including government), TAMWA organised a three-day workshop involving national and local administrators, members of parliament, the police, traditional healers, religious leaders and journalists. Together these groups developed a three-year plan of action (2000–2003) to address the killings of elderly women because of witchcraft beliefs.[12]

Like TAMWA, Sancharika Samuha (Forum of Women Communicators) has focused on using the media to address violations of women's human rights in Nepal. For example, the question of equal property rights has dominated public debate in the country over the past decade. From the outset the mainstream media campaigned against granting women the same rights to inherit property as men. Sancharika runs a regular women's features service called 'Serial on Women', which is distributed free to more than 150 newspapers and magazines throughout the country. The articles focus on all kinds of issues affecting rural and urban women in Nepal, and have a very high take-up rate. For six months in 1997 this service was used to place articles on equal property rights in the press. The group produced and aired radio jingles and a television advertisement, distributed posters, held workshops with journalists and NGOs. This campaign still continues. In 1999 Sancharika organised a national workshop on equal property rights, and agreed to set up a media monitoring project on the topic. Although the issue remains unresolved in terms of legislation, Sancharika believes this to have been one of its most successful initiatives.[13] The links created between concerned NGOs and sympathetic journalists mean that mainstream media are no longer implacably hostile to the notion of equality for women in what is a fundamentally important domain. As a result there is a new awareness among the general public about women's side of the story.

Men, the Media and Violence against Women

> People often ask me what men are like in South Africa. Well … consider that more women are raped in South Africa than any other country in the world. That one out of three women will be raped in their lifetime in South Africa. And perhaps, worst of all, that the rest of men in South Africa seem to think that rape isn't their problem. It's not that easy to say what the men in South Africa are like. Because there seem to be so few of them out there. (Text of advertisement broadcast on South African television, 1999)[14]

In October 1999 this advertisement, aimed at making the public aware of the high incidence of rape in South Africa, was taken off the air by the Advertising Standards Authority (ASA). The ad had been running for three months, and had been seen by over sixteen million people. The ASA received two letters of complaint, one of which was signed by thirty men. They objected that the advertisement accused all South African men of being rapists. Although the ASA decided that this was not what the ad suggested, they nevertheless ruled that it must be withdrawn because 'the context of the advertisement as a whole creates a negative perception among viewers that the men not included in the category of rapists are all complacent'.

There was immediate and widespread opposition to the ban from many women's activist groups. The campaigners who had produced the ad announced that they would appeal against the ASA ruling on legal grounds and to defend freedom of speech:

> This is the first of a series of advertisements and it is essential that freedom of speech should be defended. Ironically, the very point that the advertisement was making – that rape is endemic in South Africa because so few men take it seriously – has been borne out by this decision … The ASA committee is saying to men who complain because they are accused of doing nothing (about the problem of rape) that it is okay to do nothing, except complain.[15]

The Commission on Gender Equality took up the case. An appeal hearing ruled in favour of the anti-rape lobbyists and ordered that the advertisement be reinstated.

The anti-rape advertisement touched a very raw nerve in some sections of South African society. Until that point most attempts to deal with the problem of rape had focused on changes to the criminal justice system and on improving the treatment of rape survivors. This was one of the first initiatives to place the responsibility for preventing rape back with those men who perpetrate or support it, and to try to engage men in the process of change. So it was especially troubling that the views of a small group of men should take such prominence, and should be supported by the statutory body responsible for advertising regulation. But the final outcome illustrated both the power of organised action and the power of advertising to shape public opinion. The issues raised by the incident led the Commission on Gender Equality to pursue closer liaison with the ASA, and to broach future changes to its Code of Practice and complaints procedures.[16]

Notes

1. United Nations (1995), *Beijing Declaration and Platform for Action*, para. 236: www.un.org/womenwatch/daw/beijing/platform

2. UNIFEM (1999) *Women @ Work to End Violence: Voices in Cyberspace*, available at: www.undp.org/unifem/w@work2.htm

3. Women's Media Watch (1998), 'A pilot study: violence in the electronic media', unpublished report.

4. For instance, the British Advertising Standards Authority estimates that almost 30 million print advertisements are published annually in the UK, as well as 100,000 ads on posters and 2.8 billion items of direct mail (www.asa.org.uk/guide/general3.htm). About 28,000 separate, individual commercials are shown on British television each year (www.itc.org.uk/about/ann_report_99). It is estimated that urban North Americans are exposed to between 1,500 and 3,000 promotional messages each day (www.mediawatch.ca/industry/advertising).

5. Some of these issues are taken up in *It's About Time ... To Break Free of Violence* (1999), a ten-minute video produced by Women's Media Watch, Kingston, Jamaica.

6. Lesley Sachs, personal communication, July 2000.

7. 'Media portrayal of domestic violence objectionable', *action Bulletin*, summer 2000: 1.

8. Masami Saitoh, personal communication, February 2000.

9. Independent Broadcasting Authority, 'Position Paper on the Revision of the IBA's Code of Conduct for Broadcasters', 9 April 1999; available at: www.iba.org.za/broad.html

10. Commission on Gender Equality, 'Submission to the Independent Broadcasting Authority on the Code of Conduct for Broadcasters by the Commission on Gender Equality' December 1998, section 4.2; available at: www.cge.org.za/subs/conduct.htm

11. The 16 Days of Activism against Gender Violence take place annually from 25 November (International Day against Violence against Women) to 10 December (the anniversary of the Universal Declaration of Human Rights). Co-ordinated by the Center for Women's Global Leadership in the USA, the 16 Days Campaign has been adopted by activists around the world as a framework within which to direct public attention to their priorities on violence against women. Campaign tactics are determined at local or

national level, but typically include marches, street theatre, posters and other public information materials. Media coverage has been a key element in the success of 16 Days Campaign activities.

12. Information from Tanzania Media Women's Association (TAMWA), Annual Reports for 1998 and 1999.

13. Untitled report on the first four years of Sancharika Samuha activities, 2000.

14. 'Anti-rape ad pulled off air by ASA', *Making Waves* (Women's Media Watch Newsletter), No. 10, 1999: 6–7.

15. 'Anti-rape lobbyists press release', *Making Waves* (Women's Media Watch Newsletter), No. 10, 1999: 9.

16. 'ASA sees the light', *Making Waves* (Women's Media Watch Newsletter), No. 10, 1999: 8.

8

Diversity in Media Content

If you are white, male, a businessman or a politician or a professional or a celebrity, your chances of getting represented will be very high. If you are black, or a woman without social status, or poor or working class or gay or powerless because you are marginal, you will always have to fight to get heard and seen. This does not mean that no one from the latter groups will ever find their way into the media. But it does mean that the structure of access to the media is systematically skewed in relation to certain social categories. (Hall 1986: 9)

Ethnic Minorities and Immigrants

If women are under-represented or misrepresented in media content, this is doubly so for those women who are not members of the dominant national culture. For example, a study of television news, drama and sitcoms in Malaysia – a multi-ethnic society – concluded that while major ethnic groups were represented, minority ethnic groups such as the Orang Asli (aboriginals) were marginalised on the small screen. Not surprisingly, women from these minority communities were almost invisible. But democratising access to the media means ensuring that all ethnic groups are given equal opportunity to 'express publicly their ideas, and anxieties and fears even, so as to provide them with a sense of being part of a nation' (Anuar and Kim 1996: 277).

Several media monitoring groups have taken up these issues through research or advocacy or both. A study of Canadian drama and news by MediaWatch (1994b) found that, compared with men from ethnic minority backgrounds, women fell well behind – especially in news, where they were almost invisible either as reporters or as news sources. Ethnic minority women constituted 3 per cent of all news sources (compared with 25 per cent for women in general, and 8 per cent for ethnic minority men). In drama, ethnic minority women were likely to be cast in minor, traditionally stereotyped roles (poor, lawbreaker, drug addict and so on). In news they usually appeared in the context of a racially or culturally specific story and were likely to be identified as mothers or victims of violence. Yet ethnic minority groups are the fastest growing segment of the Canadian population. For instance, according to MediaWatch, projections claim that by 2001 49 per cent of people in the province of Ontario will be from these groups. Moreover, studies show that Canadians respond positively to seeing the country's diversity reflected in the media. So if broadcasters have a long way to go in catching up with Canada's demographic reality, public opinion seems to support such a move. Commenting on the data, MediaWatch noted that although it would have been useful to look at trends in the portrayal of women from different ethnic groups, their near invisibility on the television screen made this impossible (MediaWatch 1994b).

This issue takes on quite another dimension in a country like South Africa where, although the vast majority of the population is black, black women and men are severely under-represented in media content. A monitoring study of television, radio and print media carried out for Women's Media Watch in 1999 identified 66 per cent of women appearing in the media as white, and only 25 per cent as black. Other racial groups – Asian and coloured – made up the remaining 8 per cent (Media Monitoring Project 1999c). White dominance was most marked in television – a finding linked to the fact that many programmes are imported – but in the press, too, the overall pattern prevailed. Only one newspaper, the *Sowetan*, had a higher percentage of black (65 per cent) than white (28 per cent) women in its coverage. Racial stereotyping in news topics was disturbing. White women dominated in every topic except politics and government, in which there was an equal balance of blacks and whites, and corruption, where black women were mentioned seven times more than whites.

Looking at the roles in which women were found, the single positive point for black women was their slight predominance as politicians. The only other roles in which blacks outnumbered whites were as sex-workers and housewives. This media snapshot presented a picture of a society deeply divided in terms of race, with black women in marginalised roles. The dominance of white women as programme presenters (65 per cent, compared with 25 per cent black women) was a further indication that the South African media still use a white face and voice to represent a nation that is largely populated by blacks.

The same study showed clear racial divisions in the portrayal of women in advertising. White women dominated overall, with 69 per cent of portrayals. No black women were found in ads selling luxury products and services such as cars or travel. The combination of racism and sexism is a particular problem in South African advertisements. Women's Media Watch has taken up a number of such cases. For instance, in 1998 a television advertisement for a bank credit card showed a white couple waiting for their dinner guests. The doorbell rings. A black man is at the door, with a woman whom he introduces as his wife. Then another woman comes in, whom he introduces as 'my second wife'. She is followed by another, and another. The white couple looks shocked and then relieved when the 'most recent wife' is introduced. Glancing at the dining table, which is laid for four, the white man takes out his credit card and suggests they go out for dinner.

WMW objected that this exploited culture in an unrealistic and divisive way, using the controversial practice of polygamy as the butt of a joke. The body language of the black women portrayed them as obedient and subservient. WMW found this insulting, perpetuating a stereotype of black women as weak and under the control of their husbands. In a complaint to the Advertising Standards Authority, WMW asked for the ad to be withdrawn, 'and that the advertising house which produced it should explain what message they intended to put across and what they will do in future to ensure that their advertisements are not racist, sexist or culturally exploitative'. The ad was indeed withdrawn, with little fuss, although the advertising company did not respond to the challenge put to it by Women's Media Watch.[1]

This combination of racism and sexism is present as a continuous undercurrent in most societies. But it may surface in an acute form at specific times, for instance when war or civil disturbance produces a sudden influx of refugees or economic migrants from one country to another. One example is the case of Israel, which between 1990 and 1997 experienced its largest ever wave of immigration. During that period 710,000 citizens of the former Soviet Union settled in the country. This amounted to 8 per cent of the total Israeli population at the time, and there were serious problems in the absorption process. Female immigrants experienced particular difficulties. Most were highly educated and had held positions of status in their own country. Moving to Israel entailed a severe economic, professional and often psychological cost for most of them. Yet popular media portrayals seemed to assume that many – if not most – of these women were sex-workers. Disturbed by this, and by public sentiment that appeared to echo the line emerging from the media, in 1997 the Israel Women's Network commissioned a qualitative content analysis of the popular press and a telephone survey of public opinion (Lemish 2000).

The newspaper analysis examined over 100 items published from 1994 to 1997. Two dominant images of the women were found, both negative: as a supplier of sexual services (by far the most common representation) and as 'alien' – not 'one of us'. A third image of the 'exceptionally successful immigrant' occasionally appeared, helping to reinforce the normality of the other two. Many reports blurred the distinction between women trafficked for prostitution (who were not immigrants) and immigrants *per se*, the majority of whom were well educated and had enjoyed high status in their own country. Headlines compounded the problem, with decontextualised, sensational eye-catchers. The findings from the telephone survey, which covered over 500 people, were quite consistent with the content of the popular press. About 65 per cent of the respondents held negative attitudes towards these female immigrants, most commonly associating them with the sex industry. Personal acquaintance with the immigrants was related to positive attitudes towards them. Only 31 per cent of those who knew one or more immigrants agreed with the statement that they provided sexual services, compared with 52 per cent of those who were dependent on the media for their information.

These findings suggested that popular press coverage had helped to reinforce a situation in which female immigrants would find it extremely difficult to be accepted by and to become integrated within Israeli society. The IWN then launched a solid public campaign to lobby for these women. It produced a widely distributed calendar with photographs to illustrate the diversity among female immigrants, and organised courses for the women. Although this effort was limited by lack of funds, the IWN did focus public attention for the first time on many ignored aspects of the situation of this group of female immigrants.[2]

Sexuality and Homophobia

The issue of sexuality is still something of a taboo in many countries and, as yet, scarcely any media advocacy groups have publicly engaged in this debate. Women's Media Watch in South Africa is one of the few to have declared a commitment to fight homophobia and the absence of non-heterosexual images and relationships in media portrayal. The exclusion of gays and lesbians in media content is taken up in the WMW video *Who's News?*, and the 1999 monitoring study it commissioned also looked at the representation of sexuality (Media Monitoring Project 1999c). This analysis found that of 973 items in which sexuality could be determined, only twelve (1 per cent) featured lesbians. These women appeared in television drama, in magazine programmes and in self-promotional adverts. The tiny number of cases made it impossible to analyse patterns in the portrayal of sexual identity, but this in itself made a statement about the very limited spaces available to non-heterosexual members of society.

In Croatia, B.a.B.e has also taken up the question of sexual identity. In 1999 it carried out a two-month monitoring study of the portrayal of gays and lesbians, covering the six largest circulation dailies, the most popular weeklies and magazines. All texts and illustrations that discussed or mentioned homosexuality were collected and analysed. The research produced sixty pages of material with tables and comments. Not a single article dealing with homosexuality was found on front pages in 'serious' sections of the monitored newspapers. All were found in the sections on culture and entertainment or in letters to the editor. Only 30 per cent of the material dealt with Croatian citizens; the rest focused on people from other countries. A distinction was found in the way the issues were handled by Croatian and foreign journalists. When translated from foreign newspapers, the articles were relatively neutral and informative. When written by Croatian journalists, almost all (80 per cent) of the reporting was classified as negative, mocking or hostile.

In the context of its overall focus on human rights, B.a.B.e believes it important to draw attention to the fact that homosexuality is neither understood nor sanctioned in Croatia. When the group questioned publicly the fact that the new Family Law recognises no form of homosexual partnership, reactions in the media were uncompromisingly negative. There are two lesbian NGOs in the country, but they keep a very low profile. B.a.B.e plans to network with these and any other groups willing to lobby for and advocate change in the existing situation.[3]

Disability

Are we saying that people with disabilities don't drink coffee, don't fall in love, don't have careers, don't laugh? Because this is what you see. And if you're not validated in the media, you internalise that invisibility and you think yes, I'm *not* good enough to be part of 'out there'. (Shelley Barry, Equity Officer, e-tv South Africa, in *Who's News? Women and the Media* 1999)

People with disabilities are almost invisible in the media. And when they are seen, they tend to be portrayed very differently from able-bodied people, in ways that usually do not match their own experience of reality. This was the starting point for the Forum of Viewers with Disability, which came together as part of the Delhi-based Viewers' Forum established by India's Media Advocacy Group in 1998. The forum works to persuade the electronic media to mainstream issues related to disability, and to find ways of increasing the presence of people with disabilities in fiction and news programmes. The group has two major criticisms of typical media content. One is that by depicting disabled people as being in need of special treatment, existing media portrayals reinforce an image of helplessness and despair that the disabled are constantly trying to break away from. The second is that because the perspectives of disabled people are almost never included in media discussion of general issues such marriage or sexuality, the disabled are rendered invisible when it comes to 'normal' life. For the disabled community, this can add to a sense of psychological isolation.

The Forum of Viewers with Disability tries to bring these matters into the public arena and to the attention of media people. For example, in a talk show about depression how could it be possible for no disabled person to be included? Yet even here, the implication is that depression is the prerogative of the able-bodied, whereas in fact depression is part and parcel of the lives of many disabled people. Invisibility is only part of the problem. For instance, when media people become aware of the invisibility of people with disabilities in the media one common response is to make programmes that focus on the achievements of disabled people. In some ways this is a step forward. Yet what disabled people really long for is a fully rounded representation in the media, one that highlights achievements and failures, and emotional as well as physical issues.[4]

Body Image and Women

As a short-waisted woman under five feet two inches with a D cup, all I could do was dream of being tall and thin – dream and feel insufficient with myself for not measuring up to fashion's image. Fortunately, I grew up and out of that belief system. (Miftah Leath, media literacy educator, About-Face, USA)[5]

Box 2   Some Do's and Don't's on Portraying Disability

Don't equate disability (by implication or unconsciously) with villainy, evil, disease, menace.

Don't use stammering, deafness, blindness to evoke humour or ridicule.

Don't use figurative language like 'blind as a bat', 'stone-deaf' and so on.

Don't always depict the disabled in settings such as rehabilitation centres, hospitals and so on.

Do place them in the home, the workplace and other 'normal' settings.

Do emphasise the rights of the disabled.

Do promote natural, everyday integration.

Forum of Viewers with Disability, New Delhi, *Viewers' Voices*, October–November 1998.

In the late 1990s the phenomenon known as 'girl power' led to a new emphasis on young girls as an attractive youth market for products. This new segment, dubbed the 'tween' (11–14-year-old, female) market, emerged as the focus of considerable media attention. In North America and many Western European countries, health professionals began to point to media portrayals of girls that promote physically unattainable ideals of femininity as a factor influencing eating disorders among young women. Activists too, began to focus on this newly emerging area, and on the relationship between media content and self-image among women.

In 1999 MediaWatch commissioned a focus group study with Canadian tweens to explore media influences on body image and self-esteem. Body weight was clearly a concern for this age group. 'The multitude of comments on body image, weight preoccupation and self-esteem issues illustrated that these issues are central to the lives of these young women' (MediaWatch 2000: 8). The media were frequently cited as reference points: 'Because I like her and she's a good actor I think that I am going to lose 15 pounds to be just like that. I don't really know anyone who has done that,' said one. And another: 'I think that girls that look at that ad and don't have a great self esteem may think oh maybe I should do it and like start worrying about it even more' (MediaWatch 2000: 9). The tweens also felt under pressure from their male peers who, they feared, compared them with the models in fashion advertisements: 'Well, the more guys that see this, or the more guys who have it up on their locker or whatever, you try to be like that' (MediaWatch 2000: 10).

While these young women readily acknowledged that the most common images of women in the media are unrealistic and unhealthy, this did not prevent them from criticising themselves in the light of the images they condemned. Many of them felt powerless against the organisations, companies and networks that create the images, and had never taken any action.

In the United States several actions have been mounted since the mid-1990s. The National Organisation for Women (NOW) launched its first Love Your Body Day in 1998. It was hugely successful and has become an annual event in the NOW calendar. Across the country NOW's 600 local chapters and other women's organisations hold rallies, video screenings, discussions, and organise pickets and letter-writing campaigns to speak out against media images that promote unrealistic and unhealthy beauty standards. For Love Your Body Day in 2000 actions were targeted at fashion and advertising companies in New York, beer advertisers in Milwaukee, cigarette advertisers in Virginia, and television and film studios in Hollywood. NOW has developed a kit with fact sheets, resource materials and ideas for action. Its video *Redefining Liberation* is a major tool in the Love Your Body Day campaign. This analyses the tactics used by the tobacco, fashion and alcohol industries to appeal to women and girls, and the links between advertising messages and women's body image, health and self-esteem. One of the positive sides of the campaign is an annual poster competition for school and college students. The winning entry is adopted as the Love Your Body Campaign for that year.[6]

To coincide with the campaign, each year NOW organises a Body Survey in which members say which advertisement or image or character most represents an oppressive beauty standard, and which positive images they have seen. The results are illuminating. In the offending category there is wide agreement. For example, Calvin Klein advertising, Ally McBeal (the waif-thin heroine of a television drama series) and 'Baywatch' are named by substantial numbers. Affirmative body images are apparently much harder to find. Members' responses do not group around a single positive image or set of images; each year many simply answer 'none'. If it is so difficult to identify affirming female body images in the media, there is clearly a huge divide between the idealised, unreal and often technically enhanced female bodies promoted in a certain strand of media output, and what women see when they look in the mirror.

Helping women to explore and understand this divide is one of the goals of About-Face, a media literacy organisation that encourages girls and women of all ages, sizes, races and backgrounds to think positively about their bodies. The organisation was born in San Francisco in 1995, when a particular Calvin Klein advertisement was being widely displayed on billboards and buses all over the city – and indeed the world. The ad – for the perfume Obsession – showed the supermodel Kate Moss reclining nude, her bones accentuated, looking terribly gaunt. For Kathy Bruin, who was to become executive director of About-Face, the ad was the last straw in her increasing frustration with this kind of imagery: 'I wanted to make a statement that would be louder than just writing Calvin Klein a letter ... I wanted to do something big enough that ... other people might be motivated to do something too.'[7] She decided to create a satire of the Obsession ad, and chased after buses for weeks to get a good photograph of it. Then she changed the text to read 'Emaciation Stinks' (a reference to the perfume promoted in the ad) and 'Stop Starvation Imagery' (see Plate D). A thousand posters were produced and displayed all over the city.

The posters immediately galvanised public opinion and received widespread media coverage. Since then About-Face has built up a volunteer team with skills spanning public health, clinical psychology, counselling, community activism, advertising, and website development. The About-Face team lectures in schools and community groups, teaches critical media skills, and provides resources and materials that are used by students and

PLATE D Reproduced by courtesy of Kathy Bruin/About-Face, USA

professionals. A big part of the work is done via its interactive website that provides a gallery of media images, including some from outside the United States. Each image is accompanied by a brief comment, a set of facts relevant to an analysis of the image, and a list of contacts for people who want to take action. The approach is not to impose an interpretation (indeed, About-Face believes that there are no absolute right or wrong answers) but to guide people to become critical thinkers in their own right.

Other parts of the About-Face site include an open forum, information for parents and teachers, and suggestions on ways to escape from the fixation with body image that is promoted in so many media representations of women and girls. The overall message that About-Face communicates is that, despite the power and resources of the media, change is possible. The entire operation started with a single poster, and the organisation continues to make good use of this medium.

Some of the brightest people in the world are creating ads to grab our attention. In the face of this very effective barrage, it is virtually impossible for any of us as individuals to compete, to offer a criticism or opinion of the images or an alternative image that might make an impact. How far can one get if all she has is a xerox? After all, we tend to believe that the producers of the glossy images know what they are talking about, and that the people passing out xeroxed copies on the corner are a little 'off'. [The] goal in using posters is to make a public statement using a medium that is familiar. They are stylish and big, and out in the streets with the other images. And the rebellious nature gets people's attention.[8]

The About-Face approach has many lessons to offer in terms of how individual action, using basic but creative tools, can develop into a social movement. About-Face works from the same premise as almost all media and advocacy groups, motivated by a belief that 'someone else' is making the rules that limit women's lives, that the rules need to be questioned, and that those who make them need to know what women think. The About-Face slogan, 'It's time to throw our weight around!', might not be what activists in every country would say, but it is probably what most would think.

Notes

1. 'Complaint about Standard Bank advertisement', *Women's Media Watch Newsletter*, No. 7, 1998: 8.

2. Orit Sulitzeanu, personal communication, July 2000.

3. 'Portrayal of Gays and Lesbians in Croatian Media', in BaBe Annual Report, 1999: 6; available at: www.babe.hr/eng/reports/annual1999.htm

4. 'Can TV become a disability sensitive medium?', *Viewers' Voices*, November 1999: 2.

5. See About-Face website: www.about-face.org

6. Information from NOW website: www.now.org/issues/media/index.html

7. Kathy Bruin, 'Enough is enough'; see: www.about-face.org/who/bios/kathy.html

8. Ibid.

Part III

Approaches

9

Studying Gender in the Media

Experience has shown us that a body of sound research helps make the case for gender equity in the media irrefutable. (Cishecki 1998: 6)

Some activist groups like MediaWatch in Canada and the Centre for Media Advocacy and Research in India have, since their inception, relied heavily on research data to back up the positions they take *vis-à-vis* media output. Others such as Women's Media Watch in South Africa and Women's Media Watch in Jamaica based their initial work more on critical observations than on the findings of empirical research. For some activist groups, research may seem impossibly expensive, time-consuming and even intimidating. Yet as the 1995 Global Media Monitoring Project demonstrated to many, straightforward data can be collected relatively easily. Despite the limitations of simple monitoring exercises, the information they generate can add weight and authority to criticisms that may otherwise be dismissed as personal and unsubstantiated points of view. Since the mid-1990s more and more activist groups have turned to some form of data collection, even on an occasional basis, to document their critiques and strengthen their arguments.

Asking Questions

There are countless ways of studying gender in media content. The focus will depend on which aspects are to be highlighted in the individual piece of analysis. Women's Media Watch Jamaica, in its training manual on media analysis, runs through some of the simple formal and informal methods that are available (Women's Media Watch, 1998). As it points out, one of the best ways to start looking critically at the media is by asking questions. Some questions will be determined by particular cultural concerns, but many are universally relevant. The following ten-point checklist (adapted, with permission, from Michielsens 1995) was developed as a guide for media practitioners in Belgium to help them focus on differences in the portrayal of women and men in television programmes and advertisements.

It is a useful starting point for anyone interested in the overall patterns of gender representation in the media.

1. *Count the women and the subject areas in which they appear.* Are they evenly distributed, or is the balance skewed?
2. *Women speaking.* Are they represented in a way that allows them to speak with dignity and authority?
3. *Gender roles.* Are traditional gender roles reinforced – for example in relation to portrayal of family life or occupation outside the home – or avoided?
4. *Superwoman stereotype.* Are active, independent women represented as if they are 'superwomen'?
5. *Natural woman stereotype.* Does the content reinforce the stereotype of women as innately docile, emotional, non-analytical, technically inept etc.?
6. *Sex-object stereotype.* Are women represented primarily as objects of male desire?
7. *The beauty myth.* What physical attributes apply to male and female participants – for example in relation to age, body weight, skin tone, clothes?
8. *Violence against women.* Does the material normalise violence? Does it suggest that women accept or enjoy violent treatment? How are female victims of violence portrayed?
9. *Multi-dimensionality.* Does the representation encourage us to understand women's many dimensions in terms of personality, capabilities, tastes, preferences etc.?
10. *Diversity.* Does the material reflect the diversity of age groups, social classes, ethnic groups, physical characteristics of women and men in the community as a whole?

Counting and Categorising Media Content

For absolute beginners, the quarterly journal *Media Report to Women* in the United States has published a very simple guide on how to monitor newspapers. The approach goes no further than counting female and male bylines, photographs and references. But for those who have never tackled a quantitative analysis, this can be a useful way to begin (see *Media Report to Women* 2000a). Going beyond these simple counts M. Junior Bridge, who carried out annual studies for Women, Men and Media in the United States between 1989 and 1996, gives examples of the questions that can be asked to extend simple quantification and to deepen the assessment of gender coverage in newspapers:

- How are females described – by their marital/parental status, by their appearance, by their occupation? How are males described?
- In what kinds of story are females quoted or referenced or left out? In what kinds of story are males quoted or referenced or left out?
- How are females portrayed in photographs? Are males portrayed differently? If so, is there a valid reason for the differences?
- Are proper names or pronouns used for repeated references to a female in the same proportion as are references to males?
- Are there pages with no female references, bylines, or photos? Are there pages with only female or predominantly female references, bylines and photos?
- Are issues of special concern to women, such as reproductive rights or breast cancer, being covered? If not, why not? If covered, is it adequate coverage? Where is such coverage – in news briefs, in major articles; in editorials or commentaries; in cartoons? In what sections of the newspapers are they covered?
- In news of general interest, such as the economy, the job market, war, day care and education, are women's viewpoints, experience and expertise included? Is female commentary being sought out as frequently as male commentary? Are males excluded in the coverage of certain topics, such as teenage pregnancy and childcare? If so, why?
- Are the accomplishments of females covered in the news? If so, how and where? How does this coverage compare to coverage of the accomplishments of males?
- Are female reporters assigned to all topic areas? If not, what are they reporting on, and why are they limited to certain subjects? What are the subjects? (Bridge 1995: 27–8)

Questions like these can also be asked to get behind and beyond more elaborate quantitative news coding schemes such as those used in the Global Media Monitoring Projects of 1995 and 2000. The utility of the GMMP system, designed by the Canadian team Erin Research Inc., has been proven by groups all over the world. Because the scheme is intended for use in many different countries, not all of its coding categories are completely appropriate in specific national contexts. However, as an overall approach it provides an excellent starting point from which groups can develop more specific tools, adapted to local and national circumstances.[1]

In Trinidad and Tobago the Gender Media Monitor (GEMM) has adapted the Global Media Monitoring Project model not simply for its own analysis of news, but also for the study of cartoons and advertisements in print and on television. Although the format of the grid is similar to that used in the GMMP news analysis, most of the coding categories are of course quite different. Apart from basic data on the type of product or service advertised, the grid collects information on the characteristics of the people portrayed in the ad and on whether sex or sensuality is used to sell the product. Another more unusual aspect covered is 'dramatic technique' – the advertisement's marketing approach. The categories suggested by GEMM include demonstration, testimonial, 'slice-of-life', sex, and lifestyle (e.g. enhancing, modernising). Technical aspects of the marketing approach – use of animation, humour, music, voice-over – are also coded. Clearly, some of the categories in this schema are specific to Trinidad and Tobago and will not be applicable elsewhere. But groups looking for a relatively simple approach to advertising analysis will be able to adapt the basic model to fit their own needs. The system was designed for a media literacy project carried out in secondary schools in Trinidad and Tobago in 2000, and GEMM found that students had very few problems in using it.[2]

One of the most tried and tested sets of categories for the quantitative content analysis of gender portrayal in advertisements was developed twenty-five years ago by Leslie McArthur and Beth Resko in the United States. Since then these basic categories have been used in studies in every world region (see Furnham and Mak 1999). The McArthur and Resko system covers seven characteristics of the central figure/s in adverts. Central figures are defined as those who play a major role by virtue of either speaking or having prominent visual exposure.

- Gender of the central figure.
- Basis for the credibility of the central figure: product user, authority.
- Role of the central figure: spouse/partner, parent, homemaker, worker, professional, real-life celebrity, interviewer/narrator, boyfriend/girlfriend, other.
- Location of the central figure: home, leisure/outdoors, work/occupation, other.
- Arguments given by the central figure: factual/concrete/scientific, opinion/testimonial/non-scientific, no argument.
- Rewards offered or reaped by the central figure: social enhancement (approval, advancement), personal enhancement (attractiveness, health, cleanliness etc) practical (saving time, labour, money), other.
- Type of product associated with the central figure: body products, home products, food products, cars and sports products, services, other. (McArthur and Resko 1975: 211–12)

The most notable omission in this system is a code for mode of presentation. For example, many studies have found gender differences depending on whether the central figure provides voice-over or is simply

depicted visually. This and other less important additions have been made
in later research into gender portrayal in advertising (see Furnham and
Mak 1999). However, the basic framework provided by McArthur and
Resko still endures.

Exploring the Structure of Media Messages

Standard coding of numbers, roles, occupations and other relatively
straightforward aspects can yield only a very limited understanding of
gender portrayal in media content. The complexity and subtlety of most
media messages tend to be lost when analysis is restricted to attributes that
can be readily quantified. It is usually necessary to dig more deeply to
reveal the nuances that contribute to particular patterns in gender representation. One approach is to analyse the implicit assumptions that underlie
the way in which events are represented. Close attention to the choice of
words and images can help bring to light the values being used to construct
a particular message. Sometimes known as discourse analysis, this pro-
cedure can be applied in rather complex analyses of the various layers
within message construction.[3] But the general approach can also be used
in relatively straightforward ways, to move beyond the simple story told by
quantitative data.

For instance, in a 1998 study of media coverage of violence against
women (VAW), the Media Monitoring Project in South Africa developed
a set of 'propositions' to analyse the range of themes found in news reports.
These propositions were based on findings from earlier research carried
out by the MMP. Each macro-proposition represents a range of propositions, not all of which would necessarily be present in any one item (see
Box 3). More than one macro-proposition might be identified within a
single item.

This approach can be applied to many areas of media content. However,
it usually requires a multi-stage development. For example, a sample of
material would first be scanned so as to identify some broad propositions.
Next the usefulness and relevance of these would be explored in relation
to a wider body of content. This would lead to a final set of propositions
to be examined in the definitive stage of the research.

A more quantitative instrument for measuring the implicit values in
media messages is the Gender Discrimination Index (GDI), developed by
the Korean Women's Development Institute (KWDI) in 1996.[4] The basic
coding categories of gender, age, occupation, role, setting, marital status
and relationships are similar to those used in most studies of content.
Beyond these, the GDI aims to quantify the values that produce gender
discrimination in news reporting and in drama (Kim and Min 1997). To

Box 3   Values, Arguments and Media Messages

Macro-proposition	Proposition
1. Victims	Women need to be protected by men for their safety; the system fails to protect women; women are sexually passive.
2. Reduced responsibility	Stimulants reduce responsibility in men and/or in women; childhood sexual trauma reduces responsibility; stress or pressure leads to abuse; being powerful or famous reduces responsibility.
3. VAW as lovers' quarrel	Domestic violence is just a lovers' quarrel; emotional abuse is not as serious as physical abuse; domestic violence is dramatic; domestic violence is about love triangles and jealousy.
4. VAW and masculinity	Violence against women is men's way of expressing love/passion; violence is a way for men to discipline unruly women; rape is a crime of lust over which men have no control.
5. VAW as perversion	Violence against women is committed by psychopaths; men who rape or sexually abuse women are sick perverts; gang rape is a form of male hysteria.
6. Women look for trouble	Physical attractiveness increases the potential for rape; women ask for it by going to places they shouldn't, walking alone at night, dressing provocatively.
7. Culture/tradition justify VAW	Culture/tradition should not be disrupted by modern or foreign values; husbands are entitled to abuse their wives.
8. VAW as criminal/ human rights abuse	Violence against women is a human rights abuse and a crime; there is no excuse for spousal abuse, either sexual or physical.
9. Women as survivors	Victims of violence against women have courage; survivors are entitled to dignity.

Adapted from Media Monitoring Project 1998c: 4–5

do this, coders are provided with operational definitions that are continually reviewed and revised throughout the analysis, so as to increase validity. Examples of the definitions used in the study of news include:

- condoning/accepting preference for boys
- accepting notions of male superiority
- putting women down
- making hostile remarks towards women
- implying that women are responsible for sexual violence or harassment
- projecting over-exposure of women's bodies
- over-emphasising the wise-mother-and-good-wife ideology
- under-valuing domestic work
- unfair/hostile treatment of the women's movement
- not providing gender-segregated data in reporting survey results[5]

In news analyses twenty-one elements were scored, giving one point if the element is not present and two points if it is. This gives a possible 'gender discrimination score' in the range 21 to 42 points. The first news analysis showed an average score of 38 on the GDI. When applied to two drama series, scores of 43 and 44 (out of a possible 50) were recorded (Lee 1999).

The authors of the GDI admit the difficulties in setting standards of measurement, given the complexity and diversity of media content (Kim and Min 1997: 205), and the limitations of this method almost certainly hide many important subtleties in gender representation. But the GDI could be a useful starting point for those who favour a quantitative approach and who, for example, want to compare items within a given genre or to compare a particular genre across different media organisations within their own country.

Analysing Patterns and Interactions

A great deal of media monitoring concentrates on news analysis. While other types of media content such as popular drama or talk shows are very important in terms of gender portrayal, until now they have been relatively unexplored by activist groups. In these genres, the standard coding categories normally applied in news analysis – role, age, occupation and so on – tend to be of very limited use. Much more important are the interactions between characters, the patterns of authority and credibility established in terms of who speaks when and about what, the use of technical devices such as camera angles, lighting and sound to create specific effects. All this presents quite a complex analytical problem, for which activists are not usually prepared by experiences of news monitoring.

For instance, the Media Advocacy Group in India found that its early work in monitoring news was of limited help when it came to studying popular drama. The following issues emerged from a first pilot study:

- Apart from strictly quantitative aspects, fiction cannot be studied in terms of predetermined categories as news can.
- Given the nature of fiction, both the larger and the smaller picture have to be studied. There were many variations even within individual dramatic episodes.
- The challenge of not simply recognising shifts or trends in character portrayal, but determining whether these are credible or simply superficial.
- For the purposes of advocacy, making recommendations is a more difficult task in fiction than in news. (Media Advocacy Group 1995a: 8–9)

As a result of the pilot, the MAG identified certain aspects of popular drama that deserve attention from a gender perspective:

- Portrayal of women in terms of the interplay of their personal and professional relationships. For example, when a woman is portrayed as working outside the home is she also portrayed as strong in terms of her personal relationships, or is she depicted as weak, confused, in need of male support?
- Where women are portrayed as protagonists in 'new' roles, for example as police officers, what is the gender environment? For example, is she simply a female cipher in a male-determined setting?
- How is the family structure depicted? Who is the focus of family life and activity? Is there a difference between the roles of female and male characters in the family?
- In a conflict situation, how are women and men portrayed – for example in terms of emotions or approaches to conflict resolution? (Adapted, with permission, from Media Advocacy Group 1995a: 8–9)

While other more specific aspects are bound to emerge in relation to the particular drama to be analysed, the MAG has here identified some of the key features that occur in a good deal of television fiction.

For those seeking a flexible coding structure for the analysis of drama and talk shows, the work of the NOS Gender Portrayal Department in the Netherlands may be a useful starting point. Variations of its approach have been used to highlight the subtle patterns of gender stereotyping that recur in radio and television programmes. For example, the department's analyses of talk shows and interviews have found that women are more often interrupted than men, that men are more often invited to speak than women, and that female guests are addressed in a more familiar and casual way than male guests (NOS 1996a and 1996b). In drama programmes men tend to take the initiative and to be invested with authority, not just in terms of how their parts are scripted but also through the use of camera angles (NOS Gender Portrayal Department 1994). Findings like this, that go behind the straightforward results of most content analysis studies, enable the Gender Portrayal Department to work with radio and television programme-makers to examine why these patterns occur and to explore alternative ways of doing things.

One of the most sophisticated tools for analysing gender interactions in television is the Profile Time developed by the Centre for Women's Studies at the University of Antwerp. This computer software program allows coders to enter information directly into a database while watching a video recording. It can chart straightforward quantitative data quickly for large numbers of programme participants – for example in talk shows and panel discussions, or in drama programmes. And it can map almost every conceivable facet of interaction patterns: who talks when, in response to whom, about what, for how long. The software produces graphic computer representations of these interactions, and can graphically illustrate the structure of the television programme itself (see Spee and Carpentier 1999).

The Profile Time is a powerful research tool, intended for detailed analysis of gender interaction in all its complexity. In 2001 the Centre for Women's Studies launched a project called MEER (Media Emancipation Effect Report) to adapt the sophisticated Profile Time for use by groups whose analysis needs are more general. The aim is to develop a user-friendly software application and a manual that will allow activists and media practitioners to assess gender elements and interactions in television easily and quickly.

Studying Media Employment Patterns

Systematic monitoring of gender employment patterns in the media presents a real challenge for activists. It can be extremely difficult to obtain raw, first-hand employment statistics. Many organisations consider employment data to be confidential, and are reluctant to hand over information. In some countries organisations simply do not keep statistics that are differentiated by gender. When the Peruvian group Calandria tried to do a detailed study of women's employment in the country's media in 1997, it encountered both of these problems. Few organisations had information that distinguished between women and men on the staff. The novelty of the enquiry 'provoked considerable surprise and many fears among the people we interviewed. So we reduced our ambitions for the quantitative side of the study and focused more on the qualitative aspects' (Alfaro 1997: 61).

Calandria did manage to get responses to its questionnaire from a small number of organisations, though 'it took many months to get the responses and we almost had to beg the respondents' (Alfaro 1997: 62). The group decided to supplement these replies with an analysis of television programme credits for thirty of the most important nationally produced programmes. In fact, this is a reasonable way of obtaining at least approximate data on the numbers of women and men engaged in certain kinds of media work. Usually the approach is more productive for television than for radio since, in general, radio programmes do not list extensive credits. By listening to the credits read out at the end of a radio programme, one might learn who the producer or director was, but it would be less usual to give a credit to other important categories such as researcher, writer, production assistant, sound technician, studio manager and so on. Similarly with newspapers, it is possible to get some idea of the numbers of male and female reporters by counting bylines. However, categories such as editorial director, desk editor, sub-editor, layout artist, illustrator – to name just a few – will not be covered.

Even with television, there are usually big variations between programme types in the range of jobs included in credits. In some countries, no credits at all are given for news programmes. While drama programmes may list a very wide spectrum of people, spanning almost every professional contribution to production, in sports and current affairs programmes the list of credits is usually much more limited. It is extremely unusual to include administrative, sales or commercial staff in the credits for any programme, although these are employment categories in which women often predominate. So if the only option is to analyse television programme credits, it is important to do some pre-research to get an idea of which professional categories tend to crop up in different kinds of output. This can guide decisions about which job categories and which programmes to select for the analysis.

With this type of approach – analysing newspaper bylines, radio or television credits – it is important to remember that the figures produced will only give an approximation of the real gender breakdown in the media workforce. For example, Calandria's analysis of programme credits produced a figure of 27 per cent women while the information provided directly by the television channels showed that 22 per cent of their staff were women. Such differences are inevitable, partly because not all employment categories are listed in programme credits but also because the picture provided by the analysis of credits reflects specific programmes transmitted on specific days. So it is wise to extend the analysis over a reasonable period of time – perhaps a week – to try to get a broader panorama. It also makes sense to cover a range of programme types, as women and men tend to be concentrated in different programme-making areas. However, this presents another problem in that the same job title – for example producer – may entail quite different levels of responsibility from one type of programme to another. So it can be hazardous to make comparisons between programme areas without knowing something about the produc- tion hierarchy in each one.

When choosing job categories for analysis, it is useful to include a few technical positions – for example, camera and sound operation – as these are often highly paid jobs in which very few women are employed. Some of the most obvious jobs to cover would be: executive (senior) producer; producer; director; researcher; designer; scriptwriter; video/film editor; camera operator; sound operator. The gender breakdown of other cat- egories such as reporters, journalists, programme hosts can of course also be monitored by watching or listening to a selection of programmes.

There are two other major limitations of analysis based on the study of credits and bylines. The first is that it cannot adequately show women's place in the media management structure. While it may be possible to distinguish between levels of seniority in certain job categories – for example, senior producers and producers – it cannot trace women's place within the overall media hierarchy. It may be possible to piece together some of this information from annual reports or yearbooks, where they exist. The number of women on any external decision-making bodies can usually be tracked down through professional or statutory bodies. But internal management data are extremely difficult to obtain without the co- operation of the organisation concerned. The second major limitation is that some of the most important issues that define and limit women's employment in the media cannot be tackled. For example, type of contract (permanent, part-time, occasional), basic salary and real income (the two are often very different in certain media jobs), working conditions and training opportunities, rates of promotion. There may be important differ- ences between female and male employees in all these areas (Gallagher 1995a).

Clearly, then, monitoring employment patterns in the media is not an undertaking for the faint-hearted activist. Yet there are ways forward. In many countries, the first step is actually to persuade media organisations to keep gender-differentiated employee data that show the number of women and men in each occupational category and at each hierarchical level. Activists can work with professional associations and trades unions to put pressure on the media to provide these data, at least in summary form, on a regular annual basis. In countries with small media systems, it may be possible to access at least the basic data without too much difficulty. For example, Asmita Women's Publishing House in Nepal has been able to get useful data from both government and private media (Maskey 1998). Sometimes professional associations have the right contacts to obtain reasonably comprehensive data across even large media systems. The Korean Press Institute and the Korea Women Journalists' Club have both carried out extensive studies (see Lee 1999); the All-China Journalist Association and the Chinese Academy of Sciences collaborated in a national survey of women journalists (1995). In some cases university researchers with media connections can access solid data, and their analytical skills help to bring out the nuances sometimes missed by others. Good examples here come from the Caribbean (de Bruin 1994), Japan (Muramatsu reported in Miyazaki 1999) and South Africa (Goga 2000). Activists must explore these and other alliances as potential partners in collecting detailed employment data. For instance, public media organisations may be more likely to release employment information if the request comes from, or is supported by, a statutory or semi-official institution – for example, a gender commission, a parliamentary committee, a media regulatory body. Backing from such bodies will carry less weight with commercial media companies. In these cases, good professional contacts will probably be the most effective key.

If anything, this area will become even more complicated to monitor in the future. The new multi-media industries require a 'multi-skilled' workforce that is very different from the 'single-skilled' employees (journalists, directors, editors) of the traditional media industries. Already digital technology is affecting jobs and employment structures in radio and television. Journalists and producers/directors now edit their own material, without the need for a technician, and this has an impact on women's career possibilities. The emerging multi-media industries depend greatly on computer-based skills such as interface design, graphic modelling, website development, interactive design – all central tasks in the production of digital media products. With the convergence of media industries, it is becoming more and more difficult to define distinct categories of media employment and to trace career paths within the media. For example, an attempt to map employment in the British audio-visual industry in 2000 defined twenty-two broad occupational groupings (e.g. radio broadcasting, animation, new media), over ninety professional roles (e.g. production, graphic design, news-gathering) and almost 300 examples of job titles (creative director, web editor, interface designer).[6] In this new media world, counting the number of reporters or producers may no longer tell us the most important story about women's employment and potential influence in the media industries. As the nature of media production changes, monitoring will need to shift some of its focus on to women's role in these new centres of multi-media design and decision-making.

Finding out About Audiences

Information about audiences, and the female audience in particular – how they react to media content, what their preferences are – is an important tool in successful lobbying. In most countries these days, media organisations must pay attention to what their audiences think. This is still a relatively unexplored area for feminist media activists, although within the academic community a good deal of research into the female audience has been carried out over the past decade. Two strands within this academic research may be of particular interest to media activists.

The first is a relatively straightforward attempt to document audience reaction to gender portrayal in media content. Studies carried out in the 1990s have shown that both women and men are critical of the sometimes exploitative and simplistic images of women. For example, a survey of 1,000 German television viewers found that 70 per cent were critical of the deprecating and discriminatory portrayal of women on television (Röser 1995). Other studies indicate that women tend to be more critical than men (Cobo 1991). Research also shows that there are specific areas of media content which women find particularly offensive, including certain kinds of advertising (Millwood Hargrave 1994), 'erotic' television programmes (Grivaz 1994) and televised violence (Schlesinger et al. 1992). All this raises the question of whether media organisations are adequately informed about their female audience, whose judgements may be more sophisticated than is usually suggested by the bland statistics provided by standard audience research measures.

Monitoring and advocacy groups that have put special emphasis on collecting and using audience feedback include the Centre Advocacy and Research (CFAR) in India and MediaWatch in Canada. One of the earliest activities of CFAR – then known as the Media Advocacy Group – was an audience survey to assess viewer response to representations of sex and violence on film and television (Media Advocacy Group 1994a). The findings were included in a submission by MAG to a government-convened consultative committee, set up to consider the incidence of sex and violence on the screen. This was the first time that systematically collected audience data were available as an input to policy decision-making in India.[7]

One of the decisions that emerged from the consultation was that women should have 50 per cent membership of the Central Board of Film Certification. The importance of the move was to be felt in subsequent rulings, one of the most notable occurring in late 1998 over Deepa Mehta's film *Fire* which depicted a lesbian relationship. Initially passed for release without comment by the board, the film provoked violent protest by the conservative Shiv Sena, which argued that it offended Indian culture. When the government requested it to consider the film again, the board – headed by a woman, Asha Parekh – defended its initial decision and released the film for a second time. The episode provoked tremendous debate in the media around questions not just of freedom of expression, but just why this particular film had aroused such conservative outrage.[8] At the time of its release the MAG study had been attacked in the press for 'encouraging censorship' by drawing attention to audience reactions to sex and violence. But its feminist motivation – to promote a more equitable and open media system – was evident in the way the group pursued the use of its findings. The case is a good illustration that the collection, interpretation and use of all data are highly gender-determined – a point that monitoring groups need to remember when, for example, media organisations argue that 'their' research findings contradict those of advocates.

At about the same time that the Media Advocacy Group was carrying out its first audience reaction study in India, MediaWatch set out to 'fill a gap in the existing research' in Canada (MediaWatch 1994a: 5). A telephone survey asked women across the country about their television viewing habits, preferences and concerns. One of the major preoccupations of these women was television violence. Asked if there were any television programmes or types of programme they avoided, 36 per cent said they shunned shows with violent themes. No other category of programming provoked anything like this level of avoidance among women. Almost three-quarters of the women said that they were occasionally (41 per cent) or often (32 per cent) offended by sexist portrayals. More than half (53 per cent) said they had refused to buy products from advertisers who offended them.

MediaWatch has used these and more recent findings as part of its lobbying efforts. For instance, in spring 2000 the organisation commissioned a national poll of community attitudes to standards of taste. The poll covered both women and men. It showed that when Canadians are offended by something they see or hear in the media 53 per cent report they would switch to another channel, and 41 per cent say they would switch off. These data were used as part of a MediaWatch submission to the Canadian Radio-television and Telecommunications Commission in April 2000 in an attempt to demonstrate that offensive media content – in this case the Howard Stern Show – is bad business for channel operators. When the audience react negatively, argued MediaWatch, the competitor wins.[9]

A second important strand of research is concerned with the extent to which audiences identify with different characters, roles and relationships in media content. Several studies have found that both women and men are more inclined to identify with competent, attractive television characters – irrespective of gender (NOS 1995). As content studies have shown, such characters are more likely to be male than female. So women in the television audience have fewer opportunities than men to identify with characters of their own gender. This partly explains why media such as television soap opera and women's magazines, in which strong female characters are common and whose themes reflect the day-to-day pre-occupations of many women, play an important part in the daily lives of the female audience. This does not mean, of course, that women are in some way innately programmed to prefer this material. It simply reflects women's lack of opportunity to identify with strong female protagonists in other types of content – including news, sport and factual programmes of all kinds. According to one recent study of female audiences, 'genres do not matter as such. Rather women choose specific programmes … in which they find connections to their own realities of everyday life. At present, these programmes seem to be predominantly fiction or entertainment-oriented. This is partly because programming policies rely very much on basic audience ratings and take for granted the underlying, traditional gender division by genres' (Aslama and Jääsaari 2000: 123). In other words we have a chicken-and-egg situation, in which women watch what media planners think they want. In fact women want the issues and themes they care about to be reflected across the full spectrum of media output.

These are not simple matters for research and study. To get useful answers, the questions must be based on a detailed knowledge of the media content itself. This needs to be linked with an understanding of the characteristics of the audience, or groups within the audience, so that feedback can be interpreted sensitively. Thirdly, the findings need to be relevant to the current concerns and priorities of media producers. An example of how this can work comes from the Centre for Advocacy and Research/Media Advocacy Group in India. In 1995 the group carried out two comprehensive monitoring studies of soaps and serials on Indian television. One looked at female role models; the other examined the portrayal of violence (Media Advocacy Group 1995a and 1995b). Each study monitored the public television broadcaster Doordarshan as well as a number of new satellite channels. It was a very significant period for the electronic media in India as, with the arrival of cable and satellite, programmes for Indian television were being developed on a massive, previously unknown scale. Also for the first time, programme schedules were being determined by the channels' ability to sell programme space to advertisers. In such a competitive milieu, gaining audience attention and loyalty was crucial.

Against this background, the MAG used detailed findings from the monitoring studies as the basis for a series of group discussions. Organised in three different cities, the groups included students, homemakers and working women from a wide spectrum of social and economic classes. Wherever possible, media professionals – scriptwriters, producers, planners and researchers – were also present. These discussions, highly innovative within the Indian media context of the time, threw up some important insights into the ways that women relate to television. Although working women and students found soaps and serials compelling to watch, they were critical of many of the representations, which they regarded as exaggerated and lacking in credibility. There were marked differences in the ways that working-class and middle-class women related to the depiction of violence, including sexual violence, on the screen. For middle-class viewers, the inclusion of themes such as domestic violence and rape in soaps and serials had helped to stimulate family discussion around such issues. For the viewers from poor homes, these representations were perceived as unrealistic and alienating. Their own reality was far more intense and threatening than anything depicted on the screen. Countless other observations of this kind led to one very broad conclusion: that the new channels in particular were catering almost exclusively to middle- and upper-class urban viewers while low-income, disadvantaged groups felt marginalised (Media Advocacy Group 1997b). Doordarshan's original commitment to education and development was being overtaken in Indian television's rush to join the 'entertainment marathon' (Sinha 1996: 319).

The findings were distributed not just to the media, but to a cross-section of opinion-makers including trades unions and professional associations, so as to launch a public debate around the issue of inclusion and exclusion in media content. This in turn led to an extensive advocacy campaign by MAG, to highlight the achievements and life situations of grassroots women, both rural and urban. Invited as editorial consultants to a new weekly television programme called 'Sampark', produced by Doordarshan from a gender perspective, the MAG team was able to give voice to women's development issues such as health, human rights and political representation.

The finding that viewers may persist in watching television content – or in reading newspapers and magazines – of which they are highly critical is documented in numerous academic studies (for example, Seiter 1999). This is important, because the most common response of media organisations and advertisers to audience data presented by advocacy groups often seems difficult to refute: 'If people don't like it, why do they go on watching, or buying it?' For example, when the Women's Media Centre in Cambodia published a poll in December 1997 showing that 80 per cent of respondents considered pornography in newspapers to be a problem, the information fell on deaf ears. Editors insisted that pornography sells (Sarayeth 1998). In a commercial media environment, the bottom line is certainly market share. But it is important to know, and to be able to argue, that the audience's relationship with media products is extremely complex. The power of the media lies precisely in their ability to seduce, while at the same time affronting – or perhaps just boring – the audience. That is why it is important to question media content. On the other hand, research does show that audiences do not necessarily give much thought to issues of media portrayal (for example, Millwood Hargrave 1994), a finding which points to the need for media education, as well as to the need for careful interpretation of audience data.

Successful use of audience data as a lobbying tool can be problematic for media advocacy groups. Many media organisations have their own audience research units that produce ratings tables and appreciation indexes on a daily basis. Often these will paint a very different picture from the one that media advocates put forward. Advertising agencies, which may spend millions on pre-testing their messages, will need a lot of convincing that they are out of step with a significant sector of the population. For citizens' monitoring groups, a sound research design is essential to ensure that the audience data they present have credibility. For example MediaWatch commissions this kind of research from Canadian universities or public opinion firms. The Media Advocacy Group's 1994 audience study was carried out in collaboration with a mass communication research centre in Delhi. While the media industry may use its own prerogative to cite anecdotal evidence or personal opinion to support a particular position, citizens' groups must constantly prevent their arguments from being undermined on the grounds that they are not properly representative.

Interpreting Images, Presenting Data

> There is no universal message. Each viewer can find a point of view, a spokesperson [role model] and a solution. So there is no consensus. (Media Advocacy Group 1997b: 19)

In Jamaica in 1994 a full-page colour advertisement for Panther Stud condoms, with the picture of a nonchalant, smiling man dressed in an athletics outfit as if to run a race, appeared with the caption: 'If you want to see how fast he can run, tell him you're pregnant.' Women's Media Watch objected to the ad, interpreting it as a stereotypical representation of the irresponsible Jamaican male who has always been unwilling to accept fatherhood. The advertisement, they argued, put the blame and responsibility for safe sex and unwanted pregnancy on the female. The advertising company responded that WMW might be imposing a value system on a particular class of people who were vulnerable to the problem of absentee fathers and unwanted pregnancy. In one of WMW's public education sessions, female participants were asked to critique the ad. Although they disapproved of the type of male behaviour condoned in the text, 'they felt it was very effective in discouraging young women from carrying unwanted pregnancies'. The women were in fact reading the message in terms of their own day-to-day existence (Walker 1999: 20–2).

One of the most important points for media advocates to bear in mind when interpreting images and presenting data is that there is rarely one, unequivocal way of understanding media content. This does not mean that advocates should weaken their arguments by getting lost in 'on the one hand this, on the other hand that' types of presentation. Advocacy must be based on conviction, but conviction must derive from a realisation of the nuances in media content, from an acceptance that different people will interpret the same content in different ways, and from an understanding of the context in which media professionals work. At the heart of media advocacy is a desire to transform one-dimensional, uncreative media content into something more diverse and satisfying for audiences. This means entering into a dialogue with media professionals and policy-makers. To make such a dialogue productive, activists need to avoid terminology that is obfuscating or abstract. But it is just as important to avoid simplistic generalisations or unrealistic suggestions that media people will dismiss as naïve. There are two ways of approaching this.

First, without necessarily getting too steeped in the detail of academic feminist research, it is important that activists keep informed about developments in this now extremely rich field. The ideas and interpretative frameworks that have emerged over the past decade can spark new insights and can help advocates refine and re-contextualise old arguments. For example, much activist discussion still revolves in a generalised way around questions of stereotyping and its effects, without paying much attention to important specificities of media, genres and audience experiences. In effect, it 'assumes an unequivocal meaning and effect of media content, with stereotypical images leading more or less unproblematically to stereotypical effects and traditional socialisation patterns. The audience is thus conceptualised as a rather passive mass, merely consuming media messages' (van Zoonen 1994: 18).[10] Arguments that do not take account of the complexities of media relationships and audience interpretation risk imposing outmoded definitions of what 'all women' want and think. Gender identities and evaluations are in fact filtered through other fundamental constituents such as class, ethnicity, socio-economic position, geography and many more (see Brunsdon 1997).

Second, it is essential that media advocates pitch their arguments in terms that resonate with media practitioners. These terms will vary, depending on the nature of the medium. With commercial media, arguments based on audience consumer power may be appropriate. As one activist has put it, 'the media are not terribly interested in our views about discrimination and equality. We have to find a way of expressing these issues in terms of our rights as consumers. This is the only way to enter into dialogue with the media market' (Celiberti 1998). When it comes to public service media, reminders of their commitment to reflect the diversity of the audience may be effective. Discussions with journalists may be successful if couched in terms of concepts like balance and fairness that underpin the journalistic profession.

These are just some of the factors that media activists need to bear in mind to ensure that the media take note of what they have to say. For instance, in late 1999 Women's Media Watch in South Africa organised a three-day workshop to consider the results of its first foray into the field of structured media monitoring (Media Monitoring Project 1999c). Increasingly the group had felt the need for empirical data to back up its advocacy work, and to avoid being discounted as an unrepresentative lobby that relied on opinion rather than facts. Much of the workshop discussion centred on how to carry out monitoring in such a way that the results could not be sidelined by media organisations. One conclusion was that many monitoring studies are limited by their exclusive focus on women; representations of men and masculinity also need to be included so as to appeal more broadly to media professionals. The group also agreed that one of the most crucial aspects is to present findings in language that media practitioners can relate to. In 2000 Women's Media Watch established its own monitoring group to work on ways of framing its analyses in terms of principles that the media espouse – for example fairness, accuracy, balance and objectivity. By putting a human rights spin on these principles, WMW hopes to persuade journalists to question their own ways of working and, in doing so, to produce stories that are more inclusive and also better journalism.[11]

Notes

1. The complete set of materials used in GMMP 2000, including a news monitoring guide with instructions and examples, coding grids and categories for radio and television as well as newspapers, is available from Erin Research Inc. (www.erinresearch.com) or the World Association for Christian Communication (www.wacc.org.uk/womedia/gmmp2.htm) which organised and co-ordinated the project.

2. Natasha Nuñez, personal communication, July 2000.

3 For a useful account of the relative merits of traditional content analysis and discourse analysis in media monitoring, see Edwards et al. (1999).

4. The overall aim of the Gender Development Index was to define a set of indicators that would map out all aspects of women's relationship to the broadcast media, and that would allow quantitative comparisons. The full set of indicators covers media employees, media content and the broadcasting culture or environment (codes and guidelines, regulation, management statements etc.). See Kim and Min (1997).

5. Yanghee Kim, personal communication, February 2000.

6. Department for Culture Media and Sport/Skillset, 'Audio Visual Industry Census 2000'; see: www.skillset.org/censapp.htm

7. Akhila Sivadas, personal communication, July 2000.

8. For example, Kalpana Sharma, 'Fighting the moral police', *The Hindu*, 20 December 1998; Shobori Ganguli, 'If fire is abnormal, is rape normal?', *The Pioneer*, 16 December 1998; Manisha Vardhan, 'A fire in male territory', *The Pioneer*, 6 December 1998.

9. MediaWatch submission to the Canadian Radio-television and Telecommunications Commission, CRTC-Corus Entertainment, April 2000, unpublished document.

10. For those interested in exploring the potential and limitations of available research methods for feminist media analysis, Liesbet van Zoonen's (1994) extensive critique will be extremely useful.

11. Women's Media Watch, Final Report 1999: 3.

10

Giving Women a Voice

All gender media advocacy groups are concerned in one way or another with ensuring that women's voices are heard. Some actually create media productions designed to bring an alternative women's perspective into the mainstream media. The Women's Media Centre of Cambodia produces television and radio programmes about violence against women. These programmes aim to use positive role models to encourage behaviour change, rather than simply focusing on the negative aspects of the problem. In 1999 the WMC established Cambodia's first independent NGO radio station – Radio WMC FM102. By late 1999 the station was broadcasting fifteen hours a day (Women's Media Centre of Cambodia 1999). Radio is one the main tools of the Tanzania Media Women's Association, which uses it to inform the public about gender violence and women's issues in general. In 1998 the association achieved extensive radio coverage about the newly passed Sexual Offences Act and its implications for women – spanning more than 100 programmes on the national channel Radio Tanzania alone.[1]

Most groups do not have this degree of direct access to the media. But there are many other effective means of giving voice to women's concerns and points of view on mainstream media concerns.

Campaigns and Protests

Street campaigns and protests can be a very immediate way of focusing public attention on a problem or issue. Groups like B.a.B.e in Croatia and Women's Media Watch in South Africa decided that, at least in the early stages of their work, street actions could help to raise awareness and create interest in their concerns. In 1997, when B.a.B.e started this kind of activity – by posting large stickers reading 'this offends women', 'sexism' and 'STOP' across billboard advertisements – people in the street were rather mystified. But the guerrilla tactics got good media coverage in *Tjednik* (Weekly), Croatia's leading political magazine, and provoked a certain amount of debate. The following year B.a.B.e displayed its posters 'How to be a fabulous feminist' and 'Because women's work is never done' all over Zagreb city centre and distributed them to women's groups throughout Croatia. The group sees this as part of a long process in building awareness about sexism in the media. Gradually some people have started to understand. 'We educated a lot of women to see and understand what's wrong with the sexist approach ... Revolutions are not possible when we want to change a state of mind, habits, culture etc. It's going to be a very slow and sometimes painful process.'[2]

Offensive billboards have also been at the centre of campaigns by the National Women's Media Centre in Australia and the Gender Media Monitor in Trinidad and Tobago. The intrusive nature of billboard advertising makes it a special target for media advocacy groups. Citizens can exercise at least minimal control over advertisements in the print and electronic media. They can turn the page or not buy the publication, and they switch off the radio or television, but billboards are inescapable.

In Australia, part of the NWMC billboard campaign in 1998 focused on 'metrolites', the illuminated posters in public places like bus shelters. In the state of New South Wales, metrolites that carried underwear and clothing advertisements were identified as the worst offenders because of the risks they posed to public safety, particularly for young women. This was brought to the surface by a secondary school student who, in a forum organised by the NWMC, spoke of her experience while waiting to catch a bus in the early evening. She was accosted by two youths. They began by making gestures at the sexualised images in the ad, and moved on to the young woman herself. She said that her sense of safety in the world had been changed for ever. The testimony of this young woman was powerful enough to get the attention of the media. The government took up the issue and there were discussions with Sydney City Council, which was preparing for pre-Olympics streetscape changes. In the end, commercial interests won out: 'there are now more metrolites than ever, and the images continue to be the same'.[3] But whatever the specific outcome of such campaigns, if they help to raise public awareness and debate they can make a difference.

Campaigns and protests that use humour or involve a play on words and images can have an enduring symbolic impact. In South Africa, Women's Media Watch has mounted some highly creative events in this style. To mark the fiftieth anniversary of the Declaration of Human Rights in 1998 the group staged a protest outside Newspaper House, home of two of the country's major dailies *The Argus* and the *Cape Times*. To draw attention to the labelling and stereotyping of women by the media, WMW printed adhesive labels with common stereotypes for women – victim, whore, virgin, sexy babe, humourless feminist, man-hating lesbian, and many more. The women stuck the labels all over themselves and took to

Keeps whites whiter, colours brighter and blacks beautiful.

Only SABC TV understands what today's woman wants from her soap. Which is **SABC** why both our international and local soaps are suitable for all skin types.

PLATE E Reproduced by courtesy of South African Broadcasting Corporation

the streets, carrying placards, posters and fliers with information about the socio-economic situation of women in South Africa. Outside Newspaper House they distributed the information, talked to journalists and the public at large. To round off the protest they ripped off the labels and threw them into a big red dustbin to illustrate the notion that 'labels are rubbish'.[4]

Women's Media Watch believes that protests like this live on in the imagination, and help to define the group as one that can enjoy itself while

PLATE F Reproduced by courtesy of Women's Media Watch, South Africa

making serious points. One of its most successful creative protests was in
1997. The South African Broadcasting Corporation (SABC) had published
an advertisement for its television soap operas, claiming that only SABC
television 'understands what today's woman wants from her soap. Which
is why both our international and local soaps are suitable for all skin
types.' The SABC soap, claimed the ad, 'keeps whites whiter, colours
brighter and blacks beautiful' (see Plate E). WMW members found the
advert both sexist and racially divisive, and decided to act. They put tiny
soap cakes into boxes, with labels reading 'Wash Sexism and Racism out
of the Media'. They printed posters showing a bucket and a mop, alongside
the words 'It will take more than soap to wash racism and sexism out of
the media'. Armed with these, and with flyers explaining what WMW
stood for and why they objected to the advert, the group protested outside
the SABC building. The little boxes of soap and the flyers were distributed
to SABC employees and to passers-by (see Plates F and G).

    There was an on-the-spot reaction from the SABC, with WMW repres-
entatives invited to take part in two different programmes. Officials from
the company, though at first bemused, allowed Women's Media Watch to
distribute the soap boxes and flyers inside the SABC building itself. But
the effects of the protest were more enduring than the event itself. WMW
sees this kind of action as empowering in a lasting way for the people who
take part. If well staged, it will also make news, putting the 'offending'

PLATE G Reproduced by courtesy of Women's Media Watch,
South Africa

party in an uncomfortable position from which it must redeem itself. It can
also be a good way of attracting the support of journalists and other media
people. Even if they didn't know it beforehand, many of these may find
themselves in sympathy with an issue that is presented in terms of images
and symbols that strike a chord with the media's own way of doing things.[5]

To be effective, a public protest or demonstration must be well planned
and organised. In its Media Activist Kit the group Fairness and Accuracy
in Reporting (FAIR) gives some useful guidance (see Box 4).

Effective Complaint Strategies

What do you think writing a letter would do? Nothing. Those guys wouldn't
even read it. (Twelve-year-old girl, Vancouver, in MediaWatch 2000: 11)

In a study of eleven- to fourteen-year-old girls carried out in spring 2000,

Box 4 How to Organize a Demonstration

Before you demonstrate Make sure you have a convincing case. Unfounded criticisms serve only to undermine your cause as well as future attempts at media reform.

When and where to demonstrate The best place to demonstrate is in front of the media outlet itself. Choose a time that makes it convenient for as many activists as possible to attend, and when most employees at the media outlet can see the demonstration – early morning, lunchtime, late afternoon.

Publicity Try to allow at least a week to publicise your demonstration. Advertise through flyers, local community forums, newspapers and radio stations, other activists and newsletters.

Placards and signs Distil the gist of your case and recommendations into a few pithy phrases and slogans. Most passers-by don't have time or inclination to chat with demonstrators, so it's important that your placards catch their attention and convey the message. Once you have their attention, they are more likely to take your fact sheets and other information.

Press packets and information sheets Call the press well in advance, so that your protest gets reported. Don't burden the press with excessive information, but make sure your case is backed up with sound evidence. Prepare a one-page fact sheet that summarises your main points and if possible some recommendations (e.g. an apology from the editor or director, an opportunity for your group to make its case on-air). More detailed documentation – photocopies of articles, letters to the media outlet, replies, statistics – can be included to support your case.

Slogans and chanting Catchy chanting and slogans can attract attention. Try not to sound belligerent. Think about the impression you are making on the targets of your protest and on passers-by. Make your point in straightforward language that gives the greatest number of people the opportunity to agree with you. You want to show that you are reasonable and principled. Make it clear that you are not calling for media censorship but for constructive change.

Spokespersons Brief one or two articulate activists to be spokespersons when the media ask for interviews. Be clear on what your main message is, and make sure that everyone who is interviewed stresses it. (Adapted, with permission, from FAIR's Media Activist Kit: www.fair.org/activism/organize.html)

MediaWatch discovered that although the young women were able to imagine strategies for voicing their concerns about media images, many felt sceptical that action would do any good. 'If you write a letter what they are probably going to do is that they are either going to throw it out, or if they're not busy they will write a letter back to you and say either turn it off or we don't care what you think or something like that' (MediaWatch 2000: 12). The media's own standard definition of freedom of choice – 'if you don't like it, you don't have to buy it' or 'you can always switch off the set' – has been accepted by these young women. Asked what they would do if they saw something they found offensive, a frequent response was they would just ignore it: 'Turn the channel, I mean ignore it, turn the page … look away.' Yet the minority who had taken action appeared to have been empowered as a result, regardless of the effect or lack thereof.

Through its many-layered efforts to promote consumer advocacy, Media Watch constantly emphasises the feeling of satisfaction that accompanies taking action. In one audience survey of women, they found that almost 85 per cent said they would take the time to complain if they thought that doing so would have an impact. But although the majority had at some time been offended by sexist media content, only 13 per cent had ever formally voiced their concerns about an advertisement by phone and only 8 per cent had ever done so by letter (MediaWatch 1994a).

In its early years, MediaWatch urged people to fill out complaint forms and send them to MediaWatch, which would then direct them to the appropriate organisations. The industry failed to take these complaints seriously, assuming that they were generated by MediaWatch itself, rather than by individuals. So this was replaced by a system of direct consumer contact with the industry. To make it effective, MediaWatch developed a guide to writing a complaint letter (see Box 5). Still an excellent model, the letter writing guide has been adapted for use by groups in many countries.[6]

In most countries the process of lodging a complaint is tortuous. There may be several complaint mechanisms, each one dealing with a different type of media content. One of the services provided by advocacy groups like MediaWatch and the National Women's Media Centre in Australia is to help people find their way through the maze of regulatory bodies responsible for the different areas of the mass media. The MediaWatch and NWMC websites give addresses, e-mail, phone and fax contacts for the organisations to be contacted with complaints about advertising, direct marketing, television and radio programmes, and material in the press.

The NWMC also runs an advertising complaints hotline, where women can lodge their complaints. The centre keeps a register of complaints, helps women to frame them in line with relevant codes, and forwards complaints

Box 5 Writing an Effective Complaint Letter

1. *Write as soon as possible* after seeing or hearing the offending media. The information will be fresh in your mind. Encourage others to write also.

2. *Direct your letter to the appropriate contact.* These might include regulatory bodies, advertising agencies, product manufacturers, television stations, radio stations, press councils. If not already known, addresses can be found in guides and telephone directories. For newspapers and magazines, publishers' and editors' names and addresses are usually listed within the publication. For outdoor advertising, if possible contact the billboard leasor.

3. *Identify yourself.* Include your name, address, telephone number and e-mail address. Anonymous letters are not taken seriously.

4. *Identify the medium and format.* Include all the details – what did you see or hear? Where? When? For print material, attach a copy when possible.

5. *Write persuasively.* Be clear and specific about what you find offensive and why. You want the reader to respect your viewpoint and to take action.

6. *Criticise constructively.* Focus criticism on the issue, not the organisation or individual.

7. *Give praise where it's due.* If there is anything positive to say, add these details. This way, the reader is more likely to be open to your criticism. Suggest alternatives. Some media producers are unaware of the issues and appreciate positive and specific suggestions.

8. *Remind them of what's at stake.* You, your family, colleagues and friends make up an important market that the advertiser, broadcaster, newspaper or magazine editor wants to reach. If you are considering a boycott, mention that in your letter.

9. *Ask for a response.* Follow up with another letter or phone call if necessary.

10. *Copy and circulate.* Who else might be interested? For example, a school board, trade union, professional association, member of parliament, local government official, community group or other NGO.

Adapted, with permission, from MediaWatch, Canada:
www. mediawatch.ca/involved/voice

to the advertising industry's system, the product owner, the media carrier (publication, radio or TV station), and relevant members of parliament. An online media complaint form is provided on the NWMC website. One of the points stressed by the NWMC is the need to express concerns in terms that are covered by the relevant code of practice for that section of the media. Complainants are advised to state clearly if the material:

- Portrayed women in a fair and accurate manner
- Was not discriminatory, or ...
- Discriminated against women by ...
- Demeaned the role of women by ...
- Did not realistically reflect the role of women in the community because ...

The NWMC also offers advice on draft complaints, to ensure that they have the best possible chance of being upheld.[7]

Advocacy groups can do much more than simply help individuals to frame and channel complaints appropriately. In most cases a single complaint, however justified, will have little impact on any media organisation. But by building strategies that involve other individuals and organisations in the complaint process, advocacy groups can enhance the likelihood that the media will pay attention. One example of how this can work comes from South Africa, where a member of the public telephoned Women's Media Watch to say that she had heard wisecracks about violence against women on a Saturday-night radio talk show. Listeners had been asked to call in with jokes. The first caller shared his: 'Question: How do you know when your wife is dead? Answer: Well, nothing much changes but the dishes mount up.' The presenter laughed and then told his own joke: 'Question: What do you say to a woman with two black eyes? Answer: Nothing, you've spoken twice already.'

The woman asked WMW to take up her complaint. They suggested she put her concerns in writing, and in a six-page letter to the radio station she explained how these so-called jokes normalise and promote violence against women. WMW took the position that though a presenter cannot be held responsible for what callers say, presenters are definitely responsible for their own response to any caller. They contacted the station, pointing out that the first joke should not have been laughed at, and certainly should not have been 'bettered' with another joke about violence against women. They asked for an on-air apology, suggested gender training for presenters and programme planners so that this kind of mistake would not be repeated, and proposed that the station draw up a policy on gender representation in programmes.

Word spread through the network of women's crisis centres and other organisations working on violence against women about the 'jokes' episode. When the station manager called several of these groups to ask them to take part in a programme about violence against women, their response was unanimous: first deal with the WMW complaint. In the face of this apparently high level of mobilisation, the managing director of the radio station telephoned WMW. He agreed to go on air during the programme in question and to apologise on behalf of the station. WMW were invited to be there, to accept the apology on behalf of women. The station also agreed to work with WMW on developing a gender policy.

The episode is a good example of how a coalition of partnerships can contribute to an effective result. In this case, the individual listener would almost certainly have evoked no response from the station. WMW itself did not at first get a satisfactory result. The station manager's solution – to make a programme about violence against women – was a fairly typical media response that ignored the need for a more thorough examination of the company's policy and practice in relation to gender issues. It was only when it became clear that a number of high-profile organisations felt strongly enough about the issue to refuse to co-operate with the station, that the managing director agreed to the WMW proposals.[8] For advocacy groups the lesson is that if they *seem* capable of mobilising a broad range of groups across different sectors in support of a complaint or action, media organisations are more likely to pay attention.

Elsewhere, groups use various kinds of 'snow-balling' techniques to maximise the number of complaints generated. In Croatia B.a.B.e sets in motion a chain of letter reactions activated through a 'phone tree'. The letter chain was used successfully in late 1998 when the Christmas catalogue for the supermarket chain Konzum used a cover picture of a seductive blonde woman, tousling her hair and wearing a red dress with a zip down the front that seemed to invite readers to pull it down. The picture carries the words 'See you ...' (B.a.B.e 1999: 12–13). The B.a.B.e-inspired letter campaign threatened to boycott all Konzum shops. In a change of heart, the next catalogue (Easter 1999) had a man dressed up as an Easter bunny, bringing his female partner breakfast in bed. Later catalogues have not used any human models, just pictures of food, which is what the super-market sells.[9]

Particularly in cases where there is no effective regulatory mechanism, and where complaints have to be addressed directly to the media or advertising industry, numbers can be very important. This is the situation in Israel where, although there is a body charged with overseeing the content of commercials, fear of legal suits by advertisers, allied with a very general code that merely says content should not 'offend the feelings' of the audience, renders it ineffectual (Sappir 2000). Frustrated by this situation,

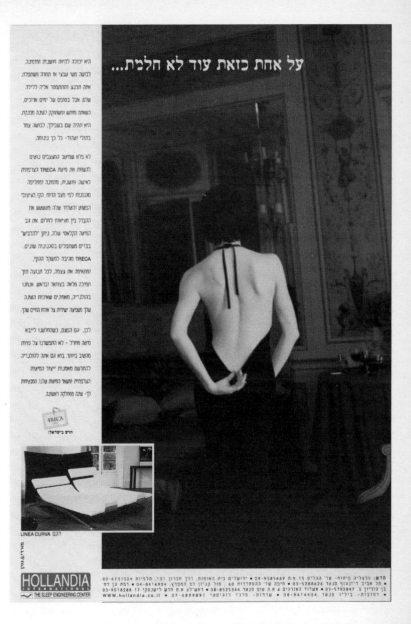

in 1997 the Israel Network began to assemble a list of 'media ambassadors'. By 2000 there were about 120 names on the list. When there is a protest to be mounted, or a complaint to be taken up, the IWN writes a letter and sends it to the ambassadors as a guide, advising them to write their own letters. The list is compiled from the names of people who contact the IWN about anything to do with the media. Not all of these are members of the IWN. The main thing is that they are active. A core group of about twenty 'ambassadors' is extremely dynamic. The strategy has brought results.

In 1999 a full-page advertisement for a bed was published in *Ha'aretz*, one of Israel's most prestigious dailies (see Plate H). Three-quarters of the ad showed a woman in a dimly lit boudoir setting, her back to the camera, in a very low-backed evening dress that she appeared to be about to unzip. The picture of the bed occupied about one-tenth of the page. The headline read: 'You've not yet dreamt about this one.'[10] In the advertisement text, the woman-bed is portrayed as 'sensual and tempting', 'changing styles according to her moods', she 'responds to body weight and adapts herself to every move'. The advertisement appeared next to a story about three women who had been victims of incest. Through the IWN media ambassadors' network and other contacts, 150 letters of complaint arrived on the desks of the managing director of the manufacturing company, the advertising company and the Israel Consumer Commission. The letters pointed out that the ad was written in male language, that it objectified women by blurring the distinction between the bed and the woman, and that it could encourage violence against women. A boycott of all the company's products was threatened.

Almost immediately the manufacturers replied that they had asked the advertising agency to 'change its style so as not to offend you or other women – something which (we) never intended'. The media ambassadors each received the gift of a pen from the company concerned. The recipients smiled wryly, but there was a more serious sequel. The advertising agency asked the IWN for its reaction to a new advertisement for the bed. The second ad shows a sleeping baby whose head is cradled in the hands of a female adult (see Plate I). The headline reads: 'You can't remember when you last slept as well as this.' The text continues: 'The last time you slept like this was in your mother's lap, her soft hands covering your body and supporting your head, so that it wouldn't come to harm.' And so on. The 'you' addressed by the ad is still a man. The bed is still a woman, but this time a mother rather than a seductive temptress. The IWN let it go. They had achieved something, but the episode confirmed there was a long road ahead.[11]

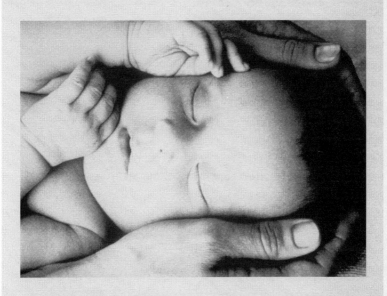

את כבר לא זוכרת מתי ישנת טוב כל כך...

Soriree M.Thum

הפעם האחרונה שישנת כך הייתה
בחיקה של אימך, בידיה הרכות העוטפות
את גופך ותומכות בראשך, שלא יגרם לו
שום נזק.

אחרי שנתיים של מחקר הצליחו החוקרים
שלנו ב״סרקה פריד״, ליצור את המיטה,
שתחזיר לך את יכולת השינה הזאת, שינה
בריאה, נוחה וטהורה...ממש כמו שישנת אז.
הקוים המתומטכים של מיטת ״טרקה״ נעים
בטעגלים, ללא זוית חדות, כמו גלים רכים
המתאימים עצמם לקוי המתאר של הגוף

שלך ולתמוחה המועדפת עליך, תוך תמיכה
מלאה בצוואר ובראש.

אנחנו בהולנדיה מאמינים, שאיכות השינה
שלך משפיעה ישירות על אורח החיים שלך.

לכן, גם הפעם, כשהחלטנו לייבא מיטה
מחו״ל - לא התפשרנו על פחות מהטוב
ביותר.

את לא יכולה לזכור מתי ישנת טוב כל- כך?
בואי גם את להולנדיה להתרשם מאמנות
ייצור המיטות הצרפתית ומשאר המיטות
שלנו.

HOLLANDIA
INTERNATIONAL
THE SLEEP ENGINEERING CENTER

חדש: הרצליה פיתוח - שד' הגלים 15, א.ת. 09-9585669 • ירושלים - דרך חברון 101, בית האומות, תלפיות.
02-6731524 • תל אביב - דיזנגוף סנטר, 03-5288628 • חיפה - שד' ההסתדרות 60, סול קניון לב המפרץ.
04-8416924 • רמת גן - רח' בן גוריון 5, 03-5792847 • אשדוד - האורגים 6, א.ת סול סיטי 10,
08-8525344 • ראשל״צ-לישופקי 17, א.ת חדש, 03-9518288 • רחובות - ביל״ו סנטר, 08-9414404 • שדרות- פרכן
לוגיסטי, 07-6899891 • www.hollandia.co.il מרכז מידע והזמנות: 1 - 800 - 744 - 844

Accessing the Media

How often have we decided not to give an interview, or not to go on television, out of fear that we'll be confronted by wily questions on a crucial subject? Or out of apprehension that our remarks will be quoted out of context or misinterpreted? We need to know the different amounts of time to expect from radio, television and the press. To understand that in a couple of minutes you have to say everything. Difficult? Of course, but politicians have learned how to do it … Unless we learn the language of the media, our journey will become even slower than the one we've already been travelling. (Portugal and Torres 1996: 13)

Speaking in public, particularly in the increasingly 'sound bite' context of today's media, can be an ordeal for most people. Many advocacy groups

---

Box 6   How to Handle Media Interviews

- *Keep it simple, sister!* (The KISS principle.)
- *Stick to one main point* (no more than two or three), *and keep using it.* You may feel that you've said it a thousand times, but your audience is likely only to start hearing your key message around the time you are sick of saying it.
- *Be prepared.* You will be asked for an interview at short notice. Organise your resources, clarify your group's aims to yourself and make sure you have your facts at your fingertips.
- When the producer contacts you, you should *ask how long the interview will be and the topics to be covered.*
- *Listen to or watch the programme* before the interview, to find out what the interviewer is like and to get an idea of the style of the programme.
- If you have the time, *rehearse some key phrases* that will catch people's attention and stay in their minds. With a bit of practice, you can get a long sentence down to a few short words.
- Once the interview is underway, *stay cool and answer questions clearly*, but at a comfortable pace, stating your conclusion rather than your argument first. This way you will always get your main point across.
- *Talk to your audience.* Make your message relevant with phrases like: 'Every woman at home knows what it's like to …' or 'This affects everyone – if not you, then someone in your family, a friend, a neighbour …'

have developed materials and training workshops to help women develop the confidence and the media skills to put their points of view effectively. The National Women's Media Centre in Australia places a lot of emphasis on this. It provides a great deal of guidance, both on its website and in face-to-face training sessions, for people who want to use the media to get their message across but who may be afraid of saying the wrong thing.

Other groups tackle various practical aspects of message delivery for different groups, and in different ways. In India the Centre for Advocacy and Research has a training module on media advocacy for NGOs and community-based organisations. Through print, slides and video it sets out the steps involved in using the mass media to advance a social or public policy issue. In its training manual on gender analysis of the media, Women's Media Watch in Jamaica includes tips on lobbying and how to organise a

---

- *Remember whom you are talking to.* The total audience might be very big, but in reality you are simply talking to one or two people listening or watching at home.
- *Express opinions with conviction.* Confident, assertively voiced ideas are convincing. Let your passion come through.
- *Be specific with your comments.* Use anecdotes and examples to back up your argument. Ground your talk with facts. This way you won't appear to be hedging.
- *Control the interview* rather than letting it control you. If you are not happy with a question, then restructure it to bring it into line with the real issue. You can pull this off by using bridging clauses such as, 'Let's look at the broader issue here' or 'Before I answer that, I think we should discuss this aspect ...'
- *Question the interviewer* to make them clarify the question if you are not sure what is being asked, or if you do not like the question. For example, replying 'What do you mean when you say ...?' gives you time to think, and also forces the interviewer to make the question more specific.
- *Pre-recorded interviews*: you always have a second chance – if you say the wrong thing, just ask to do it again.
- *Take care about throw-away lines.* Too often they are the only bits that get used.

Adapted, with permission, from National Women's Media Centre: www.nwmc.org.au/Action/Resources/interviews.htm

presentation (Women's Media Watch 1998). Women's Media Watch in South Africa, many of whose members have little or no formal education, runs a series of workshops on basic topics like writing skills. Canada's MediaWatch has an extensive online Media Skills package covering how to write a news release, organise a news conference, and handle an interview. It also has a Speakers' Guide, with tips on how to give presentations, and a reading and resource list. A particularly useful section gives ideas on how to handle some of those awkward comments – 'the media simply reflect reality', 'news is news', 'men are stereotyped too', 'freedom of speech is better than censorship' – that can be difficult to parry convincingly.[12]

There are of course many less traditional ways of getting a message across in the media. Trying to explain to people about sexism and stereotyping through a conventional interview or discussion may sometimes seem very abstract. The use of popular media formats can help to concretise the same ideas in ways that audiences will talk about and remember. In 1998, for the 16 Days of Activism against Gender Violence, B.a.B.e made a music video with Scats, a young female rap group. CDs were sent to radio stations throughout Croatia. The rap, 'It's not worth it …' received excellent media coverage and publicity. It tackled difficult issues in an upbeat and entertaining way and 'these two young women are now role models for many young women and girls' in the country.[13] For 1999 B.a.B.e made a video clip with a well-known Croatian jazz singer, 'I am a woman for all times'. In developing the story line, the group asked men what they thought a powerful woman would look like. The men could only imagine an 'amazon'. As it was election time, B.a.B.e decided to make a video with a female president and ministers, showing them making changes to policies on violence, media, the economy and reproductive health. The video had media coverage at its launch, and has been widely used since then.[14] Together with other activities, these videos have helped to break down some taboos. It now seems to be easier to talk about difficult issues like sexism, and sympathetic media have understood the links between political issues and gender violence.[15] Sometimes the truly contentious gender problems can be addressed most effectively in less traditional formats.

Gender activists also need to keep in mind that many important ideas are conveyed not just through serious media content, but also through highly popular or populist formats that may promote conservative and sexist ideas. Although women often find these types of media objectionable, and therefore shun them, it may actually be particularly important to 'colonise' the very media that are most distasteful. This is the thinking behind the National Women's Media Centre's 'Talkback Radio Campaign'. Talkback is sometimes known as phone-in programming. In Australia talkback radio commands the largest audiences of all media, and it expresses a narrow range of views that are often sensationalised and anti-women. It is also often used by decision-makers as a measure of community opinion on major policy issues. The NWMC campaign encourages women to listen to the programmes they almost universally avoid. This helps them to become informed about the issues that are raised as well as those that never get covered, and to understand the methods used by commentators. It urges women to air their own views on talkback radio and, to help them, it provides 'Seven Easy Steps' for action (see Box 7).

As the NWMC points out, if activists and other groups who are critical of commercial talkback radio keep avoiding it, audiences have little chance

---

Box 7 Accessing Talkback Radio

1. Work out one or two points you want to make. Jot down some catchy ways of saying them.
2. The first challenge is to get on. Perseverance is the key. Talkback is a hit-and-miss affair really. Just keep pushing the redial button.
3. You've got the dial tone – they are answering. Usually you will get the producer first. They will screen you by asking what comment you want to make. If you sound interesting and coherent, they will put you through to the presenter and flash up some of your key words on the screen in the studio. So – be passionate or coolly analytical, whatever is appropriate. But be interesting.
4. If you want to record your moment of glory, put a tape in and turn the volume down to minimum. If you try to hear yourself over the radio as you speak, the producer will get 'feedback' – that screechy noise – and they will cut you off.
5. Speak clearly right into the mouthpiece. Your telephone handset doesn't reproduce the voice very clearly, so you need to help the technology along.
6. Right! You're on and giving it all you've got. But the presenter interrupts you in mid-flow. The moment the presenter speaks into the microphone, technology works against you. Your voice is cut off and only the presenter can be heard by listeners.
7. All you need to do is stop speaking, listen to what the presenter is saying to you, and either continue your line of thought if that's appropriate or answer their question once they have stopped speaking. The technology won't allow you to interrupt the presenter. But you still have some control. You don't have to answer questions if you don't want to. Just say something like, 'that's a very good point – but first let me tell you about ...' (National Women's Media Centre: www.nwmc.org.au/Action/Resources/talkbackradio.htm)

of understanding the wider picture. That is why women with something important to say must start using this powerful medium.

Women's Expert Opinion

> If it were not so sad, it would be funny to see that (even) on topics that are usually considered 'women's topics' … the media interviews men. When we began asking why, the answer we usually received was that there were no women experts. (Sachs 1996: 65)

During the 1990s, many monitoring and advocacy groups realised that one way to combat the widely used excuse 'we'd like to, but we can't find a female expert on this topic' was to provide the media with names and contacts for women. Canada's MediaWatch was among the first in this field with its *Media Directory of Women: A Resource for Broadcast and Print Journalists* (1992). Others soon followed. The Israel Women's Network *Bank of Talent* originally consisted of 200 names, and was distributed to all editors of radio and television programmes, newspapers and magazines in the country. Feedback from the media shows that it was appreciated and used (Sachs 1996). Regularly updated, the listing now has 450 names across just about every professional field. The IWN uses its website to invite contacts from women who would like to be part of the list.

One of the challenges with this type of listing is to ensure that it is kept up to date, and here the Internet has opened up new possibilities. In South Africa the Commission on Gender Equality has developed a database that is constantly updated – the *Gender and Media Directory* – available in booklet and electronic format.[16] It includes contacts for women who can provide perspectives on topics including affirmative action, AIDS/HIV, criminology, defence, domestic violence, media, pornography, reproductive health, customary law, parliament, welfare and many more. Good publicity is important so that the information gets to the right people in the media, and is used. Simply mailing out a listing, or informing people that it exists, will rarely be enough. In 1999 the CGE launched its directory at a workshop for journalists – a good opportunity to get people involved, create commitment, and demonstrate the use of the directory as an online resource. Journalists were able to talk about the constraints they face, and why they have particular problems in getting access to female expert opinion. The directory was presented as an innovative resource that could help journalists do a better job, rather than something they 'must' use.

Assembling these directories can be time-consuming. Women's Media Watch in Jamaica reports that its listing *Women Resources/Speakers* took a very long time to develop, one of the problems being women's shyness. It is not always easy to persuade women that they do indeed have valuable

expertise that is worth sharing. Sometimes, providing rudimentary interview training can help to convince women that they are quite capable of
holding their own in public. The National Women's Media Centre in
Australia did this as part of the process of compiling its *Directory of Media
Spokeswomen*. Training was offered partly to boost women's confidence,
but also so that media people would not be disappointed in the contacts
they made, and would value the directory as a source of 'good talent' and
keep using it.

The NWMC directory was developed in direct response to the findings
of the 1995 Global Media Monitoring Project, which had shown that only
20 per cent of interviewees in the Australian media were women. The
Centre searched Australia for women who were willing to be expert commentators on a wide range of issues including human rights, management,
agriculture and sport. With over 300 entries, including women from non-
English-speaking backgrounds, Aboriginal women and rural women, the
directory was first published in book form in 1998. It was distributed to
journalists and other media practitioners, and was updated at the end of
1999. Key media people were contacted directly, and the purpose and uses
of the directory were explained to them. During 2000 the Centre developed
an online version, to be available as a searchable database.

The NWMC is convinced that these tools really can make a difference.
Although the Centre did not have resources to do a systematic monitoring
of impact, gender counts on some programmes before and after they were
sent directories showed some positive changes. The whole process was said
to be an eye-opener.

> Women who would never have put their hands up acknowledged that they
> had expertise they could share in the media, sometimes with a bit of inter-
> view training first. Journalists and commentators could be seen to cringe
> when we slapped them with the GMMP statistics on women interviewees.
> Many 'did better', many more were 'helped to do better' by their women
> researchers or producers once they were armed with the directory.[17]

Building Media Alliances

> Develop links from the outset with a few media persons, build up your allies
> – even a few – and keep them as your allies. (Walker and Nicholson 1996: 100)

After several years of lobbying and public education, Women's Media
Watch in Jamaica noted that these alone were not enough. It was also
important to build better alliances with the media. This is not always easy.
When WMW hosted a two-day national consultation on Gender and Media
Development in 1993, input from the major media outlets was poor. This

led the group to reflect on its ability to influence the mainstream media. Lobbying for the removal of an advertisement was much easier, it concluded, as businesses fear the bad publicity that accompanies such public outcry. From 1993 onwards, Women's Media Watch set about building alliances with journalists and broadcasters. Gradually this paid off. Three years after the national consultation that the media had largely ignored, the grouping of heads from all the media houses in Jamaica invited WMW for the first time to one of their monthly meetings (Walker and Nicholson 1996).

The strategy of building alliances brought results. WMW set about commending journalists and broadcasters for gender-sensitive articles and programmes, and sending them data, sources, story ideas and names of possible speakers. Using international event days – international day against violence against women, international women's day, international health day – they worked to galvanise media interest in covering salient issues. As part of this process, WMW also made a concerted effort to raise its own profile and status by collaborating on projects with agencies such as the Commonwealth Broadcasting Authority, UNICEF and others. These alliances give credibility, and mean that the media pay more attention to an organisation they regard as mainstream rather than a fringe pressure group.

Building sensitivity and alliances was also helped by the courses Women's Media Watch has taught at the Caribbean Institute of Media and Mass Communication (CARIMAC) since 1994. The students include not just aspiring journalists, but experienced practitioners. WMW also began to provide in-house gender-sensitivity seminars for some of the media organisations. Gradually some results could be seen, not just in terms of invitations to contribute a gender perspective to specific programmes but to bring that perspective into the discussions of media bodies such as the Press Association and the Cinematograph Authority. Links with individual sympathetic journalists also pay dividends. In 2000 a senior editor of *The Gleaner*, Jamaica's longest-established daily, asked WMW to help with ideas for a features series about violence. They brought together a small group of women from different sectors, with varying points of view, for a half-day discussion with the editor. Out of this came a number of articles, including a series about violence and definitions of masculinity written by a male journalist.[18]

One problem with which advocates have to deal constantly is the lack of depth in most media coverage. However well intentioned individual journalists may be, time and market constraints mean that there is little place for in-depth analysis. Yet the issues taken up by gender activists are often complex and cannot be answered with a yes or no. A typical example might be the legalisation of prostitution, a complicated and controversial topic. When this question surfaces in public debate, feminist activists will invariably be asked by the media to take a position, for or against. But often no definitive position can be presented. For example, the Israel Women's Network found itself on difficult ground when this issue surfaced in Israel in the mid-1990s. The subject was due to be raised in parliament and the IWN wanted to launch a public debate ahead of the parliamentary discussion. However, the network found it impossible to come out with a categorical statement or slogan as it had done on previous issues – for example, with 'No More Violence in the Family'. It wanted the public to consider the consequences and angles of legalising prostitution and wanted the women who work as prostitutes to be included in the debate. At the same time, it had decided to avoid sensationalism. So rather than giving interviews or generating a media 'event', the IWN organised a seminar. But this was not appreciated by the media, who 'warmed to the subject but not the way we were willing to present it ... We managed to receive quality media coverage but not the quantity' (Sachs 1996: 63–4).

With time the IWN discovered that one of the best tools to get through to the media was to have updated data and, if possible, exclusive information. It now has a resource centre that houses an extensive body of information on all subjects within its mandate. 'Thus the moment one of "our" subjects comes up in the media, we can provide comparative statistics with other countries and of course within Israel' (Sachs 1996: 64). Providing timely and solid information to sympathetic media professionals is indeed a good way of capitalising on alliances and pushing for improved coverage. In India, the Centre for Advocacy and Research has developed a number of kits for media practitioners. These cover issues such as violence, trafficking of women and malnutrition. The idea is to help media professionals get to the core of the issues easily, and to help them focus on context and causes so as to bring new perspectives into media content. For instance, in relation to trafficking of women, the usual tendency is to focus on the women who are trafficked. But equally or even more important are the people who do the trafficking. These are the ones to focus on, if there is to be real change. Moreover, reporting the topic from this perspective shifts the emphasis from sex and sensationalism to economics and power and leads to a more substantive analysis. So as part of its advocacy programme, CFAR works with NGOs to explore new angles on women and development issues and to try to bring these on to the media agenda.[19]

Awards for good – and bad – practice can be another way to create links with mainstream media and advertisers. When Women's Media Watch gave its first Media Appreciation Award, the group was taken by surprise at how much Jamaican media practitioners seemed to care about it. In Canada, MediaWatch issues an Annual Report Card. This is a humorous end-of-

year review intended to give the media, the advertising industry and
consumers an overview of the worst and best 'memorable media portrayals'
over the past year. For instance in 1999 the 'Giving Free Speech a Bad
Name' Award went to *Hustler* magazine for a photo display and text inviting
readers to send in descriptions of the sexual acts they would like to engage
in with Canadian Heritage Minister Sheila Copps. The 'Boys Will be Boys'
Award for hormonally-inspired news judgement went to the *Vancouver
Province*, for giving priority to a picture of country singer Shania Twain's
legs rather than to coverage of the appointment of Beverley McLaughlin
as the first female Chief Justice of the Supreme Court of Canada. These
and other 'awards' are delivered in tongue-in-cheek style that draws attention to the absurdity of the portrayals. The Report Card also gave kudos
– for example to 'Advertising Standards Canada for buying billboard space
to let members of the public know where to send their complaints about
offensive or irresponsible advertising'.[20] However, as MediaWatch's 1999
Report Card demonstrates, even after twenty years of activism on media
and gender in Canada, the pool of candidates for 'worst' portrayal is still
immensely greater than the potential nominees for 'best' awards.

Strong media alliances may take years to build up. But if well nurtured,
they can be highly influential and productive. In Italy, national media
monitoring activities beginning in the early 1990s included the creation of
a 'Female Image Desk' (Sportello Immagine Donna) under the auspices of
the National Commission for Equal Opportunities (Longo 1995). The desk
was intended as a focus and a channel for citizens to express their points
of view on images of women in the Italian media, and it attracted an
enormous response, partly because of the publicity it received from sympathetic journalists who had been linked with the project. When the desk
and the project came to an end because of lack of funding, the seeds for
an informal network of journalists had been sown. Over time this network
developed, with the formation of various round-tables of women journalists
who worked to support later monitoring initiatives.[21] Eventually in 2000,
partly through the influence of these journalists, the parliamentary radio
channel of RAI (Italy's public service broadcaster) proposed the establishment of a 'Women and Media Observatory' (Osservatorio Mediadonna) to
monitor radio and television news, entertainment and cultural programmes,
and advertisements.[22] Under the direction of the Faculty of Sociology at
the University of Rome, the Observatory was conceived as both an educational and a media awareness-raising activity that would link schools and
universities (responsible for the monitoring) and journalists (responsible
for discussing and publicising the findings, and for proposing alternatives).

The significance of the Women and Media Observatory was that for
the first time a powerful media organisation – with the ability to mobilise

relevant media policy-makers and advertising institutions – was centrally involved in a national monitoring activity in Italy. This gave the Observatory the status and potential to ensure that its findings were listened to. However, the engagement of RAI was not coincidental. It was the result of a decade of alliance-building between feminist researchers and journalists who, as the Female Image Desk struggled to gain a public profile, could not have foreseen the eventual ramification of that early monitoring project.

Notes

1. TAMWA (1999: 23–4).

2. Sanja Sarnavka, personal communication, June 2000.

3. Helen Leonard, personal communication, July 2000.

4. 'Women's Media Watch protest against gender labelling', *Women's Media Watch Newsletter*, No. 11/12, 1998: 8–10.

5. Gabrielle Le Roux, personal communication, July 2000.

6. For a Spanish adaptation of the guide, see 'Guia para escribir una carta' (Silva 1998a), produced by Sur Profesionales in Chile.

7. National Women's Media Centre 'How to write your complaint': www.nwmc.org.au/Action/Complaints/howtowrite.htm

8. 'Building working partnerships out of conflict', *Women's Media Watch Newsletter*, No. 1, 1998: 11–12.

9. Sanja Sarnavka, personal communication, June 2000.

10. Hebrew grammar classes nouns and pronouns according to gender. In this advertisement, the 'you' in the original Hebrew text is masculine while the 'one' he hasn't dreamt about is feminine.

11. Orit Sulitzeanu, personal communication, July 2000.

12. See MediaWatch website: www.mediawatch.ca/involved/speaking

13. Kristina Mihalec, United Nations online consultation on women and the media, 15 November 1999.

14. 'I am a woman for all times', *B.a.B.e. up-date*, No. 8, 2000: 9.

15. B.a.B.e, *Annual Report, 1999*: 2000, 13.

16. Electronic format available via Women's Net, an Internet support programme for women in South Africa: www2.wn.apc.org/cge

17. Helen Leonard, personal communication, July 2000.

18. Hilary Nicholson, personal communication, July 2000.

19. Akhila Sivadas, personal communication, July 2000.

20. 'MediaWatch Out-Take Awards Highlight: Memorable Media Portrayals of 1999', MediaWatch news release.

21. Gioia Di Cristofaro Longo (1996) 'Osservatorio Immagine Donna', unpublished report for the Commissione delle Elette, Comune di Roma.

22. Gioia Di Cristofaro Longo (2000) 'Osservatorio Mediadonna', unpublished paper, July 2000.

11

Building Media Literacy

> Media literacy is the ability to read and analyse images and implicit messages in all types of media content. Being media literate is the first step to understanding media and to becoming an active media consumer. Be in charge of your media consumption! Be media literate! (Media Watch, 'Media literacy': www.mediawatch.ca/media)

Almost all media monitoring and advocacy groups are emphatic about the need for critical media skills. Media literacy is often perceived as the bedrock on which other approaches can take root. For example, a media literate public can help to ensure that policies and codes of practice are implemented, that monitoring studies are given credence, and that complaints and protests are listened to. Above all, an informed and media literate audience is in a position to evaluate media content, to make its opinion known, and to push for change.

In many countries, political and institutional instability can make it difficult for advocates to work in a sustained way with media policy-makers. In the media industry, too, staff changes are often rapid and unpredictable. Good relationships may be built up, and commitments made, only to be swept away in an unexpected restructuring of the organisation. Thus the work of media advocates at policy and media institutional levels is often precarious, and much effort can be expended without any lasting reward. Initiatives that build on grassroots participation, on the other hand, promise more enduring transformational potential. This was the conclusion of India's Centre for Research and Advocacy in the mid-1990s. Reflecting on its intensive efforts to influence media policy in an increasingly volatile political and media environment, the group concluded that 'an incremental approach would not suffice: one more audience survey report, one more monitoring study, etc. We had to rethink our tactics and focus attention on the mechanisms that would sustain and strengthen our advocacy ... Thus it would be necessary to build citizens' initiatives and make our advocacy broad-based.'[1]

Other groups, such as the Women's Media Centre in Cambodia, believe that media literacy programmes offer a better alternative than legislation or codes of practice which, in a society without well-developed structures for policy implementation, could simply strengthen the power of government to close unfriendly media in an arbitrary way. In newly emerging media democracies, the spectre of censorship is very real. Thus the WMC believes that the best solution is media education – with programmes aimed at the general public, the media and relevant policy-makers – to help build a climate in which there is real understanding of the cultural assumptions that lead to stereotyping and women's oppression. These assumptions about women's low status and traditional role are widespread, and the media play a special part in reinforcing them. There is actually a so-called Women's Law, known as the *Chbab Srey* or 'Rule of the Lady', which all Cambodian girls are encouraged to follow. Parents, officials and other women repeat its principle to girls, encouraging them to cook good food, clean the home, speak sweetly and obey their husbands to avoid being beaten. The WMC believes that media literacy programmes must start at this level, by addressing the stereotyped beliefs held by everyone in society, not just journalists (Sarayeth 1998).

The potential of media literacy to build strong public advocacy lobbies and to deconstruct deep-seated cultural assumptions about gender attributes is obvious. But there can be a surprising amount of confusion and even outright mistrust surrounding the concept itself. In Japan the Forum for Citizens' Television and Media (FCT), one of the longest-established organisations devoted to media literacy and gender awareness, notes that the Japanese media continue to be suspicious of media literacy and the development of critical media skills. For a time the very word 'critical' seemed to be taboo. There was a breakthrough in late 1999 when the public service broadcaster NHK transmitted a television series called 'Media Literacy Education' in which a screen definition of media literacy included the word 'critical' – 'the ability to read critically, make use of, and express oneself about the media'. But the moderator of the programme 'commented that this was "a two-edged sword that cuts both ways". So, media people still tend to see media literacy as an adversary of the media' (Suzuki 2000: 11).

Although there is widespread agreement about the need for critical media skills, groups in different parts of the world obviously approach the development of these skills in divergent socio-political contexts and with varying motivations. From 'the active media consumer' of Canada to the cultural oppression inherent in the 'Rule of the Lady' in Cambodia, there is an enormous distance in terms of perceived priorities. But the overall goal – to create media literate citizens who understand how media messages are created, how they relate to the wider cultural, socio-economic and political spheres, and how they can be changed – is common to all gender monitoring and advocacy groups.

Children and Young People

> That is the girl who brought the pot.
> She carries a bucket of water on her head.
> She is singing a song.
> She is frying eggs.
> She is sweeping the floor.
>
> (English grammar drill for primary school children in Tanzania, quoted in Mbilinyi 1996: 93)

Children learn much about gender roles and responsibilities through school texts. Dorothy Mbilinyi's survey of Tanzanian school textbooks showed very strong gender stereotyping in the messages. While men and boys were portrayed as leaders, decision-makers, owners of wealth and holders of power, women and girls were shown as 'facilitators of life for others (men), not as equal partners in life' (Mbilinyi 1996: 92). These patterns are of course replicated in media targeted specifically at children, such as cartoons and comics, which in many countries are clearly divided into girls' and boys' genres. The titles alone tell their story. In Japan, the most popular girls' comic is *Ribbon*; the most popular comic for boys is *Shonen Jump* (Boys' Jump). While *Ribbon* is filled with love stories, *Shonen Jump* includes plenty of violence and sex. Some of the stories in these and other comics are linked with television cartoon programmes, with stories migrating regularly from one medium to the other (Miyazaki 1998).

A number of media monitoring groups address these issues through programmes to help children and young people dissect mass media messages. In 2000 the Gender Media Monitor (GEMM) in Trinidad and Tobago launched a media literacy project in fourteen secondary schools. Basing itself on the 1995 Global Media Monitoring Project, GEMM developed its own tools for local analysis of news, advertisements and television cartoons. The group worked first with teachers to build support for the enterprise, through workshops on gender portrayal and on the monitoring concept. The teachers then held mini-workshops in their own schools, and organised practice sessions so that the students could try out the monitoring materials. Each school concentrated on one type of media content, and when the monitoring was complete the students and teachers all came together in a common workshop to exchange experiences and ideas. Four schools were selected to make presentations to start up the discussions, and then everyone took part in exercises based on the findings.

There was a lot excitement among the students who had clearly enjoyed the whole experience.

To launch the results, a workshop for the media was held in collaboration with the Media Association of Trinidad and Tobago. Students were asked to write essays based on what they had learned and these were submitted to the *Trinidad Guardian*, the country's largest circulation daily and one of the newspapers included in the monitoring. At least one student got into print with an article headlined 'Cartoons portray women as weak' in the paper's Saturday Young Voices column. In mid-2000 this project was still continuing, with plans to produce a training manual along with audio and video material for use in schools and in the wider community. Over the longer term, GEMM wants to persuade schools to include some form of media literacy in their teaching and hopes to encourage community groups to do their own media monitoring.[2]

The inclusion of a media literacy component in the curriculum allows students to develop critical awareness skills specifically in relation to media content. But there is also the wider issue of gender representation within the educational curriculum itself. One of the few advocacy groups to have focused on this aspect of the problem is B.a.B.e, which carried out an extensive analysis of literature textbooks in Croatian primary and secondary schools from 1997 to 1999. Women were authors of only 15 per cent of the texts. The themes in the books were also male-dominated. Men were the subject matter of 42 per cent of texts at secondary level, and women 11 per cent. But when it came to family roles women appeared more frequently than men did. Only in 2 per cent of units were women mentioned as public figures, compared with 24 per cent of men. Psycho-social characteristics were heavily stereotyped. While women were portrayed as quiet, well-intentioned, sweet, devout, diligent and self-sacrificing (in that order), men were characterised as intelligent, brave, proud, ambitious and inquisitive (in that order). Overall, the textbooks conveyed to students 'an implicit message of limited possibilities for women' (Baranovic 2000: 50). For B.a.B.e, these results were 'devastating'[3] and in 2000 the group began negotiations with the Ministry of Education and the governmental Commission for Equality to carry out educational workshops for teachers and students about gender equality.

One other group that has approached the issue of gender representation in terms of its broad implications for curriculum development is Red-Ada in Bolivia. When it released the findings from its 1998 monitoring study of newspapers, radio and television news, and television entertainment (Flores 1999a), a new tertiary-level curriculum design – part of a national educational reform programme initiated in 1994 – was already underway. Red-Ada organised a one-day discussion involving many of the people responsible for the new curriculum. The idea was to get curriculum designers and textbook writers to consider the whole issue of gender representation – including the need for inclusive, non-sexist language. A working document (Flores 1999b) was later prepared, illustrating how gender is constructed – in particular through language. This document, which also includes recent international declarations on women and media, is now used in a number of the country's communication schools and departments.[4]

Groups like MediaWatch (Canada), the National Women's Media Centre (Australia) and Women's Media Watch (Jamaica) have strong traditions in providing media literacy materials and resources for students at primary, secondary and tertiary levels. In 2000 WMW ran a series of gender, media and violence workshops covering almost 800 trainee teachers in Jamaica.[5] The NWMC has a Student Pack for individual students, and a Student Resource Kit intended for university and other tertiary-level libraries.[6] MediaWatch has for many years run media education programmes, largely directed at schools. Its 1995 Project Positive Action contained three kits – one each for parents, teachers and educational administrators – designed to teach media literacy on sexism and violence to children aged four to twelve. In 2000 it launched *Double Vision: A Guide for Teaching Elementary School Children on Gender and Violence in the Media*, a flexible two- to three-week teaching unit that teachers can integrate into their own classes as and when they choose.[7]

All these materials are based on a fairly conventional pedagogical approach, assuming a standard 'teacher–student' relationship. But in 2000 MediaWatch branched out in a new direction, with its Tween Consumer Literacy Project aimed at eleven- to fourteen-year-olds. Rather than starting from the premise 'this is what we think you need', the aim was actually to involve young women in defining the kinds of information they wanted, how it should be packaged, and how it could be made most relevant to their concerns. Focus group research with these young women showed that they did want information, but differently packaged information from that currently offered by MediaWatch. It was not just a matter of style and design, but more especially a question of focus and targeting. Issues of body image and self-esteem were high on the agenda, rather than generalised questions about sexism.

In particular this group wanted information to be 'gender neutral', rather than singling out women or girls as a group needing special treatment. They distinguished themselves from what they perceived as the counterproductive standpoints of (older) feminists. One of the fourteen-year-olds put it this way: 'The thing is feminists, you start off with the right idea, that we want our equality, but it is completely wrong to get revengeful – just because you did it to us, to do that same thing back to the guys ... It incites the cycle again. We have to just rise above it and say this isn't all right. We should be equal' (MediaWatch 2000: 14). Most said they preferred a strong message to a subtle one, and they were attracted to positive messages as opposed to negative ones. The research showed a great need for young people to act as their own agents of change and, through a youth advisory committee, they are to be involved in all stages of a new specially targeted component on the MediaWatch website.[8]

Creating a Critical Media Audience

Once stereotypes have been made visible they aren't as damaging – I think they lose some of their power. I think the stereotypes we should worry about are the ones we aren't aware of. (Catherine Lumby, ASA, Australia)[9]

Media literacy and media education programmes are fundamentally concerned with making visible the invisible, apparently seamless messages of media content. With the arrival of the Internet many advocacy groups can now do this at a distance, using their websites to analyse images and to invite comments and feedback from users. This can be extremely stimulating. Ideally, however, critical media skills are most effectively developed in the process of discussion and face-to-face exchanges. That is certainly the conclusion of Japan's Forum for Citizens' Television and Media (FCT), one of the oldest and most active groups in the media literacy field.[10] Its principles are rooted in a belief that media literacy will empower citizens who live in today's 'media society'. The group organises an open forum three or four times a year, during which people from all walks of life can join in media literacy workshops and discussions about current media themes.

In 1998 the FCT started a television monitoring project known as TEMO in which anyone could participate, in their own homes, using analysis sheets available from the FCT. The idea was simultaneously to collect data and develop critical media skills. Several TEMO activities were held, with between fifty and seventy people taking part in each. Participants were asked to code basic categories covering gender representation and the depiction of ethnic minorities in various kinds of programme, and to analyse the visual and sound techniques that were used to produce meanings. What emerged was that although this generated useful data for the FCT, it was not a successful way of developing media literacy skills. Because most of the participants did the monitoring on an individual basis, they could not share their readings and interpretations with other people. The participants got to know something about how other people interpreted the programmes only when they read the FCT's reports, maybe six months later.

The experience of the FCT over many years is that the most effective path to critical media skills is to exchange interpretations on the spot, by talking about the differences in people's assessments, and about why these variations may exist. In each FCT forum there are people of different backgrounds, age and gender. Very divergent views may emerge between – for example – disabled people, teenagers, adult women and men towards identical programme segments. It is the dialogue between these groups that is important in creating critical viewers. The FCT has found too that the issue of gender can be an extremely useful entry point for media literacy workshops on a broad range of topics. Many women can easily recognise and read how women are depicted and given 'meaning' by the media. This awareness can be built on to develop media readings of other issues, and to connect women's issues with wider human rights issues.[11]

Face-to-face interaction and participation is a guiding principle for the Women's Media Watch (Jamaica) public education programme. WMW uses popular theatre, skits and role play, film screenings, discussions and multi-media workshops. The idea is that the experiences of the participants should guide the development and procedures of the gathering. The approach seems to work. People quickly become aware of their taken-for-granted ways of seeing (or not seeing) the media, and start to come up with their own examples as the workshops develop.[12] Women's Media Watch (South Africa) also stresses personal experience and expertise in its regular workshops for members. The sessions aim to develop basic media analysis skills, and at the same time to build awareness of specific issues such as pornography, reporting on violence against women, advertising and so on.

These workshops are framed so as to build bridges between different constituencies. Journalists are invited to explain their side of the issue – for example, they may track the development of a specific story, the constraints they commonly face, the decision-making layers within a news-room. NGOs are asked to present case studies, to give facts and figures, or to talk about legislation. The aim is to break down the 'us' and 'them' gap between NGOs and journalists. 'We always tell our NGO members not to attack journalists, even if they seem prickly or cynical. If they bother to come to such a workshop, they are potential allies.'[13] These exchanges can be invaluable, not just in giving people on each 'side' new insights into the constraints within which the other operates; they can also break down barriers and create the basis for useful working relationships.

Breaking down barriers between audiences and media is at the heart of one of the most ambitious citizen-based media literacy efforts, the Viewers'

Forum established by the Centre for Advocacy and Research in India. A series of focus group discussions held in the early days of the Centre's work demonstrated not just the diversity of views that people in the community held about television, but how much people *wanted* to talk about the medium. In acknowledgement of this, the Viewers' Forum was established in three cities – Delhi, Ahmedabad and Lucknow – in 1995. To avoid the discussions becoming locked within an urban middle-class perspective, in 1998 a forum was established in the rural centre of Mau, which at the time was barely reached by cable and satellite. Meanwhile in Delhi the original group gradually sub-divided into three: a forum of low-income viewers, a forum of viewers with disability, and a forum of middle-class viewers. The forum is open to everyone, but women are its most active and vocal participants.

The basic idea is to develop channels for dialogue between citizens and media practitioners. This is done in two ways. One is the development of media literacy, through regular neighbourhood meetings – at least eight per year – that provide viewers with a structure in which they can analyse and discuss some aspect of television content. These sessions have also dealt with media regulation and the media production process, the aim being to give citizens an awareness of their rights as media consumers and of the various possibilities for intervention. The second route is the organisation of theme-based workshops that bring together viewers and invited panellists from the media industry. Helped by a number of prominent media professionals on its advisory board, the Centre for Advocacy and Research has been extremely successful in attracting media practitioners – producers, directors, scriptwriters, sometimes even actors – who, if not always easy to convince, have been ready to enter into dialogue with the viewers' groups. The high-points of these discussions are summarised in the forum newsletters, distributed to the media in English (*Viewers' Voices*) and Hindi (*Nazariya*), as well as on its interactive website. Training for forum organisers was expanded in 1999 and 2000, so as to build up second- and third-line leadership that could help to expand membership and participation in the years to come.

Like MediaWatch in Canada, CFAR sees media literacy as a tool for citizen empowerment. The ability to critique media content and the opportunity for dialogue with media professionals provide members of the Viewers' Forum with a sense of identity in today's often faceless media environment, and with an awareness of their rights as consumers. Members of the forum contribute to many of CFAR's other activities such as helping to set up audience panels or collecting viewer feedback for monitoring studies. For CFAR the Viewers' Forum is both a starting point for citizens' interventions in broadcasting, and a logical culmination of the group's

initial incursion into advocacy which began with monitoring gender representation in the media.[14]

Towards Gender-sensitive Media

One of the ideas (we) had was to create an organisation that would do studies
and create roundtables and seminars around the country that would discuss
the issues, to get opinions about what needed to be done, and to make the
press more aware of how to do this job of covering women. Hopefully, in
having those conversations, we would be able to promote change. (Nancy
Woodhull, quoted in Gibbons 2000: 260)

The year was 1988, the country was the United States, and the idea was
novel. Frustrated by lack of change in media portrayal of women despite
organised protests stretching back to the early 1970s, feminist author and
critic Betty Friedan and founding editor of *USA Today* Nancy Woodhull
created Women, Men and Media. The approach was innovative, particularly in the context of its time. The aim was to carry out regular studies
to track progress in how women were being portrayed in the media. By
releasing the findings at conferences and symposia around the country the
plan was to link together 'journalists, media executives, film critics, screen
writers, academics, social activists and other creative thinkers in a network
of discussion and debate about how to improve media treatment of women'
(Gibbons 2000: 256).

With their national reputations and media connections, Friedan and
Woodhull were actually in a position to achieve this. Over the next ten
years Women, Men and Media commissioned studies ranging from women's
images in advertising and in magazines, to the work for which it was to
become best-known – women's representation in the news. Panels and
roundtables were organised to debate the findings, and the Women, Men
and Media Breakthrough Awards were launched to give recognition to
individuals or companies that had helped to cross boundaries or change
stereotypes in gender portrayal. Women, Men and Media collaborated with
other organisations including Women in Film, Women in Communications
and Women in Cable. It sponsored public discussions on topics such as
women's coverage in politics, abortion and family issues, and the impact
of male-dominated talk radio (Gibbons 2000).

The high-profile nature of the participants helped to attract good press
and media coverage for Women, Men and Media events. But did media
portrayal of women itself change? News studies were carried out every
year between 1989 and 1996. The 1996 study showed that, for the second
year running, news references to women were declining and that women

in power – in both public and private sectors – received very little coverage, either as news-makers or as sources of information (Bridge 1996). With the results showing little change, these general studies were abandoned in favour of research into more specialised topics such as news coverage of women in sport (Women, Men and Media 1998), business and the economy (*Media Report to Women* 2000b) and the armed forces (*Media Report to Women* 2000c). Speaking in December 1999, on the release of the study of women in business and economic news, Betty Friedan seemed despondent: 'Progress is slow. The results are, depressingly, not very much improved. It's still shocking … I wish we could have more sensational progress to report but at least we've helped create a consciousness of a big blind spot' (*Media Report to Women* 2000b: 1).

Perhaps it was too much to expect sensational progress in the monolithic US media system, even after a decade of activity led by such media-savvy activists. What can be said is that the annual studies 'pushed newspaper organisations to examine themselves. A number of them began using the Women, Men and Media analysis model to assess their own progress … Other groups began conducting their own assessments of their local news-papers' (Gibbons 2000: 262). In most cases the results paralleled those of the Women, Men and Media studies, suggesting that there were still plenty of 'big blind spots' to be addressed. Despite its aspiration – reflected in the name Women, Men and Media – to include men in the process of change, getting men around the table was often the hardest thing to do. Women, Men and Media programme director Sheila Gibbons summed up its legacy as 'giving women in the news media tools to take back to the office and use to show editors and news directors how obviously they were short-changing women … It's harder now for news executives to stick with the status quo.'[15]

Trying to move the media towards the adoption of gender-sensitive journalistic and production values is probably the most formidable of all tasks undertaken by gender monitoring and advocacy groups. Indeed, until relatively recently it was a challenge that many avoided meeting directly, opting instead for more oblique ways of influencing media content. Women, Men and Media's establishment in the late 1980s was an exceptionally early attempt to create a structure in which activists and media profes-sionals came together to interrogate critically the values and priorities that result in the patterns of gender representation we find in the media. It signalled a new development, and the realisation that without dialogue – between researchers, activists, advertisers, journalists, radio and television producers – there could be no way out of the impasse in which the debate about gender portrayal appeared to be locked. At the heart of many gender monitoring and advocacy initiatives since the mid-1990s has been a search for data, concepts and language capable of involving media practitioners in discussion, and of stimulating them to think about gender as a factor in the choices they make and the representations they produce.

A *sine qua non* for dialogue is that activists should understand the professional and institutional contexts in which media people operate. And in any discussion media practitioners must have space to express and explain the implications of these, without being made to feel that they are simply making excuses. For example, more than 100 journalists were involved in workshops organised by Red-Ada to consider the results of their 1998 monitoring study in Bolivia. An important point to emerge was that while many journalists were concerned by the results and wanted to improve the situation, they felt constrained by the weight of day-to-day professional pressures. These include the need to present the news in a way that attracts readers, is palatable, easily and quickly absorbed. A journalist usually must cover different sources within one day and has little time for research. Journalists' scope for action is oriented by editors and information chiefs, by chance events and by whom they happen to come across, by the themes of the moment, by ability and salaries, by the ideological orientation of the newspaper, and by the priorities of the owners (Flores 1999a: 129).

This battery of professional and institutional constraints does not, of course, mean that journalists and other media practitioners work within a complete straitjacket. Journalists exercise many individual choices that have an impact on gender representation, from the selection of guests and interviewees, to interview locations and settings, to the style of questioning, to camera movement, to commentary and voice-over. Programme-makers in genres such as drama and entertainment have an even wider range of choices including characterisation, role relationships, casting, music and sound effects, lighting, camera positioning and so on. So although media professionals do operate under constraints, there is often considerable scope available to those who want to break away from gender stereotypical conventions. However, one of the problems is that in the media, as in every sector, the accepted way of doing things is usually also the easiest. The challenge for activists is to convince media professionals that the easiest way is not necessarily the best – in terms of the quality of their output, or its appeal to the audience.

This can be an uphill struggle when there is at best only a superficial awareness of gender issues in most countries, and in most media systems. Even people who produce programmes for women often have little understanding of what needs to be done. In their analysis of women's programmes on Chinese television, Bu Wei and colleagues (1999) conclude that many producers assume that showing women's images or reflecting women's issues on screen is enough in itself. Yet such a simple 'representation' does not necessarily guarantee a progressive effect. Although these programmes often deal with violations of women's rights – in employment, through sexual harassment or domestic violence – the abuses are generally treated as isolated, individual cases rather than as part of a deeper social problem. The solutions proposed often reproduce stereotypes about gender roles: for example, suggesting that women should improve themselves in various ways, wear plainer clothes, or be nicer to their husbands. So while it may be true that these programmes offer greater diversity of female images, they offer little in terms of women's empowerment. According to this research, too many women's programmes in China reflect women from the perspective of a male-defined power culture.

Breaking free of that normalised male-defined perspective to achieve 'gender consciousness', and adopting what is sometimes called a 'gender perspective', is of course not a simple transition. People who work within a gender perspective usually know what this perspective means. But explaining it to others – particularly to media professionals – is not always easy. Posing the fundamental question 'what is gender consciousness' in programme-making, the authors of this Chinese study suggest that it revolves round a sensitivity to gender inequality 'in terms of situation, interests and power' and to gender differences in 'observing, analysing and handling things', and that it includes a readiness to take 'measures and actions' to promote gender equality (Wei et al. 1999).

While it may be unrealistic to imagine that more than a few people working in the media will develop this kind of gender consciousness, many media professionals do have an acute awareness of social inequality that activists can connect with. For instance, interviews with women media professionals in Peru concluded that they did not have a gender consciousness in the sense of being motivated actively to promote change. But they did have clear ideas about violence and sexual discrimination, a realisation that women have not achieved equality as citizens, sensitivity towards women who suffer and struggle, a wish for greater openness between women, a sense of their own personal fight for equality, and a deep recognition of the importance of women's political participation. (Alfaro 1997: 94). Though they may not add up to a gender perspective, such ideas do offer contact markers for advocates intent on pursuing dialogue with media professionals. At the very least, they can be starting points for the development of media content centred on specific areas of gender inequality.

Bringing gender, as a concept, into focus within inscribed media practices and priorities or within the day-to-day frame of reference used by media professionals is, however, a much more daunting enterprise than pushing for the coverage of particular gender-related issues. Groups like B.a.B.e in Croatia, Women's Media Watch in Jamaica and CFAR in India have organised workshops for journalists and other media practitioners to analyse standard portrayal patterns in different types of content from a gender perspective and to explore alternative approaches. In South Africa, media professionals themselves have initiated this kind of activity.

The South African National Editors' Forum (SANEF) is an influential grouping of senior editors from all media sectors in the country. One of its objectives is to redress racial and gender stereotyping in and through the media, and since its establishment in 1996 it has worked hard to be a front-runner on these issues, creating links with like-minded groups including the Commission on Gender Equality and Women's Media Watch. At the invitation of SANEF, in 1999 Women's Media Watch organised a workshop on Gender and Diversity. The idea was to launch a debate on how issues such as gender violence are portrayed in the media, and how journalists can provide a more holistic reflection of South Africa and its people. Using its video *Who's News?* as the main workshop resource, WMW was able to put a human face on issues that media people sometimes find remote and difficult to grasp – the media invisibility of poor and disadvantaged women, the representation of sex-workers, disabled and gay women, coverage of rape and domestic violence, the portrayal of women in politics. The workshop was so successful that SANEF decided it should be repeated in all nine provinces in the country.[16] For WMW, getting the attention and support of media decision-makers is important as it creates relationships that can be built on later at the media organisational level. It is also a way of making concrete the gender portrayal guidelines that exist in many South African media organisations, but which even people at the top rarely seem to know about.[17]

Other advocacy groups have concentrated their efforts on changing specific media practices. For instance, in Japan the Workshop on Gender and Media (GEAM) has successfully focused attention on questions of journalistic language and style. Their non-sexist guidelines to eliminate discriminatory language in descriptions, adjectives and job titles (Ueno et al. 1996) were the result of seven years of monitoring newspaper content and journalists' style manuals. In 1993 this Toyama-based group published the results of its first newspaper monitoring study. It began to hold workshops with local print and television journalists, and with journalists' unions, to discuss the impact of language and other aspects of presentation on people's perceptions of women and men. Partly through contacts between these local media and their national parent companies, interest developed at national level. After publication of GEAM's guidelines in 1996, over the next three years influential media including the daily newspaper *Asahi*

Shimbun, the Kyodo News Agency and the public service broadcaster NHK gradually revised their style manuals or issued their own guidelines on non-discriminatory language. Until that time, words such as *shujin* ('master') had routinely been used when referring to a woman's husband (*otto*) or partner (*tureai*). Women, whatever their status, were commonly referred to as *shufu* ('housewife'). So this relatively recent development implies an important shift in ways of describing, and representing, women in the media in Japan.[18]

For Sur Profesionales in Chile, a focal point has been to try to widen the conventional definition of news. A news monitoring project by the group in 1997 led to the conclusion – reached by many others – that women's poor representation is linked to the fact that 'news' is understood primarily as something referring almost exclusively to the public sphere, and in particular to the world of politics and government. The entry of more women into public life should, at least in theory, lead to a greater visibility for women in the news. But this in itself does not address the more fundamental limitation – the fact that news priorities result in the over-exposure of a privileged few, and the exclusion of the majority, in public discourse. From this point of departure, Sur Profesionales produced a manual for media professionals (Silva 1998b). The aim was to introduce new themes and new ways of portraying women and men in media content. There are comprehensive tips on how to avoid common traps in the kinds of question asked, the assumptions made, the use of language, the implicit evaluations used in portraying women and men. Beyond this, the manual suggests a number of themes that deserve greater attention in the Chilean news media – for example masculinity, the changing relationships between women and men, women and work, domestic violence, sexual violence and harassment, sexuality, reproductive health, divorce and abortion (neither of which is legal in Chile). The manual gives a brief orientation to each theme, as well as contacts to organisations with expertise in the different areas.

As the first of its kind, the manual has been in great demand. Two years after its publication, it was still being distributed throughout Latin America and even further afield through channels such as the World Association of Community Radio Broadcasters. What might be the impact of an initiative like this? Although in the short term it could not really be said to have produced measurable changes in media content, it did open lines of communication with media professionals and it did make a mark in terms of media and public debate. For Sur Profesionales, this in itself was a step in the right direction, even if lack of funding meant that only limited follow-up was possible.[19]

People working in the media inherit a whole battery of professional routines that carry within them traditional assumptions about gender.

Changing these routines begins with persuading programme-makers to reflect critically on the decisions and choices they make. This approach guides the work of the Gender Portrayal Department (GPD) that was established within the Netherlands Broadcasting Corporation (NOS) in 1991. Originally conceived as a five-year project, the department's impact both nationally and internationally has been such that in 2000 the NOS management board decided to give it a permanent place within the organisation. Not only was this a brave decision, given that it meant taking on board a critical watchdog; 'It is also a unique decision, because it means that public service broadcasting is now taking the initiative to build bridges between programme-makers, audiences and media critics' (van Dijck 2000: 28). In the sense that the GPD is a critical entity operating inside the media system itself, it may seem quite different from most other media monitoring and advocacy groups. But the department's insider position does not undermine its role as a critic,[20] and indeed puts it in a privileged situation in terms of contacts with programme- and policy-makers. Moreover, the GPD has always had a strong outward-looking orientation and a tradition of developing alliances with consumer and community groups, parliamentarians, researchers, students and others concerned with issues of gender portrayal.

The department sees part of its role as bringing groups like these into contact with programme-makers for discussion and sometimes programme analysis. For example, the GPD invited women's associations, ethnic minority organisations, researchers, programme-makers, managers, politicians and young journalists to take part in the second Global Media Monitoring Project on 1 February 2000. Over eighty people took part in the day-long activities which included not just filling in the coding sheets, but panel discussions and – perhaps most important of all – conversations between widely different groups. 'As the day progressed, it became increasingly clear to both programme-makers and journalists that the world inhabited by those with whom they were now engaging in dialogue was being largely overlooked by "the news". Where were all the young people, the women, the ethnic minorities?' (van Dijck 2000: 29). This very direct lesson, which illustrated in a vivid way the somewhat abstract results contained in the monitoring data, was a revelation for most of the programme-makers, many of whom decided they would continue with the monitoring within their own companies. But the Gender Portrayal Department, like the FCT in Japan, is convinced there is a world of difference between 'doing' monitoring and 'talking' about the patterns it reveals. It is in the interaction, particularly between people with different perspectives, that insights emerge and new programme-making possibilities come to light.[21]

This stress on discussion and interaction is very much at the heart of the department's work with programme-makers. Based on a series of solid and detailed research studies, throughout the 1990s the GPD documented well-established and widespread patterns of gender portrayal in Dutch radio and television programmes.[22] To make these patterns come to life for producers and journalists, the department anchors its discussion in an analysis of examples from current programme output and tries to put forward suggestions for alternatives. 'Naturally, there are no off-the-peg solutions, but almost invariably some scope exists for a more varied portrayal of both women and men' (NOS Gender Portrayal Department 1996b: 2). A key concept for the GPD is 'programme quality'. By focusing attention on gender portrayal, they argue, you get better-quality radio and television. 'More diversity, a broader view of reality, results in more interesting radio and TV fare. It offers a new perspective, and allows a different story to be heard' (NOS Gender Portrayal Department 1998a: 3).

By the mid-1990s the approach of the NOS Gender Portrayal Department had caught the attention and imagination of other European public service broadcasters. In 1997 work started on the development of an audio-visual training toolkit including research and television programme examples from Denmark, Finland, Germany, the Netherlands, Norway and Sweden. The result was *Screening Gender* (2000). This toolkit brings together video clips that illustrate common patterns of gender portrayal, demonstrate the gain in programme quality that can be achieved by paying attention to gender, and give a voice to programme-makers who explain how an awareness of gender influences their work. Following the method of the NOS Gender Portrayal Department, *Screening Gender* is especially concerned with encouraging media professionals to use gender as a starting point for exploring their working practices and routines. In workshops held during the development of the toolkit, it became clear that programme-makers find it valuable and invigorating to take a fresh look at their own and other programmes from the perspective of gender. When questions are asked about why certain programme-making decisions were taken rather than others, a producer's sense of curiosity and creativity is aroused. 'The automatic pilot is switched off for a moment, the choice of a particular approach has to be rationalised. This makes it clear what consequences pragmatic decisions have for the meaning of the images you ultimately broadcast, and hence for the story you are telling. It is precisely in these observations that the germ of change lies' (van Dijck 2000: 29).

The story of the NOS Gender Portrayal Department offers a heartening example of how a responsive media environment, allied with a fortuitous mix of creative vision and professional pragmatism, can foster critical thinking about media content. It also illustrates the importance of tenacity and strategy in ensuring a place for media advocates at the table of mainstream media decision-making. The GPD did not come into being overnight. In fact, its origins go back to 1985, when an informal group called Women in the Picture came together within the NOS. In 1990 this group succeeded in getting three sponsors to fund a five-year gender portrayal project: the NOS, the Ministry of Social Affairs and Employment and the Ministry of Education, Culture and Welfare. The future of the GPD was in serious doubt when the project funding came to an end in 1996, but by this time the department had a solid record of work, and enjoyed high professional standing with programme-makers. These were among the various factors that convinced the NOS to continue its financial support, though still on a project basis. In the late 1990s the department put much strategic effort into convincing policy-makers that project-based funding undermined the effectiveness of its work. It was not until January 2000 – fifteen years after the initial seed was planted by Women in the Picture – that the Gender Portrayal Department achieved a permanent presence in the Dutch broadcasting system. Now known as the Diversity Department, its mandate has broadened to include ethnicity and age, as well as gender, in a comprehensive programme to ensure unconditional diversity in Dutch radio and television.[23]

Notes

1. Akhila Sivadas, personal communication, July 2000.

2. Information from 'Gender Media Monitor Media Literacy Project Report', unpublished project document, June 2000; and Natasha Nuñez, personal communication, July 2000.

3. B.a.B.e, *Annual Report, 1999*, 2000: 6.

4. Patricia Flores Palacios, personal communication, December 1999.

5. 'Teacher Training College and Community College Workshops and Presentations', internal document, Women's Media Watch, Jamaica.

6. See NWMC website: www.nwmc.org.au/Publications/publicat.htm

7. See MediaWatch website: www.mediawatch.ca/resources

8. Melanie Cishecki, personal communication, July 2000.

9. Quoted in Tamara Stowe, 2 June 2000, 'That Windsor Smith Billboard'; see National Women's Media Centre website: www.nwmc.org.au/Articles/stowe.htm. Catherine Lumby is a board member of the Australian Advertising Standards Bureau.

10. The FCT was established in 1977 and was initially known as the Forum for Children's Television. Its interests gradually expanded to include gender and diversity, and it was renamed the Forum for Citizens' Television in 1992. In 1998 the word 'media' was added, to reflect the contemporary interconnected media world of videos, internet, computer games and so on.

11. Toshiko Miyazaki, personal communication, July 2000.

12. Hilary Nicholson, personal communication, July 2000.

13. Gabrielle Le Roux, personal communication, July 2000. In a more formal context, Mediaworks, the parent organisation of Women's Media Watch, offers a Gender and Communication course for community women's rights activists each year. Critical media analysis is one component, along with communication skills and creative media work.

14. Akhila Sivadas, personal communication, July 2000.

15. Sheila Gibbons, personal communication, July 2000. After the tragic and premature death of Nancy Woodhull in 1997, Betty Friedan continued to lead Women, Men and Media until spring 2000, when the organisation decided to conclude its work.

16. Judy Sandison (Secretary General, SANEF), personal communication, July 2000.

17. Women's Media Watch, *Final Report, 1999*: 3.

18. Masami Saitoh, personal communication, February 2000. This work on language has been part of a broader development to promote equality between women and men in Japan. In April 1999 the Revised Equal Opportunity Law prohibited gender discrimination in job recruitment and advertisements. Gender-neutral job titles and descriptions are one dimension of this.

19. Uca Silva, personal communication, July 2000. The Communication and Gender Project of Sur Profesionales was funded between September 1997 and March 1999.

20. For a description of the complex structure of the Dutch public service broadcasting system that makes this possible, see Brants and McQuail (1997). Despite strong competition from a growing commercial sector, principles of diversity and pluralism remain central to media policy in the Netherlands.

21. Bernadette van Dijck, personal communication, February 2000.

22. See NOS Gender Portrayal Department 1993, 1994, 1996a, 1998b for summaries in English and Dutch.

23. Bernadette van Dijck, personal communication, July 2000.

Part IV

Achievements

12

The Final Analysis

It's like riding a tiger: once you get on you cannot get off. This is a continuous process. You cannot stop it. There is no beginning, there is no end. (Manisha Chaudury, Centre for Advocacy and Research, in *Making a Difference* 1999)

The results of the second Global Media Monitoring Project, carried out in seventy countries on 1 February 2000, suggested that the news world might have been standing still for five years. On that day women accounted for just 18 per cent of news subjects, compared with 17 per cent in 1995 (Spears et al. 2000). The degree of concordance between the main results from the two global monitoring projects was remarkable. Yet it was hardly surprising. To have expected a perceptible shift in the world's news over the time period would have been naïve. The embedded nature of news values and news selection processes is such that the overall patterns detected by quantitative monitoring are unlikely to change appreciably even over the medium term.

Indeed, the apparent universality of prevailing news definitions obliges advocates to question the extent to which it is realistic to expect a fundamental 'gender shift' in news agendas and priorities. Reflecting on their 1997 news monitoring experience, Red-Ada in Bolivia did pose a number of salient questions that highlight the constraints on change. To what extent do journalists actually construct the news agenda? Is it feasible to divert news values away from coverage of government and politics? To what extent is it really possible for other actors, linked to aspects of daily life, to find a place in the news? Is it possible in the short term for the press to reflect a gender perspective and to move away from a masculine-as-universal vision of the world? To what extent can the press contribute to the construction of women as citizens, based on a vision of equality? For Red-Ada, the answer to this kind of question lies in the fact that in contemporary Bolivian society the press plays an important investigative and watchdog role on behalf of citizens – uncovering corruption, exposing people and events that contravene the law, and highlighting violations of human rights (Flores 1999a: 129–30).

For advocates in many countries, this is the crucial link. In theory at least, it should be possible to turn that critical, investigative journalistic perspective on to the issue of gender. Critical journalists do not un-questioningly accept the official line or the press release; they search for alternative sources of information not just as a check on reliability, but also to add texture and tone to their reports. It seems logical that gender – in terms of sources, priorities and perspectives – should be among the factors taken into account by journalists within this tradition. Yet it rarely seems to be. Media activists have begun to find ways of introducing this gender dimension into journalistic and indeed other media production routines. But the process is just beginning. As the experience of several media advocacy groups shows, change is likely to be achingly slow.

On the other hand, the media industries themselves develop at a ver-tiginous pace, posing ever more complex problems for gender monitoring and advocacy. Digitalisation brings countless new channels to be kept in view. Mass audiences fragment into many smaller units, each with its distinct experience and interpretation of media content. Advertisers res-pond to video time shifting and consumer ad zapping by conceiving a radically different style of commercial that is interwoven with content, rather than being separately identifiable. The Internet presents a seemingly limitless arena for new forms of imagery, as well as new channels for the transmission of traditional media content. And despite all the technological change, the same old patterns of gender representation apparently remain relatively intact. In that sense there is no sign of a radical break with the past, and there is no end in sight.

Riding the Tiger

> They keep us on our toes. A lot of times we take certain things for granted or we overlook them. (Editor-in-chief *The Gleaner*, Jamaica, speaking of Women's Media Watch; Walker and Nicholson 1996: 100)

Riding the tiger of gender media monitoring and advocacy demands skill, nerve and determination. Spills and upsets are a constant threat, while there is rarely a sense of crossing the line or reaching the finishing post. Keeping media people on their toes means being able to keep them in-terested in the issues. This involves a constant search for new angles and discussion points. Progress is hard to measure. And even with the best planning, unexpected hazards can undermine gains already made.

As an essentially political activity, media monitoring and advocacy is almost inevitably affected by shifts in the wider political and economic environment. Sometimes these can overturn, almost overnight, painstakingly developed alliances. In a highly publicised meeting in January 1996 held in collaboration with the Indian Women's Press Corps, three years of effort by the then Media Advocacy Group were rewarded by a commitment from the director-general of India's state television organisation Doordarshan. He agreed to the development of gender guidelines or a programme code for television producers. But almost immediately afterwards, in anticipation of general elections to be held in May, the ruling party made critical changes in the leadership of Doordarshan. This had a tremendous impact on advocacy efforts. Not only was there no follow-through regarding the proposed guidelines, but the changes completely disrupted a complex set of relationships that had been built up over the previous three years.[1] This kind of setback can be devastating for small groups. The Israel Women's Network was jubilant when, after protracted discussions, it persuaded the Israel Broadcasting Authority – the country's public service broadcaster – to sponsor courses on women's issues for its senior staff. The agreement was regarded as a breakthrough (Sachs 1996). But only one course was ever held. Soon afterwards, changes in internal organisation meant that the necessary will and commitment at decision-making level disappeared within the IBA (Sappir 2000).

The overall political framework can have both direct and indirect effects on media advocacy work. In the mid-1990s Australia's change of government signalled a move from a system that, broadly speaking, supported regulation in the community interest to one that favoured deregulation and free market principles. This transformed the power relations between community and business groups, leaving little space for dialogue about solutions to community concerns and making it extremely difficult even to maintain the gains of the early 1990s in terms of gender-based media policies and codes. An organisation like the National Women's Media Centre is affected by this kind of shift in political climate not just at the level of strategy – in terms of the available options – but also at the level of day-to-day practice. Like many advocacy groups, the NWMC depends on a high level of voluntary input. Much of this comes from media students. They learn something in return, so it is also a way of passing on the knowledge and skills that can bring about change. But the problem for the NWMC is that the brightest voluntary workers move into junior media jobs where they can no longer be active advocates – not because of lack of time, but because they must protect their career prospects. 'Whereas a few years ago there was often no problem, now even liberal media ask employees what affiliations they have. So for women wanting a media career, it's not viable to stay on in any "community activist" capacity.'[2]

For Women's Media Watch, Jamaica, dependence on voluntary effort also puts the organisation in a vulnerable position. The country's deteriorating economic situation means that, to make ends meet, most people have two or more jobs. Inevitably, the volunteers are less involved than they used to be. Without a car, getting around Kingston is often difficult and dangerous at night for women. So the mere question of how to get home after an evening workshop with a youth group is a problem. 'People think we are a big agency, but we run with two part-time staff and a semi-paid volunteer. We have to struggle to run the programmes properly, because we can't pay qualified people. It's hard to raise seed money for capacity building, and the work (i.e. educational work) cannot generate income.'[3]

Finance is without doubt the most fundamental obstacle faced by most monitoring and advocacy groups. The battle to raise core funding for even a skeleton staff is constant. The NWMC in Australia currently relies almost entirely on member support to keep going. Funding cuts have forced Canada's Mediawatch into an intensive restructuring process, cutting full-time staff from three to two and making changes to the way they work. The group began a fund-raising strategy, including a direct mail fund-raising programme, applications to foundations and private funding sources for various projects.[4] Organisations may spend endless time on funding applications, only to have them rejected. And without a clear fund-raising policy, there is the risk that groups will allow their activities to become too dispersed by succumbing to 'donor temptation' (TAMWA 2000: 43). Project-based funding for specific monitoring activities can be useful, but it usually limits the amount of follow-up that is possible. Good work is started, but there can be no continuity. Projects tacked on to existing structures, or added to individuals' workloads, can result in burn-out and wasted effort. Momentum is built up, and then there is frustration.[5]

The scarcity of funding makes partnerships crucial. MediaWatch points out that funding for related activities such as media literacy or violence prevention can sometimes be obtained in association with another agency, on the understanding that gender portrayal issues will be a central part of the work. But partnerships are important in many other ways too. MediaWatch has devoted much time to building partnerships with organisations that work in the areas of violence in the media, media literacy and diversity issues. This brings them in-depth information and resources that they would not be able to get with their own limited means. In return, MediaWatch can add a gender perspective to the work of partner organisations. China's Media Monitor Network for Women co-hosts meetings with other women's NGOs such as the Women's Health Group, East Meets West Group, the Women's Psychology Consulting Centre and the Women's Legal Assistance Centre of Beijing University. These activities not only provide new information and resources for women journalists, but also strengthen co-operation between the Network and other organisations.[6]

The Tanzania Media Women's Association builds alliances through networking, the media and community outreach. Besides the media institutions themselves, TAMWA works with the Ministry of Community Development, Women's Affairs and Children, the Ministry of Constitutional Affairs and Justice, the police force, as well as other women's NGOs such as the Tanzania Women Lawyers Association, the Tanzania Gender Networking Programme and the Women's Legal Aid Centre. These and other partnerships with, for example, the Legal and Human Rights Centre and the Tanganyika Law Society, help TAMWA to meet its objectives; a wide cross-section of society is made to feel accountable, and thus gives support to TAMWA's activities. For its part TAMWA, through its access to the media, can play the role of 'mouthpiece' for the concerns of sister NGOs (TAMWA 1999).

Both the National Women's Media Centre in Australia and Women's Media Watch in South Africa work co-operatively with organisations with similar aims. As the only national women's voice on media policy and practice, the NWMC supports and networks with other local and state groups, trying to help them stay afloat and united during what has been a particularly difficult time to bring about change. The very different political climate of South Africa offers Women's Media Watch more scope for intervention. WMW believes that regularly raising gender issues with media authorities such as the Independent Broadcasting Authority, the Advertising Standards Authority, the Press Ombudsman and the Broadcasting Complaints Commission of South Africa helps to keep gender on their agenda. 'It has a tendency to slip off when they are not actively confronted with it.'[7] Its links with interest groups can add weight to a complaint or action and can be a useful strategy in raising awareness. For instance, WMW works with NGOs such as the Network on Violence against Women, and with national decision-makers including the Commission on Gender Equality, the Parliamentary Committee on the Improvement of the Quality of Life and Status of Women, the Parliamentary Women's Caucus and the ANC Women's Caucus. For Women's Media Watch these contacts have proven helpful in putting pressure on media producers to make changes.

The issue of links and partnerships becomes even more central in the context of new technologies and the Internet. Many monitoring and advocacy groups already have websites, some of them interactive, often containing an enormous amount of information and providing links to other similar groups nationally and elsewhere. Through their websites media advocates can reach infinitely more people than ever before – both nationally and internationally. This area of activity is bound to increase, and groups need to be ready to manage the change. Canada's MediaWatch found that with the rise of new technologies, the scope of their work increased dramatically. Yet they had fewer staff than ever in their history. To meet the challenge MediaWatch has turned to the new technologies themselves for help. In 2000 it launched MOVE (MediaWatch Online Volunteer Education), a pilot project to use online tools to train and support a nation-wide network of volunteers. Much of what MediaWatch has achieved over the past two decades has been due to a dedicated network of volunteers who are involved in all aspects of its operations. The MOVE project is designed to allow this network to expand and flourish.

The Impact of Media Monitoring and Advocacy

It is essential to remember that change is slow and takes time. Every success is important, no matter how small it might appear. (Melanie Cishecki, MediaWatch)[8]

The specific achievements of gender media monitoring and advocacy are relatively easy to identify. The development of codes and policies, successful complaints procedures, workshops and discussions with the media industry, training in critical media analysis – there are many examples. However, it is more difficult to assess the impact of these efforts, the extent to which they have influenced practices and mentalities in an enduring way. Until now there has been little systematic research or evaluation, though, with the passage of time, groups themselves are increasingly in a position to reflect on their perceptions of change. The Centre for Advocacy and Research in India has watched exchanges between members of the Viewers' Forum and media professionals becoming sharper, and audience perceptions becoming keener. Looking back over almost a decade of debate, it seemed that gradually all the passion about how television was threatening Indian culture was largely forgotten. Instead, more down-to-earth discussion about media representations of the family, male–female relationships, the institution of marriage, and the marginalisation of specific groups in media content took over.[9] The extent to which viewers can in fact exercise control, or influence media decisions may be unclear; but CFAR remains convinced that 'informed viewer opinion and activism is the only way to enlarge the area of viewer choice'.[10]

Assessing the extent to which feminist advocacy has succeeded in re-defining media agendas is 'work in progress'. It requires retrospective study covering many years, and as yet few comprehensive analyses have been possible. However, some recently published research has begun to throw light on the impact of feminism over the past two decades. A detailed analysis of the media strategies of the National Organisation for Women (NOW) in the United States between 1966 and 1980 concludes that the organisation was able to transfer at least some of its key issues and frames of reference into the American news agenda. In the period covered by the study, the issues that came to be taken most seriously by the media – for example the Equal Rights Amendment and sex discrimination – 'did not begin as clear-cut public issues but were made into issues over time by feminist communications' (Barker-Plummer 2000: 153). Initially, for instance, journalists did not see the issue of sex discrimination as a legitimate framework for women's experiences and treated many claims of discrimination with ridicule. It was not until the mid-1970s that the work of NOW and other feminist strategists to persuade journalists that the general, systematic framework of 'discrimination' fitted women's experiences, as it had fitted those of minorities previously, bore fruit in the 'institutionalisation' of sex discrimination as a serious news topic. Similarly, media acceptance of sexual harassment as a political issue in the 1980s was the result of continual feminist communication and framing that moved the topic from 'personal' to 'political' over time. The overall conclusion of this study is encouraging for media advocates. Although news management fulfils an ideological function by 'sorting' and prioritising issues for audiences – particularly in terms of a public–private categorisation – 'the influence of other discourses and actors can move some topics from one of these categories to the other' (Barker-Plummer 2000: 147).

Some confirmation for this comes from a twelve-country study of news coverage of the four world conferences on women, spanning 1975 to 1995. This also detected positive movement and change in the nature and content of reporting, with a marked reduction in simplistic, sensationalist and sexist coverage over the period. The sheer number of editorials published in 1995 (sixty-five, compared with seventeen in 1975) was some indication of how far the issues of the women's movement had moved up the news agenda in the course of twenty years. The point was directly addressed in a 1995 *Washington Post* editorial describing the international women's movement as 'one of the striking social developments of recent decades. It has given voice and a measure of coherence to a previously neglected set of global and cultural concerns' (Gallagher 2000: 16). It would be difficult to find a better example of the shift – in both media perceptions and political reality – that had taken place since 1975.

Like the broad concerns of the women's movement, it takes time for issues raised by media monitoring and advocacy groups to gain legitimacy. When the NOS Gender Portrayal Department began its work in 1991, 'gender portrayal in the media was widely seen as making a mountain out of molehill, not something to fuss about in the emancipated nineties' (NOS

Gender Portrayal Department 1996b: 14). Gradually this perception changed. An evaluation carried out five years later showed that the department's research and presentations had been an eye-opener to most programme-makers. By 1996 the department could claim that 'the standpoint that "the way women and men are portrayed is one of the professional aspects that determines the quality of a programme" is now widely accepted. The favourable reactions we have received from various quarters makes it clear that a process of change has been set in train' (NOS Gender Portrayal Department 1996b: 15).

It seems undeniable that, at the very least, the process of media monitoring has an impact on the way people 'see' or understand the media. According to one of the Canadian monitors in the 1995 Global Media Monitoring Project:

> I'd been studying in this area for some time, but things really hit me that day that hadn't hit me before. A lot of news stories that could have included gender information didn't ... Since that monitoring day, I've noticed myself looking at the media differently. I look at what's not there as much as I look at what's there, and I notice what makes for the gap between what's there and what's not. (Tindal n.d.: 11)

Or, in the words of one of the young Dutch journalists involved in the 2000 GMMP: 'It's as if the news suddenly tipped on one side, as if you were reading the newspaper through 3-D spectacles' (van Dijck 2000: 29).

Whether monitoring and advocacy initiatives have helped to bring about change in media performance itself is a much more difficult question to answer unequivocally. Reflecting on the first five years of the NOS Gender Portrayal Department, Dorette Kuipers, the first head of department, put it as follows:

> We hope we've gained more gender portrayal awareness in programme-makers through our work, though it's hard to measure ... because we're working on a change of mentality ... For instance, at a recent 50th anniversary celebration for the United Nations, the news presenter noted that there were 180 people in attendance from all over the world – of which only eight were women. Adding that sentence is becoming more a rule now than an exception, drawing attention to imbalance ... We suspect we've played a role in this. (Tindal n.d.: 17)

Another example from the Netherlands points in the same direction. Amateur cyclist Rudi Kemna won the Dutch championship for the third time in a row. After the race, in an interview with senior journalist Jean Nelissen, he was asked whether he now planned to join the professionals. No, replied the cyclist. He was a 'househusband: I do the housekeeping and a bit of cycling'. 'So you do the cooking? ... And house cleaning as well?' Nelissen asked in astonishment. Back in the studio, the programme anchor joked gently that his veteran colleague was 'hearing for the first time that men also cook and clean' (*Screening Gender* 2000: video 1, item 9).

Such small gains – the addition of a sentence, a comment of appraisal – may seem negligible. But if they spring from an awareness that gender representation in the media is something to be questioned rather than taken for granted, they have the potential to transform public perceptions.

Gender is Not a Women's Issue

Gender is *not* a women thing. (Placard used in 'Labels are rubbish' protest, Women's Media Watch, South Africa, 1998)

The example of the Dutch cyclist contains some lessons for gender media monitoring groups. How would an item like this be coded in a straight-forward monitoring exercise? No woman appears in the story. The news subject, reporter and studio announcer are all male. The story topic would be classified as sports, as would the occupation of the news subject. The standard coding grid would reveal an item with three men, in a story about sport. Yet this story is very centrally 'about' gender issues, and this is precisely what the coding fails to register. The fact that the cyclist describes himself as a 'househusband', the amazement of the reporter at the inter-viewee's preference for 'house cleaning' rather than professional cycling, and the wry comment of the studio anchor on his colleague's attitude (in turn implying that the anchor himself has a different point of view), are all hidden behind the numbers. Here we have an extremely clear example of the limitations of quantitative monitoring. Percentages and distributions may seem very clear and precise. In reality they usually hide a quite complicated pattern of gender representation, whose attributes are often extremely difficult to fit into predetermined categories.

This is not to say that the figures produced by quantitative analysis of media content are 'wrong' or that this kind of monitoring should not be carried out. On the contrary. As groups in many countries have discovered, these overall figures are invaluable in sketching out the broad parameters of gender portrayal. They provide inescapable evidence of the imbalance in media representations of women and men – in terms of status and authority, and indeed just sheer numbers. They can be extremely useful as a wake-up call, forcing those who maintain that 'things have changed' to face reality. Studies of this kind will always be needed, to keep track of general trends and patterns, but they are not sufficient to change media representations of gender.

Faced with the fact that only 18 per cent of news subjects are women, what can an individual media professional do? At best, she or he may make an individual effort to shift the balance in specific programmes. But numerical imbalance is only one small facet of the overall problem. Gender representation in the media is constituted in countless, more subtle ways: through the angle from which a story is approached, the locations in which women and men are shown, the choice of questions, the type of interview style adopted, and much more besides. Looking at the issue from this perspective, it becomes clear that the focus of research and action on 'women' as opposed to 'gender' is extremely limiting. It is in the comparison of how women *and* men are portrayed in the media that insights emerge, and change can ensue. 'Gender is *not* a women thing.' As a concept, it actually depends on an interpretation of the relationships between women and men. As an analytical tool it needs to be applied to the study of both masculinity and femininity. As a platform for advocacy, men as well as women must adopt it.

From the perspective of gender media monitoring and advocacy, therefore, the old question 'do women make a difference?' – for instance, to media content – is not the most relevant one. More crucial is the question of how to involve the maximum number of citizens, women and men, in recognising the imbalances in gender portrayal in media content. Most central of all is the question of how to persuade the maximum number of media professionals, women and men, that fair and diverse gender portrayal will contribute to higher-quality output, which is likely to appeal to a wider range of audiences. The involvement of men in gender monitoring and analysis is important, not just in the sense of getting them 'on board' but, more critically, because their readings and interpretations need to be debated. Recent monitoring projects such as the Gender Media Monitor in Trinidad and Tobago and the Women and Media Observatory in Italy have made a point of including boys and young men on an equal basis with girls and young women.

This seems an obvious next step for media advocates because, if gender representation is to change, that implies the representation of men as well as women. Male stereotyping is also an issue, as Justice Mlala of South Africa has put it: 'We men are trapped in a dark and secret world called Men Talk, where we swop tales of conquest and plunder but never of failure or perceived failure' (Le Roux 1999: 24). During the 1990s, within the academic world a small field of men's studies began to explore issues of masculinity and male identity. But as yet these questions hardly feature on the agenda of media monitoring and advocacy groups, a matter of concern to the young women in MediaWatch's 'tween' consumer literacy project: 'Like there is so much stuff for girls … That is great. But why don't guys have any stuff like that? Why don't they say like you need help with *your* self-esteem? Like guys aren't perfect. They don't have a wonderful life' (MediaWatch 2000: 13). Of course, it is true that prevalent representations of femininity and female sexuality maintain unequal power relations in a way that is particularly pernicious to women. But one way of ensuring that men, as well as women, understand this is to analyse the construction of both masculinity and femininity in media content and to debate the differences. As long as 'gender representation' remains synonymous with 'women's representation', gender media advocates will find it difficult to make the media alliances that are necessary to bring about lasting change.

Alliance-building with other public interest groups does not require the abandonment of principles or objectives. But it may provide more leverage in pursing them. In mid-1998 the National Organisation for Women in the United States created a task force to research and develop a Feminist Communications Network – a television, cable, radio and web broadcast network – to deliver news, talk shows and content delivered from a feminist perspective. A dream nurtured for decades, this had proven elusive. After almost a year of deliberation and consultation, in May 1999 NOW announced the launch of its Digital Broadcast Project. The organisation had concluded that the opening up of new channel space through the digital spectrum offered 'an unprecedented opportunity to make a dramatic change'.[11] Nation-wide access might at last be possible for non-commercial, public service media such as the feminist communications network envisaged by NOW. But this access depended on a statutory requirement that the broadcasters already licensed to operate the digital channels should – by reason of their 'public interest' obligations – set aside channel space for public service media. The 1996 Telecommunications Act that had opened up broadcasters' access to digital television did reaffirm the 'public interest' principles of American broadcasting, but did not legislate on specific public interest obligations. When the Gore Commission, set up in mid-1997 to determine what obligations DTV owed the public, reported in December 1998, the report was excoriated in the press. 'Almost none of the debate about the report or the process that created it occurred in public view, because television stations – perhaps fearing regulation – kept the issue off the local and national news.'[12] Not surprisingly, the broadcasters had no interest in sharing their channels, or in reducing their advertising revenue.

Through its Digital Broadcast Project NOW joined forces with People for Better TV (PBTV), a coalition of over 100 groups pushing for clearly defined and enforced public interest obligations for broadcasters in the digital television era. Although the Federal Communications Commission (FCC) had started issuing digital licences in 1997 and some operators began digital transmissions in late 1998, it had shown no signs of taking up the question of how DTV broadcasters were to be held to public service obligations. Throughout 1999 NOW and the other organisations involved in PBTV pushed hard – for example via letters to Congress – for the FCC to be required to convene public hearings so that citizens could express their views. Finally in December 1999 the FCC announced that it would seek public comment.[13] Buoyed by their success in getting the attention of the FCC and of Congress, PBTV members planned a very extensive series of actions in the run-up to the 2000 national elections.

This promised to be a lengthy struggle. But whatever the outcome for NOW, the decision to link up with a broader social movement whose public interest goals could encompass its own was strategically sound. In the context of American broadcasting, it promised a better chance of success than might have been expected if NOW had single-handedly pursued an exclusively feminist agenda. As the business and commercial interests controlling the media continue to concentrate and coalesce, riding the tiger of gender media monitoring and advocacy will increasingly call for such alliances among public interest groups, not just within but also across national boundaries.

Notes

1. Media Advocacy Group, 'Consolidated Three-Year Final Narrative Report, 1995–1998': 8.

2. This and other information in the chapter comes from Helen Leonard, personal communication, July 2000.

3. This and other information in the chapter comes from Hilary Nicholson, personal communication, July 2000.

4. This and other information in the chapter comes from Melanie Cishecki, personal communication, July 2000.

5. Uca Silva, personal communication, July 2000.

6. Media Monitor Network, 'Annual Narrative Report', 1999.

7. Women's Media Watch, *Final Report, 1999*: 4.

8. Melanie Cishecki, personal communication, July 2000.

9. Akhila Sivadas, personal communication, July 2000.

10. 'Understanding Media – A Training of the Trainers', *Viewers' Voices*, November 1999: 6.

11. 'NOW Foundation broadcast project': see www.nowfoundation.org/communications/tv/project.html

12. Mark Huisman (1999) 'Take Back Our TV'; see People for Better TV website: www.bettertv.org/takebacktext.html

13. 'FCC begins proceedings to seek comment on public interest obligations of television broadcasters as they transition to digital transmission technology', FCC News release, 15 December 1999: see www.fcc.gov/Bureaus/Mass_Media/News_Releases/1999/nrmm9030.html

Appendix: Some Gender Media Monitoring and Advocacy Groups

Australia

National Women's Media Centre Australia, PO Box 123, Civic Square, ACT
    2608, Australia
website: www.nwmc.org.au
tel: +61-2-6257.0670
fax: +61-2-6247.4669
e-mail: nwmc@ozemail.com.au
contact: Helen Leonard, Convenor

Belgium

ZORRA, UIA – Centrum voor Vrouwenstudies, Universiteitsplcin 1, B-2610,
    Belgium
website: http://women.uia.ac.be/zorra
tel: +32-3-820.2850
fax: +32-3-820.2882
e-mail: zorra@uia.ac.be
contact: Corinne Van Hellemont, Co-ordinator

Cambodia

Women's Media Centre, PO Box 497, Phnom Penh, Cambodia
tel: +855-23-364.882
fax: +855-23-364.882
e-mail: wmc@forum.org.kh
contact: Tive Sarayeth, Co-director

Canada

MediaWatch, #204-517 Wellington Street W., Toronto, Ontario, Canada,
    M5V 1G1
website: www.mediawatch.ca
tel: +1-416-408.2065
fax: +1-416-408.2069
e-mail: info@mediawatch.ca
contact: Melanie Cishecki, Communications Manager

China

Media Monitor Network for Women, 103 Di An Men Xi Da Jie, Beijing
    100009, People's Republic of China
tel: +86-10-6617.6066
fax: +86-10-6617.6066
e-mail: fengyuan@public.bta.net.cn
contact: Feng Yuan, Co-director

Croatia

B.a.B.e (Be active, Be emancipated) Women's Human Rights Group, Prilaz
    Gjure Dezelica 26/11, 10000 Zagreb, Croatia
website: www.babe.hr
tel: +385-1-484.6180
e-mail: babe@zamir.net
contact: Sanja Sarnavka, Media co-ordinator

India

Centre for Advocacy and Research, C-100/B Kalkaji (1st floor), New Delhi
    110019, India
website: www.viewersforum.com
Tel/fax: +91-11-629.2787
fax: +91-11-643.0133
e-mail: cfarasam@del6.vsnl.net.in
contact: Akhila Sivadas, Executive Director

Israel

Israel Women's Network, PO Box 53186, Jerusalem 91531, Israel
tel: +972-2-671.8885
fax: +972-2-671.8887
e-mail: iwn@netvision.net.il
contact: Rina Bar-Tal, Chairperson

Italy

Osservatorio MediaDonna, Catedra di Antropología Culturale, Facoltà di
    Sociologia, Università di Roma 'La Sapienza', via Salaria 113, 00198 Roma,
    Italy
tel: +39-06-4991.8351
fax: +39-06-4404.987
e-mail: gioia.dicristofaro@uniroma1.it
contact: Gioia Di Cristofaro Longo, Scientific Director

Jamaica

Women's Media Watch, 14 South Ave, Kingston 10, Jamaica, West Indies
tel: +1-876-926.0882

fax: +1-876-929.7079
e-mail: wmwjam@cwjamaica.com
contact: Hilary Nicholson, Programme Co-ordinator

Japan

FCT Forum for Citizens' Television & Media, Nagae 1601-27, Hayamacho,
    Miura, Kanagawa, Japan
website: www.mlpj.org/index-e.html
fax: +81-45- 941.8214
e-mail: tomiyaz@attglobal.net
contact: Toshiko Miyazaki, Co-ordinator

Workshop on Gender and Media (GEAM), c/o Masami Saitoh, 7–9 Kanebo-
    machi, Takaoka City, Toyama Pref. 933-0856, Japan
website: www.nsknet.or.jp/~saitoh/index.html
fax: +81-766-233.929
e-mail: saitoh@p1.tcnet.ne.jp
contact: Masami Saitoh, Co-ordinator

Latin America – Southern Cone

Grupo de Comunicadoras del Sur, c/o Isis Internacional, Casilla 2067, Correo
    Central, Santiago, Chile
website: www.isis.cl/grupo_de_trabajo.htm
tel: +56-2-638.2219
fax: +56-2-638.3142
e-mail: isis@terra.cl
contact: Ana María Portugal, Co-ordinator

Nepal

Sancharika Samuha, PO Box 13293, Kathmandu, Nepal
website: http://sancharika.nepalonline.org
tel: +977-1-538.549
fax: +977-1-547.291
e-mail: sancharika@wlink.com.np
contact: Bandana Rana, President

Netherlands

Diversity Department, NOS, PO Box 26444, 1202 JJ Hilversum, Netherlands
website: www.meervananders.nl
tel: +31-35-677.3478
fax: +31-35-677.2461
e-mail: bernadette.van.dijck@nos.nl
contact: Bernadette van Dijck, Head of Department

South Africa

Media Monitoring Project, PO Box 1560, Parklands 2121, South Africa
website: www.sn.apc.org/mmp
tel: +27-11-788.1278
fax: +27-11-788.1289
e-mail: mmp@wn.apc.org
contact: William Bird, Director

Women's Media Watch, Mediaworks, 6th Floor, Norlen House, 17 Buitenkant
  Street, Cape Town 8001, South Africa
tel: +27-21-461.0368
fax: +27-21-461.0385
e-mail: mediawat@mediawks.co.za
contact: Lene Øverland, Co-ordinator

Spain

Observatorio de la Publicidad, Servicio de Comunicación e Imagen, Instituto
  de la Mujer, Condesa de Venadito 34, 28027 Madrid, Spain
website: www.mtas.es/mujer/observpub.htm
tel: +34-91-347.7908/9/10
fax: +34-91-347.7998
e-mail: inmujer@mtas.es
contact: María Jesús Ortiz, Jefa de Comunicación

Sri Lanka

Women and Media Collective, 12 1/1 Ascot Avenue, Colombo 5, Sri Lanka
tel: +94-1-597.738/595.224
fax: +94-1-595.224
e-mail: womedia@sri.lanka.net
contact: Kumudini Samuel, Co-ordinator

Tanzania

Tanzania Media Women's Association, PO Box 8981, Dar es Salaam, Tanzania
tel: +255-22-213.2181/211.5278
fax: +255-22-211.5278
e-mail: tamwa@raha.com
contact: Leila Sheikh, Executive Director

Trinidad and Tobago

Gender Media Monitor (GeMM), PO Box 410, Port of Spain, Trinidad and
  Tobago
website: www.thenetwork.webprovider.com
tel: +1-868-628.9655
fax: +1-868-628.9655

e-mail: network@wow.net
contact: Hazel Brown, Co-ordinator

Tunisia

Centre for Research, Studies, Documentation and Information on Women, Av.
du Roi Abdelaziz Al Saôud, rue 7131, El Manar II, 2092 Tunis, Tunisia
tel: +216-1-874.911
fax: +216-1-874.911
e-mail: Directeur.General@credif.rnrt.tn
contact: Emna Atallah Soula, Director of Information and Communication

USA

About-Face, PO Box 77665, San Francisco, CA 94107, USA
website: www.about-face.org
tel: +1-415-436.0212
e-mail: kathy@about-face.org
contact: Kathy Bruin, Executive Director

Fairness & Accuracy In Reporting (FAIR), Women's Desk, 130 West 25th
Street, New York, NY 10001, USA
website: www.fair.org/womens-desk.html
tel: +1-212-633.6700
fax: +1-212-727.7668
e-mail: jpozner@fair.org
contact: Jennifer Pozner, Director

National Organization for Women (NOW), 733 15th Street NW, 2nd floor,
Washington, DC 20005, USA
website: www.now.org
tel: +1-202-628.8669
fax: +1-202-785.8576
e-mail: communications@now.org
contact: Lisa Bennett-Haigney, Communications Director

References

Alfaro, Rosa María (1997) 'Comunicadoras: competencias por la igualdad', in Rosa María Alfaro and Helena Pinilla García, *Mujeres en los Medios: ¿Presencia o Protagonismo?*, Lima: Asociación de Comunicadores Sociales Calandria, pp. 59–100.

All-China Journalist Association and Chinese Academy of Social Sciences (1995) *Survey on the Current Status and Development of Chinese Women Journalists*, Beijing: All-China Journalist Association/Chinese Academy of Social Sciences/UNESCO.

Allen, Donna, Ramona R. Rush and Susan J. Kaufman (eds) (1996) *Women Transforming Communications: Global Intersections*, Thousand Oaks, CA: Sage Publications.

Anuar, Mustafa K. and Wang Lay Kim (1996) 'Aspects of Ethnicity and Gender in Malaysian Television', in David French and Michael Richards (eds), *Contemporary Television: Eastern Perspectives*, New Delhi: Sage Publications, pp. 262–81.

Aslama, Minna and Johanna Jääsaari (2000) 'Women Audiences and Gender Portrayal on TV: a Finnish Case Study', *Screening Gender*, audio-visual training toolkit produced by YLE (Finland), NOS (Netherlands), NRK (Norway), SVT (Sweden) and ZDF (Germany), Hilversum: NOS Diversity Department, pp. 121–8.

Azhgikhina, Nadezhda (1995) 'Back to the Kitchen', *Women's Review of Books*, Vol. XII, No. 8, pp. 13–14.

B.a.B.e (1998) *Zene i Mediji* ('Women in Media'; in Croatian, with English summary), Zagreb: B.a.B.e.

— (1999) *Zene i Mediji – Samo za Tvoje Oci* ('Women in media – for your eyes only'), Zagreb: B.a.B.e.

B.a.B.e/Elektorine (2000) *Zene u Predizhornoj Kampanji* ('Women in Election Campaigns'; in Croatian, with English summary), Zagreb: B.a.B.e.

Bajpai, Shailaja (1997) 'Thoroughly Modern Misses: Women on Indian Television', *Women: A Cultural Review*, Vol. 8, No. 3, pp. 303–10.

Balaguer Callejon, María Luisa (1985) *La Mujer y los Medios de Comunicación de Masas: El Caso de la Publicidad en TV*, Madrid: Arguval.

Baranovic, Branislava (2000) *Image of Women in Croatian School Textbooks*, Zagreb: B.a.B.e.

Barker-Plummer, Bernadette (2000) 'News as a Feminist Resource? A Case Study of the Media Strategies and Media Representation of the National Organization for Women, 1966–1980', in Annabelle Sreberny and Liesbet van Zoonen (eds), *Gender, Politics and Communication*, Cresskill, NJ: Hampton Press, pp. 121–59.

Bauman, Zygmunt (1997) *Postmodernity and Its Discontents*, Cambridge: Polity Press.

Bohong, Liu and Bu Wei (1997) 'Research Report on Women's Image in TV Advertisements in China', *Journalism and Communication*, Vol. 4, No. 1, pp. 45–58.

Börjesson, Fia (1995) 'Ladies "Excuse Me" – Gender Problems in the Written Press', *Language and Gender*, Göteborg: University of Göteborg, pp. 113–22.

Brants, Kees and Denis McQuail (1997) 'The Netherlands', in Euromedia Research Group, *The Media in Western Europe*, 2nd edn, London: Sage Publications, pp. 153–67.

Bridge, M. Junior (1995) 'What's News?', in Cynthia M. Lont (ed.), *Women and Media: Content, Careers, and Criticism*, Belmont, CA: Wadsworth Publishing, pp. 15–28.

— (1996) *Marginalizing Women: Front-Page News Coverage of Females Declines in 1996*, Washington, DC: Women, Men and Media.

Brown, Mary Ellen and Darlaine C. Gardetto (2000) 'Representing Hillary Rodham Clinton: Gender, Meaning and News Media', in Annabelle Sreberny and Liesbet van Zoonen (eds), *Gender, Politics and Communication*, Cresskill, NJ: Hampton Press, pp. 21–51.

Brunsdon, Charlotte (1997) 'Identity in Feminist Television Criticism', in Charlotte Brunsdon, *Screen Tastes: Soap Opera to Satellite Dishes*, London: Routledge, pp. 89–198.

Carter, Meg, Mimi Turner and Maureen Paton (1999) *Real Women – The Hidden Sex*, London: Women in Journalism.

Celiberti, Lilián (1998) 'Monitoreando', *Cotidiano Mujer*, No. 27.

Celiberti, Lilián, Mariela Genta and Silvana Bruera (1998) *En el Medio de los Medios: Monitoreo Realizado a los Medios de Comunicación*, Montevideo: Cotidiano Mujer.

Centre for Advocacy and Research (1998) *Violence on Television*, New Delhi: Centre for Advocacy and Research.

Chang, Chingching and Jacqueline Hitchon (1997) 'Mass Media Impact on Voter Response to Women Candidates: Theoretical Development', *Communication Theory*, Vol. 7, No. 1, pp. 29–52.

Changing Lenses: Women's Perspectives on Media (1999), Manila: Isis-International.

'China: Women's Voice in Mass Media' (1998) *Women's International Network News*, Vol. 24, No. 2, pp. 56–7.

Cishecki, Melanie (1998) 'MediaWatch Canada: Our Lobbying Experience', paper presented at WACC Regional Conference on Gender and Communication, Kingston, Jamaica, 19–21 November.

Clarke, Judith (2000) 'Cambodia', in Shelton A. Gunaratne (ed.), *Handbook of the Media in Asia*, New Delhi: Sage Publications, pp. 242–62.

Cobo, Rosa (1991) 'La imagen de las mujeres en los medios de comunicación', in Luis Rodríguez Zúñiga (ed.), *Las Mujeres Españolas: Lo Privado y lo Público*, Madrid: Centro Investigaciones Sociológicas (Estudios y Encuestas 24), pp. 93–9.

Coronel, Sheila S. (1998) 'Media Ownership and Control in the Philippines', *Media Development*, Vol. XLV, No. 4, pp. 25–8.

Cotidiano Mujer (1993) *Los Medios del Futuro. El Futuro de los Medios*, Montevideo: Cotidiano Mujer.

de Bruin, Marjan (1994) 'Employment and Gender in Caribbean Mass Media', in Marjan de Bruin (ed.), *Women and Caribbean Media*, Kingston: Caribbean Institute of Mass Communication, pp. 6–11.

Dreamworlds II: Desire, Sex and Power in Music Video (1995), video produced by the Media Education Foundation, 55 mins, Northampton, MA: Media Education Foundation.

Edwards, Derek, Peter Golding, Dennis Howitt, Shelley McLachlan and Katie MacMillan (1999) 'An Audit of Democracy: Media Monitoring, Citizenship, and

Public Policy', in Kaarle Nordenstreng and Michael Griffin (eds), *International Media Monitoring*, Cresskill, NJ: Hampton Press, pp. 39–55.

Eie, Birgit (1998) *Who Speaks on Television? A European Comparative Study of Female Participation in Television Programmes*, Oslo: NRK (Norwegian Broadcasting Corporation).

Ekachai, Daradirek (2000) 'Thailand', in Shelton A. Gunaratne (ed.), *Handbook of the Media in Asia*, New Delhi: Sage Publications, pp. 429–61.

European Commission (1999) *Images of Women in the Media: Report on Existing Research in the European Union*, Brussels: European Commission.

Ferrer, Clemente (1995) *Nada Se Escapa a la Publicidad*, Madrid: Edimarco.

Flores Palacios, Patricia (1999a) *La Mirada Invisible: La Imagen de las Mujeres en los Medios de Comunicación de Bolivia*, La Paz: Red de Trabajadoras de la Información y Comunicación RED-ADA.

— (1999b) *El Mundo y la Cotidianidad en Femenino y Masculino*, La Paz: Red de Trabajadoras de la Información y Comunicación RED-ADA.

Frith, Simon (1996) *Performing Rites: On the Value of Popular Music*, Oxford: Oxford University Press.

Furnham, Adrian and Twiggy Mak (1999) 'Sex-Role Stereotyping in Television Commercials: a Review and Comparison of Fourteen Studies Done on Five Continents over 25 years', *Sex Roles*, Vol. 41, Nos 5/6, pp. 413–37.

Gallagher, Margaret (1995a) *An Unfinished Story: Gender Patterns in Media Employment*, Reports and Papers on Mass Communication 110, Paris: UNESCO.

— (1995b) 'Gender Portrayal in European Broadcasting: Policies and Practice', paper presented at 'Reflecting Diversity: the Challenge for Women and Men in European Broadcasting', 2nd European Commission/European Broadcasting Union Conference on Equal Opportunities, London, 3–5 May.

— (1999) 'The Global Media Monitoring Project: Women's Networking for Research and Action', in Kaarle Nordenstreng and Michael Griffin (eds), *International Media Monitoring*, Cresskill, NJ: Hampton Press, pp. 199–217.

— (2000) *From Mexico to Beijing – and Beyond: Covering Women in the World's News*, New York: United Nations Development Fund for Women (UNIFEM).

Garner, Helen (1997) *Watching Women: Election 1997*, London: Fawcett Society.

Garrido, Lucy (1996) 'En el medio de los medios', in Ana María Portugal and Carmen Torres (eds), *Por Todos los Medios: Comunicación y Género*, Santiago: Isis Internacional, pp. 131–7.

— (1999) 'Selling it better', *Lolapress*, No. 11, July–October, pp. 36–8.

Gerbner, George (1972) 'Violence and Television Drama: Trends and Symbolic Functions', in George A. Comstock and Edward Rubinstein (eds), *Television and Social Behavior, Vol. 1 Content and Control*, Washington, DC: US Government Printing Office, pp. 28–187.

Gibbons, Sheila J. (2000) 'Women, Men and Media', in Elizabeth V. Burt (ed.), *Women's Press Organizations 1881–1999*, Westport, CT: Greenwood Press, pp. 256–64.

Goga, Farhana (2000) *Towards Affirmative Action: Issues of Race and Gender in South African Media Organisations*, Durban: University of Natal, Graduate Programme in Cultural and Media Studies/UNESCO.

Goodwin, Andrew (1993) *Dancing in the Distraction Factory: Music Television and Popular Culture*, London: Routledge.

Grivaz, Guillaume (1994) 'Sexe et télévision: l'audience des programmes érotiques', unpublished DEA thesis, Paris: Institut Français de Presse/Université de Paris 2.

Groebel, Jo (1998) 'The UNESCO Global Study on Media Violence', in Ulla Carlsson and Cecilia von Feilitzen (eds), *Children and Media Violence*, Göteborg: Nordicom/ UNESCO International Clearinghouse on Children and Violence on the Screen, pp. 181–99.

Hall, Stuart (1986) 'Media Power and Class Power', in James Curran, Jake Eccleston, Giles Oakley and Alan Richardson (eds), *Bending Reality: The State of the Media*, London: Pluto Press, pp. 5–14.

Hartley, John (1982) *Understanding News*, London: Routledge.

Heo, Chul, Ki-Yul Uhm and Jeong-Heon Chang (2000) 'South Korea', in Shelton A. Gunaratne (ed.), *Handbook of the Media in Asia*, New Delhi: Sage Publications, pp. 611–37.

Hizaoui, Abdelkrim (1999) *L'Image de la Femme Dans la Presse Ecrite Tunisienne*, Tunis: Centre de Recherches, d'Etudes, de Documentation et d'Information sur la Femme.

Instituto de la Mujer (1998) *Observatorio de la Publicidad: Informe Denuncias Recogidas Año 1997*, Madrid: Instituto de la Mujer.

— (1999) *Observatorio de la Publicidad: Informe de 1998*, Madrid: Instituto de la Mujer.

— (2000) *Observatorio de la Publicidad: Informe de 1999*, Madrid: Instituto de la Mujer.

It's Time … To Break Free of Violence (1999), video produced by Women's Media Watch, 10 mins, Kingston: Women's Media Watch.

Jhally, Sut (1990) *The Codes of Advertising: Fetishism and the Political Economy of Meaning in the Consumer Society*, London: Routledge.

Joseph, Ammu (2000) *Women in Journalism: Making News*, New Delhi: Konark Publishers.

Joseph, Ammu and Kalpana Sharma (eds) (1994) *Whose News? The Media and Women's Issues*, New Delhi: Sage Publications.

Kahn, Kim Fridkin and Ann Gordon (1997) 'How Women Campaign for the US Senate', in Pippa Norris (ed.) *Women, Media and Politics*, New York: Oxford University Press, pp. 59–76.

Kim, Yanghee and Incheol Min (1997) 'Development of a Gender Discrimination Indicator for the Mass Media', *Women's Studies Forum* (Journal of the Korean Women's Development Institute), Vol. 13, pp. 197–210.

Koski, Anne (1994) *Valtiomies: valiomieheyttä ja maskuliinista virtuositeettia. Urho Kekkosen ja Elisabeth Rehn in valtiotaito kuvasemioottisessa analyysissä* ('Statesman: masculine virtuosity. Urho Kekkonen and Elisabeth Rehn in semiotic analysis'), Yleisradio report 7/1994, Helsinki: Finnish Broadcasting Company.

Lee, Chun Wah (1998) 'Feminism in Singapore's Advertising: a Rising Voice', *Media Asia*, Vol. 25, No. 4, pp. 193–7.

Lee, Kyung-Ja (1999) 'Korea', in *Changing Lenses: Women's Perspectives on Media*, Manila: Isis-International, pp. 82–92.

Lemish, Dafna (1998) 'The Ripple Effect: Pornographic Images of Women in Israeli Advertising', in Stanley G. French (ed.), *Interpersonal Violence, Health and Gender Politics*, Toronto: McGraw-Hill Ryerson, pp. 285–95.

— (2000) 'The Whore and the Other: Israeli Images of Female Immigrants from the Former USSR', *Gender and Society*, Vol. 14, No. 2, pp. 333–49.

Lemish, Dafna and Inbal Barzel (2000) '"Four Mothers": the womb in the public sphere', *European Journal of Communication*, Vol. 15, No. 2, pp. 147–69.

Lemish, Dafna and Chava E. Tidhar (1991) 'The Silenced Majority: Women in Israel's 1988 Television Election Campaign', *Women and Language*, Vol. 14, No. 1, pp. 13–21.

— (1999) 'Still Marginal: Women in Israel's 1996 Television Election Campaign', *Sex Roles*, Vol. 41, Nos 5/6, pp. 389–412.

Leonard, Helen (1999) 'Australian Codes of Conduct for Media Practitioners', paper presented at Asia–Pacific Regional NGO Symposium on Women and Media, Bangkok, 31 August–4 September.

Le Roux, Gabrielle (1999) 'The Least-reported Crime', *Rhodes Journalism Review*, December, pp. 24–5.

Longo, Gioia Di Cristofaro (1995) *Media Woman: Criticism, Analysis, Research: Emerging Cultural Models*, Rome: National Commission for Equal Opportunities for Men and Women.

Longwe, Sarah and R. Clarke (1992) *A Gender Analysis of a Narrative: The Example of Zambian Popular Song*, Lusaka: Zambia Association for Research and Development.

McArthur, Leslie Z. and Beth G. Resko (1975) 'The Portrayal of Men and Women in American Television Commercials', *Journal of Social Psychology*, Vol. 97, pp. 209–20.

Making a Difference (1999), video produced by the Centre for Advocacy and Research, 10 mins, Delhi: Centre for Advocacy and Research.

Malhotra, Sheena and Everett M. Rogers (2000) 'Satellite Television and the New Indian Woman', *Gazette: The International Journal for Communication Studies*, Vol. 62, No. 5, pp. 407–29.

Maskey, Susan (1998) 'Nepali Sanchar Madhyam Ra Mahila Sakriyata' ('Nepali Media and Women's Activism'), *Asmita*, Jetha-Asar, Vol. 11, No. 49, pp. 7–17.

Mbilinyi, Dorothy A. (1996) 'Women and Gender Relations in School Text Books', in Dorothy A. Mbilinyi and Cuthbert Omari (eds), *Gender Relations and Women's Images in the Media*, Dar es Salaam: Dar es Salaam University Press, pp. 90–104.

Media Advocacy Group (1994a) *People's Perceptions: Obscenity and Violence on the Small Screen*, New Delhi: Media Advocacy Group.

— (1994b) *Women and Men in News and Current Affairs Programmes*, New Delhi: Media Advocacy Group.

— (1995a) *Svetlana, Tara, Priya and Shanti – A Demographic Profile of Path-Breaking Women in Soaps on Doordarshan and Zee*, New Delhi: Media Advocacy Group.

— (1995b) *Violence in Soaps and Serials on Sun TV, Doordarshan and Zee TV*, New Delhi: Media Advocacy Group.

— (1997a) 'Note on The Indecent Representation of Women Act (1986)', in *Media Policy*, New Delhi: Media Advocacy Group.

— (1997b) *The Audience Speaks: Building a Consumer Forum*, New Delhi: Media Advocacy Group.

— (1998) *Assessing the Role of Television in the General Election, 1998: A Monitoring and Feedback Study*, New Delhi: Media Advocacy Group.

Media Monitoring Project (1998a) 'An Analysis of Selected Press Coverage of Violence Against Women', *Media Mask*, Vol. 3, No. 1, pp. 1–19.

— (1998b) 'Gender Coverage around Women's Day: 1998', *Media Mask*, Vol. 3, No. 2, pp. 13–32.

— (1998c) 'Monitoring Media Coverage of Violence against Women', *Media Mask*, Vol. 3, No. 3, pp. 1–19.

— (1999a) 'Biased? Gender, Politics and the Media', in *Redefining Politics: South African Women and Democracy*, Johannesburg: Commission on Gender Equality, pp. 161–7.

— (1999b) So *What's New in the Elections? Events Not Issues. An Analysis of Media Coverage of the 1999 Elections*, Johannesburg: Media Monitoring Project.

— (1999c) *A Snapshot Survey of Women's Representation in the South African Media at the End of the Millennium,* study commissioned by Women's Media Watch, Johannesburg: Media Monitoring Project.

Media Report to Women (2000a) 'How to Conduct Your Own Survey of Your Newspaper's Front Page', Vol. 28, No. 1, p. 15.

— (2000b) 'Progress in Coverage of Women and Economy, but Economic News Still a Male Preserve', Vol. 28, No. 1, pp. 1–3.

— (2000c) 'News Coverage of Military Women: More Than One Could Expect – and Also Less', Vol. 28, No. 2, pp. 4–6.

MediaWatch (1993a) *Tracing the Roots of MediaWatch,* Toronto: MediaWatch.

— (1993b) *Focus on Violence: A Survey of Canadian Newspapers,* Toronto: MediaWatch.

— (1994a) *Please Adjust Our Sets: Canadian Women Watching Television – Habits, Preferences and Concerns,* Toronto: MediaWatch.

— (1994b) *Front and Centre: Minority Representation on Television,* Toronto: Media Watch.

— (1995) *Women's Participation in the News: Global Media Monitoring Project,* Toronto: MediaWatch.

— (1998) *Women Strike Out: 1998 Newspaper Survey,* Toronto: MediaWatch.

— (2000) *Media Environment: Analysing the 'Tween' Market,* Toronto: MediaWatch.

Michielsens, Magda (1995) 'Créez une femme', in Magda Michielsens, Karen Celis and Christine Delhaye, *Les Femmes au Travers des Médias et de la Publicité,* Brussels: Ministère de l'Emploi et du Travail, pp. 7–35.

Militante, Clarissa (1999) 'Philippines', in *Changing Lenses: Women's Perspectives on Media,* Manila: Isis-International, pp. 102–12.

Millwood Hargrave, Andrea (1994) 'Attitudes Towards the Portrayal of Women in Broadcasting', in *Perspectives of Women in Television,* Research Working Paper IX, London: Broadcasting Standards Council, pp. 6–23.

Miyazaki, Toshiko (1998) 'Gender and Communication Policies in Japan', in *Engendering Communication Policy in Asia,* New Delhi/London: Asian Network of Women in Communication/World Association for Christian Communication, pp. 19–24.

— (1999) 'Japan', in *Changing Lenses: Women's Perspectives on Media,* Manila: Isis-International, pp. 70–82.

Mtambalike, Pili (1996) 'Newspaper Reporting and Gender Relations', in Dorothy A. Mbilinyi and Cuthbert Omari (eds), *Gender Relations and Women's Images in the Media,* Dar es Salaam: Dar es Salaam University Press, pp. 134–43.

Mthala, Pumla (1999) 'Small Victories for Women in the Media', *Connections,* Vol.3, No. 4, pp.10–11.

Munshi, Shoma (1998) 'Wife/Mother/Daughter-in-law: Multiple Avatars of Homemaker in 1990s Indian Advertising', *Media, Culture and Society,* Vol. 20, No. 4, pp. 573–91.

Nava, Mica (1991) 'Consumerism Reconsidered: Buying and Power', *Cultural Studies,* Vol. 5, No. 2, pp. 185–207.

NOS Gender Portrayal Department (1993) *Mieke, ho is de Stand? Research Results for 1992 of the Portrayal Department,* Hilversum: NOS.

— (1994) *Mooi of Meedogenloos: Beautiful or Bold – Looking at Dutch Drama Series,* Hilversum: NOS.

— (1995) *Who's Whose Favourite: Viewer Identification with Female and Male Characters in Television Drama,* Hilversum: NOS.

— (1996a) *Informative Programmes: Media Portrayal of Women and Men,* Hilversum: NOS.

— (1996b) *Getting Through: Five Years of the NOS Gender Portrayal Department*, Hilversum: NOS.

— (1998a) *Balanced Gender Portrayal Makes for Better Programs: Renewing Acquaintance with the NOS Gender Portrayal Department*, Hilversum: NOS.

— (1998b) *An Equal Match: Gender Portrayal in Sports Programmes*, Hilversum: NOS.

O'Donohue, Stephanie (1997) 'Leaky Boundaries: Intertextuality and Young Adult Experiences of Advertising', in Mica Nava, Andrew Blake, Iain MacRury and Barry Richards (eds), *Buy This Book: Studies in Advertising and Consumption*, London: Routledge, pp. 257–75.

Palan, Anita (1995) *Women in the Media in Cambodia*, report for the International Federation of Journalists, Phnom Penh.

Park, Myung-Jin (1997) 'Monitoring and Advocacy: Success and Obstacles in Korea', paper presented at the WACC regional conference on Gender and Communication Policy, Manila, 30 July–2 August.

Parry-Giles, Shawn J. (2000) 'Mediating Hillary Rodham Clinton: Television News Practices and Image-Making in the Postmodern Age', *Critical Studies in Media Communication*, Vol. 17, No. 2, pp. 205–26.

Phillips, Louise (2000) 'Mediated Communications and the Privatisation of Public Problems: Discourse on Ecological Risks and Political Action', *European Journal of Communication*, Vol. 15, No. 2, pp. 171–207.

Pinilla García, Helena (1997) 'La mujer como sujeto de información', in Rosa María Alfaro and Helena Pinilla García, *Mujeres en los Medios: ¿Presencia o Protagonismo?*, Lima: Asociación de Comunicadores Sociales Calandria, pp. 9–57.

Portugal, Ana María and Carmen Torres (1996) 'Introducción', in Ana María Portugal and Carmen Torres (eds), *Por Todos los Medios: Comunicación y Género*, Santiago: Isis Internacional, pp. 9–13.

— (eds) (1996) *Por Todos los Medios: Comunicación y Género*, Santiago: Isis Internacional.

Riaño, Pilar (ed.) (1994) *Women in Grassroots Communication: Furthering Social Change*, Thousand Oaks, CA: Sage Publications.

Rinke, Andrea (1994) 'Wende-Bilder, Television Images of Women in Germany in Transition', in *Women and the WENDE: Social Effects and Cultural Reflections of the German Unification Process*, Amsterdam-Atlanta: Rodopi, BV.

Röser, Jutta (1995) *Was Frauen und Männer vor dem Bildschirm erleben. Rezeption von Sexismus und Gewalt im Fernsehen*, Ministerium für den Gleichstellung von Frauen und Männer des Landes Nordrhein Westfalen.

Ross, Karen and Annabelle Sreberny (2000) 'Women in the House: Media Representation of British Politicians', in Annabelle Sreberny and Liesbet van Zoonen (eds), *Gender, Politics and Communication*, Cresskill, NJ: Hampton Press, pp. 79–99.

Sachs, Lesley (1996) 'The Missing Gender: the Portrayal of Israeli Women in the Media', in Rina Jimenez-David (ed.), *Women's Experiences in Media*, Manila: Isis-International and World Association for Christian Communication, pp. 62–7.

Samuel, Kumudini (1999) *Women's Rights Watch Year Report 1999*, Colombo: Women and Media Collective.

Sanga, Edda (1996) 'Women and Gender Relations in Radio Programmes', in Dorothy A. Mbilinyi and Cuthbert Omari (eds), *Gender Relations and Women's Images in the Media*, Dar es Salaam: Dar es Salaam University Press, pp. 105–19.

Sappir, Shoshana London (2000) 'The Israel Women's Network. Progress in the Status of Women in Israel since the 1995 Beijing Conference', paper submitted to the Beijing +5 conference, New York, 5–9 June.

Sarabia, Anna Leah (1996) 'Learning to Call the Shots', in Rina Jimenez-David (ed.), *Women's Experiences in Media*, Manila: Isis-International and World Association for Christian Communication, pp. 73–6.

Sarayeth, Tive (1996a) 'After a Long Civil War: Media Becomes a Battlefield', in Rina Jimenez-David (ed.), *Women's Experiences in Media*, Manila: Isis-International and World Association for Christian Communication, pp. 47–9.

— (1996b) *The Portrayal of Women in the Khmer Press*, first report of the Media Monitoring Group, Phnom Penh: Women's Media Centre of Cambodia.

— (1997) *How Cambodian TV Portrays Women*, Phnom Penh, Women's Media Centre of Cambodia.

— (1998) 'Violence against Women in the Media in Cambodia', paper presented at the forum on Media Violence against Women, United Nations, New York, 4 March.

Schlesinger, Philip, R. Emerson Dobash, Russell P. Dobash and C. Kay Weaver (1992) *Women Watching Violence*, London: British Film Institute.

Schröder, Kim Christian (1997) 'Cynicism and Ambiguity: British Corporate Responsibility Advertisements and Their Readers in the 1990s', in Mica Nava, Andrew Blake, Iain MacRury and Barry Richards (eds), *Buy This Book: Studies in Advertising and Consumption*, London: Routledge, pp. 276–90.

Screening Gender (2000), audio-visual training toolkit produced by YLE (Finland), NOS (Netherlands), NRK (Norway), SVT (Sweden) and ZDF (Germany); videos (total 80 mins) and text; Hilversum: NOS Diversity Department.

Seiter, Ellen (1999) *Television and New Media Audiences*, Oxford: Clarendon Press.

Seldes, George (1935) *Freedom of the Press*, Indianapolis: Bobbs-Merrill Company.

Silva, Uca (1997) *Marco Teorico del Proyecto Comunicación y Género*, Santiago: Sur Profesionales, Proyecto Comunicación y Género.

— (1998a) *Guía para Escribir una Carta (a los medios de comunicación)*, Santiago: Sur Profesionales, Proyecto Comunicación y Género.

— (1998b) *Indicaciones para Comunicar. Invitación a Establecer una Conversación entre Comunicadores*, Santiago: Sur Profesionales, Proyecto Comunicación y Género.

Silva, Uca, Carmen Torres and Teresa Caceres (1998) *Observatorio de Medios de Comunicación. Analisis de periodicos La Tercera, El Mercurio, Le Época*, Santiago: Sur Profesionales, Proyecto Comunicación y Género.

Sinha, Arbind (1996) 'Development Dilemmas for Indian Television', in David French and Michael Richards (eds), *Contemporary Television: Eastern Perspectives*, New Delhi: Sage Publications, pp. 302–20.

Siregar, Hetty (1999) 'Indonesia', *Changing Lenses: Women's Perspectives on Media*, Manila: Isis-International, pp. 56–64.

Siriyuvasak, Ubonrat (1999) 'A Thailand Country Report', report for the project Media and Gender Policy in a Global Age, Manipal/London: Asian Network of Women in Communication/World Association for Christian Communication.

Siriyuvasak, Ubonrat, Leela Rao and Wang Lay Kim (eds) (2000) *Gender Reflections in Asian Television*, Manipal: Asian Network of Women in Communication.

Skjeie, Hege (1994) 'Hva kvinnene gjör for politikken' ('Women in Norwegian politics'), in Fride Eeg-Henriksen, Brit Fougner and Tove Beate Pedersen (eds), *Backlash i Norge? Rapport fra en Konferanse om Kvinner i 90-åra*, Working Paper 1, Oslo: Norwegian Research Council, pp. 121–31.

Spears, George and Kasia Seydegart with Margaret Gallagher (2000) *Who Makes the News? Global Media Monitoring Project 2000*, London: World Association for Christian Communication.

Spee, Sonia and Nico Carpentier (1999) 'Different Voices – Different Identities. Women Participating in Audience Discussion Programmes', paper presented at 'Women's Worlds 99', 7th International Interdisciplinary Congress on Women, Tromsø, Norway, 20–26 June.

Sreberny, Annabelle (1998) 'Feminist Internationalism: Imagining and Building Global Civil Society', in Dayan Kishan Thussu (ed.), *Electronic Empires: Global Media and Local Resistance*, London: Arnold, pp. 208–22.

Sreberny, Annabelle and Liesbet van Zoonen (2000) 'Gender, Politics and Communication: an Introduction', in Annabelle Sreberny and Liesbet van Zoonen (eds), *Gender, Politics and Communication*, Cresskill, NJ: Hampton Press, pp. 1–19.

Stabile, Carol A. (2000) 'Nike, Social Responsibility, and the Hidden Abode of Production', *Critical Studies in Media Communication*, Vol. 17, No. 2, pp. 186–204.

Suárez Toro, María (2000) *Women's Voices on FIRE: Feminist International Radio Endeavour*, Austin, TX: Anomaly Press.

Suzuki, Midori F. (2000) 'Media Literacy Education and the Informed Citizen: the Development and Directions of Media Literacy Initiatives in Japan', paper presented at the International Conference on Media Education: Directions and Issues, Taipei, Fubon Culture and Education Foundation, 1–2 April.

TAMWA (Tanzania Media Women's Association 1999) *Annual Report 1998*, Dar es Salaam: Tanzania Media Women's Association.

— (2000) *Annual Report 1999*, Dar es Salaam: Tanzania Media Women's Association.

Tindal, Mardi (n.d.) *A Day in the News of the World: A Study Guide for the Global Media Monitoring Project*, London: World Association for Christian Communication.

Torres, Carmen (ed.) (2000) *Género y Communicación: El Lado Oscuro de los Medios*, Santiago: Isis International.

Trancart, Monique (1997) 'La place et l'image des femmes dans les bulletins d'information et les articles d'actualité', in Evelyn Serdjénian (ed.), *Femmes et Médias*, Paris: L'Harmattan, pp. 145–9.

— (1999) 'Médias d'information générale: le leurre féminin', in Virginie Barrè, Sylvie Debras, Natacha Henry and Monique Trancart, *Dites-le Avec des Femmes: Le Sexisme Ordinaire Dans les Médias*, Paris: CFD, pp. 17–37.

Ueno, Chizuko and Media no naka no seisabetsu o kangaeru kai (eds) (1996) *Kitto kaerareru Seisabetsu go: Watashitachi no Gaidorain* ('Non-sexist Guidelines for Japanese Mass Media'), Tokyo: Sanseido.

United Nations (2000) *The World's Women 2000: Trends and Statistics*, New York: Department of Social and Economic Affairs, United Nations.

van Dijck, Bernadette (2000) 'Changing Images: a Long Road', *Media Development*, Vol. XLVII, No. 3, pp. 28–9.

van Zoonen, Liesbet (1994) *Feminist Media Studies*, London: Sage Publications.

— (2000) 'Broken Hearts, Broken Dreams? Politicians and Their Families in Popular Culture', in Annabelle Sreberny and Liesbet van Zoonen (eds), *Gender, Politics and Communication*, Cresskill, NJ: Hampton Press, pp. 101–19.

Venkateswaran, K. S. (compiler) (1996) *Media Monitors in Asia*, Singapore: Asian Media Information and Communication Centre.

Violence against Women in South Africa: A Resource for Journalists (1999), Johannesburg: Soul City Institute for Health and Development Communication.

Viswanath, K. and Kavita Karan (2000) 'India', in Shelton A. Gunaratne (ed.), *Handbook of the Media in Asia*, New Delhi: Sage Publications, pp. 84–117.

von Feilitzen, Cecilia (1998) 'Introduction', in Ulla Carlsson and Cecilia von Feilitzen (eds), *Children and Media Violence*, Göteborg: Nordicom/UNESCO International Clearinghouse on Children and Violence on the Screen, pp. 45–54.

Walker, Melody (1999) 'Towards a New Political Paradigm in Feminist Media Activism', unpublished MA dissertation, Leeds: University of Leeds.

Walker, Melody and Hilary Nicholson (1996) 'Revisioning the Jamaican Media: the Experience of Women's Media Watch 1987–1996', in Rina Jimenez-David (ed.) *Women's Experiences in Media*, Manila: Isis-International and World Association for Christian Communication, pp. 96–101.

Wei, Bu, Liu Xiaohong and Xiong Lei (1999) 'A Research Report on China TV Programs for Women', report for the project Media and Gender Policy in a Global Age, Manipal/London: Asian Network of Women in Communication/World Association for Christian Communication.

(WERC) Women's Education and Research Centre (1999) *Code of Ethics for Gender Representation in the Electronic Media*, Colombo: Women's Education and Research Centre.

Whiteley, Sheila (ed.) (1997) *Sexing the Groove: Popular Music and Gender*, London: Routledge.

Who's News? Women and the Media (1999), video produced by Women's Media Watch, 25 mins, Cape Town: Women's Media Watch.

Women @ Work to End Violence: Voices in Cyberspace (1999), New York: United Nations Development Fund for Women (UNIFEM).

Women, Men and Media (1998) *Still No Level Playing Field: Female Athletes React to Media Coverage*, Washington, DC: Women, Men and Media.

Women's Media Centre of Cambodia (1999) *Women on Radio in Cambodia*, report of the two-year radio monitoring project by the Media Monitoring Group, Phnom Penh: Women's Media Centre of Cambodia.

Women's Media Watch (1998) *Whose Perspective? A Guide to Gender-Sensitive Analysis of the Media*, Kingston: Women's Media Watch Jamaica.

Yan, Liqun (2000) 'China', in Shelton A. Gunaratne (ed.), *Handbook of the Media in Asia*, New Delhi: Sage Publications, pp. 497–526.

Yuan, Feng (1998) 'China's Establishment Newspapers: the Gender Map and Beyond', paper written for the Centre of East and Southeast Studies, Lund University, Sweden.

— (1999) 'A Resource for Rights: Women and Media in China', paper presented at 'Women's Worlds 99', 7th International Interdisciplinary Congress on Women, Tromsø, Norway, 20–26 June.

Zabelina, Tatiana (1996) 'Sexual Violence Towards Women', in Hilary Pilkington (ed.), *Gender, Generation and Identity in Contemporary Russia*, London: Routledge, pp. 169–86.

Zarkov, Deborah (1997) 'Pictures of the Wall of Love: Motherhood, Womanhood and Nationhood in Croatian Media', *European Journal of Women's Studies*, Vol. 4, No. 3, pp. 305–39.

Index